P9-CDD-440

Twayne's United States Authors Series

EDITOR OF THIS VOLUME

Warren French

Indiana University

Theodore Roethke

TUSAS 390

Theodore Roethke

THEODORE ROETHKE

By GEORGE WOLFF

*Clermont General and Technical College of the
University of Cincinnati*

TWAYNE PUBLISHERS
A DIVISION OF G. K. HALL & CO. BOSTON

First Printing
Library of Congress Cataloging in Publication Data

Wolff, George.
Theodore Roethke.

(Twayne's United States authors series ; TUSAS 390)
Bibliography: p.139-49
Includes index.
1. Roethke, Theodore, 1908-1963—Criticism and interpretation.
PS3535.039Z95 811'.54 80-25151
ISBN 0-8057-7323-1

To Jarvis Thurston, Hazard Adams, James K. Robinson,
my parents, my wife Jo DeWeese Wolff,
and my sons Andrew and Adam

Contents

About the Author

George Wolff attended Washington University in St. Louis, Missouri, where he earned bachelor's and master's degrees in English. While at Washington University he published a poetry quarterly, *Compass Review*. His own poems have appeared in a number of little magazines. After teaching briefly at the Pennsylvania State University, he took his doctor's degree at Michigan State University, with his dissertation being written on Theodore Roethke. He has published an article on Roethke in *The Encyclopedia of World Literature in the Twentieth Century* and another one, "Syntactic and Imagistic Distortions in Roethke's Greenhouse Poems," in *Language and Style* (1973) and a note in *The Explicator* on Roethke's "Root Cellar" (1971). He is an Associate Professor of English at Clermont General and Technical College, a branch of the University of Cincinnati.

Preface

When Theodore Roethke died in 1963 at the age of fifty-five, he had been writing poetry for about thirty-five years and in that time had never ceased developing as a poet. This book looks at the two hundred and two poems in Roethke's *Collected Poems* (ignoring the previously uncollected ones) as being divided into a number of sequences. In every book that Roethke published, he arranged his poems in numbered or titled series, each of which has a unifying principle. I will have achieved a major part of my present purpose if this book explains Roethke's overall development throughout his career, clarifies the unifying principles of the sequences discussed, places each poem meaningfully within its sequence, and, finally and most importantly, gives a reasonably full explication of those poems chosen for discussion.

Roethke began his career as a poet writing within a narrowly defined tradition and ended it as something quite different—an eclectic writer with diverse poetic idioms at his command. In his early work, he joined a number of American poets of the 1930s in writing rhymed and metered poems that epigrammatically expressed the anxieties of the time through images of personal sickness and guilt. After some years of resisting associational free verse, the kind of poetry most of his peers were writing, Roethke tried to make his work looser and to give it greater symbolic depth. The publication of his second book in 1948, *The Lost Son and Other Poems*, placed him almost immediately among the foremost of the experimentalists. But when Roethke began writing free verse, he did not cease writing traditional poetry. Throughout the rest of his career, he continued to write both kinds of poetry, sometimes even mixing them in a single poem.

More important, though, than Roethke's use of various prosodic forms was his growth in philosophical depth and complexity. Two events in Roethke's life lay at the heart of this growth and, in a sense, at the heart of all the themes of his poetry. When he was fourteen his father died. For the remaining forty-one years of his life, Roethke struggled to understand and express the overwhelming love and hatred he felt for the often tyrannical old florist. Twelve years later, one month after beginning his first teaching job, Roethke was hospitalized for a manic-depressive psychosis. The unresolvable feelings associated with his father's death and the recurrent outbreaks of this emotional illness were painful, so painful in fact that Roethke needed years of what I have called "circling toward the pain" before he could confront them directly.

If one thing more than anything else made possible Roethke's growth as a poet, it was his being able to face this pain, express it, and transform it into themes of universal significance. He accomplished this transformation by making the painful absence of his father symbolize the painful absence of God from his own life and the lives of many of his contemporaries. His search for his father, or for God, also took the form of a search for his own identity: was he a lost son living in a world given a semblance of meaning only by natural processes, a world ultimately ruled by death? Or was he a divinely created son who would finally return to his Father's "happy hands"?

Roethke's mental illness was perhaps even more difficult for him to deal with than was his sense of loss. He did so, though, by associating it with the search for God and for his own identity. The depressive phase of his emotional cycle came to symbolize his lostness, his sense of being imprisoned in a stifling world, as if in a grave. The manic phase, on the other hand, came to symbolize the euphoria or ecstasy he felt when he knew his Father (i.e., God) was present. Sometimes he felt this presence by a return, in memory, to the greenhouse he knew as a child; sometimes he felt it in a deeper, more mysterious, way.

The increasing depth and complexity of Roethke's themes partially followed a line of development characteristic of many romantic poets. He explored the differences between union with nature and union with a woman. He also went more deeply into the intricacies of perception, concentrating particularly on the ability of the human mind to shape what it sees. The romantic theory of perception tied into Roethke's central themes because he often skeptically considered signs of his Father's presence as illusions created by his own intense emotional needs. In his last book, *The Far Field* (1964), published the year after his death, he extended to its fullest the theme of the symbolic landscape, describing in great detail the "true place" that made his own soul visible. His very last poems suggest a turn toward Christianity, something he had long resisted.

The explanations of individual poems offered here are simply attempts to give commonsense readings of the more difficult and the more popular poems. When common sense seems—as it often does—to go against the spirit in which a poem was written, I turn to other poems, by Roethke or poets he read, to illuminate the poem at hand. Since Roethke was one of the most diligent readers of his contemporaries and of English poets of earlier centuries, comparing his poems with theirs is frequently the most useful way to understanding.

I have tried—probably without success—to avoid the trap that Roethke critics sometimes fall into of merely juggling the explanatory terms that he himself supplied. When a poet tells his readers that "to go forward as a spiritual man it is necessary first to go back" and that "the self, once perceived, *becomes* the soul," it is almost irresistibly tempting for an interpreter to "explain" a poem by ringing variations on these axioms. Finally, I hope that in discussing the unavoidable topic of the connections between Roethke's mental illness and his poems I have not sounded absurdly clinical.

GEORGE WOLFF

Clermont General and Technical College of the
University of Cincinnati

Acknowledgments

Chronology

1908   Theodore Roethke born May 25 in Saginaw, Michigan, to
Otto Roethke and Helen Huebner Roethke.

1922   Otto Roethke sells his share in the William Roethke Greenhouse to his brother Charles.

1923   February, Charles commits suicide. April, Otto Roethke
dies of cancer.

1929   Ted Roethke graduates with honors from the University of
Michigan in Ann Arbor.

1930-   Does graduate work at Harvard. Meets Robert Hillyer.
1931

1931-   Teaches at Lafayette College in Easton, Pennsylvania.
1935   Meets Rolfe Humphries, Stanley Kunitz, and Louise Bogan.

1935   September to November, teaches at Michigan State College
in East Lansing. Suffers first mental breakdown. Hospitalized from November till January, 1936.

1936   Awarded master's degree at University of Michigan.

1936-   Teaches at Pennsylvania State College
1943

1941   Rejected by United States Army because of hospitalization
for mental illness. *Open House* published. Meets W.H.
Auden.

1943-   Teaches at Bennington College in Vermont (on leave from
1946   Pennsylvania State College.) Meets Léonie Adams, Kenneth Burke, and Reinhold Niebuhr.

1943   August, teaches at Breadloaf Writers' Conference in Vermont. Meets Robert Frost.

1945   Awarded Guggenheim Fellowship.

1947   February, returns to Pennsylvania State College; spends
summer at Yaddo writers' colony and Breadloaf. September, begins teaching at University of Washington.

1948   *The Lost Son and Other Poems.*

1950   Awarded second Guggenheim Fellowship.

1951   *Praise to the End!*

1952-   Awarded Ford Fellowship.
1953

1953	January 3, marries his former student Beatrice O'Connell. *The Waking: Poems 1933-1953.*
1954	February, his mother dies. *The Waking* awarded the Pulitzer Prize.
1955-1956	Awarded a Fulbright Lectureship to Italy. Meets René Char.
1957	*Words for the Wind* published in England.
1958	*Words for the Wind* published in the United States and awarded the National Book Award and the Bollingen Prize.
1959	Roethke awarded second Ford Fellowship.
1961	*I Am! Says the Lamb.*
1963	August 1, Roethke dies suddenly in Seattle. *Sequence, Sometimes Metaphysical.*
1964	*The Far Field* (National Book Award Winner).
1966	*The Collected Poems of Theodore Roethke.*

CHAPTER 1

Circling toward the Pain: Open House

I *Roethke's Childhood*

THE Roethke family came to the United States in 1872 when Wilhelm Roethke, his wife, and three sons left their native Prussia to settle in Saginaw, Michigan[1]. They left behind the life of minor aristocrats: Wilhelm having served as head forester on the estate of Prince Bismarck's sister, Gräfin von Arnim, and his wife having served as keeper of the wine cellar. When the family arrived at Saginaw, they built and began operating what soon became the largest greenhouse in the United States, several buildings enclosing one quarter of a million square feet under glass.

One of the three sons did not stay long in the family business; but the other two, Charles and Otto, ran the firm until their deaths in the early 1920s. The older brother, Charles, had the profit-making instincts of a good businessman, but Otto was in the business because he loved flowers. He not only grew them to sell to customers but also experimented with breeding hybrid roses. His son, Theodore, later memorialized in several poems Otto's unbusinesslike devotion to the flowers.

Theodore Roethke was born on May 25, 1908, and his sister June was born five years later. As the poems that he wrote testify, his childhood in and around the greenhouses was lonely but filled with vivid impressions of the odors, textures, and sights that he found there. He observed closely and seems particularly to have noticed the differences between the plants that flourished and the ones that died. He was aware of the different qualities of the lives and fates of the plants—the hybrid roses on which his father lavished care, the bulbs lying neglected in a cellar, and the weeds that were sought out and destroyed. What all these impressions meant to him was something that he would take the rest of his life to discover and to give expression to in his poetry.

The importance to him of his father in this greenhouse world was even greater than that of the plants. Otto Roethke was a man who demanded from his son perfection in many different forms and who punished any failure with often unnecessarily harsh words and violent shakings. The poems do not record this aspect of the father's behavior, but several prose pieces written for college assignments do. Roethke wrote of how when he once, in childish absentmindedness, spat into a cistern, his father screamed at him, calling him a filthy child, and shook him as hard as he could.[2] Another time, when Roethke was fighting with a cousin who had spoken insultingly of Otto, Ted's father caught them and punished his son and would-be defender severely.[3] Memories such as these offset the loving admiration the boy felt for the man who cultivated his roses with such care.

Otto Roethke, being the son of a highly respected forester, prided himself on his abilities as a woodsman, and he expected his son to equal his own perfection in this regard. In an elegy, "Otto," written almost forty years after his father's death, Roethke praises his father's knowledge of the woodsman's lore. And in one of his college writing assignments he records a funny but painful memory of a time when he for once lived up to his father's expectations, at least in appearance. The boy had gone fishing by himself and had taken his father's best rod. After a long day with few results he hooked a large fish—which promptly yanked the rod out of his hand into the water. Roethke rowed around after the rod, but the fish kept towing it away. Eventually, the boy decided to wait until the fish tired and then row over to the rod. The tactic worked. When he got home, the frightened boy, used to proving he was a clumsy failure, blurted out that he had dropped his father's best rod into the lake. But before Otto could punish his son, one of the greenhouse workers interceded and pointed out that it was an old trick to let a big fish tire himself by dragging around a weight before hauling him in. Roethke never forgot the praise he then received from his father.

Theodore Roethke's mother was gentler than her husband but equally demanding. She was an immaculate housekeeper who insisted that her son keep his clothes clean. It is easy to imagine how she reacted to his special interest in types of manure used around the greenhouses. It is equally easy to see how her son developed a fear of appearing a sissy and cultivated a "tough-guy" mask that he wore on occasion throughout the rest of his life.

Although the Roethke floral business was very successful, the relationship between Charles and Otto deteriorated over the years. Another of Ted's college prose pieces describes his father as a long-suffering younger brother. Charles ruthlessly took advantage of him in a number of ways. He fired hard-working members of the family whom Otto liked and hired his own friends. He took his fifty-four percent of the company profits but shared the expenses fifty-fifty with Otto. He repeatedly berated Otto in front of their employees and members of the family, and yet he could always cajole Otto into doing whatever he wanted him to. But eventually Otto could not be cajoled any longer. He wanted to leave the business, and until his wife persuaded him otherwise he was going to turn over his share of the partnership to Charles without taking any payment. But when at his wife's promptings he examined the books in order to take his rightful share of the assets, he discovered that his brother had been embezzling. Charles had used company funds to buy gifts for one of the secretaries and had continued making gifts to her family after he married her. He lent company money back to the company and kept the six percent interest himself. Even after learning all this, Otto was not angry at his older brother, but neither would he rejoin the firm. Within a matter of weeks, Otto developed a mysterious illness that the doctors could not diagnose. Soon after the sale of the greenhouse in October, 1922, the business started to fail, and in February, 1923, Charles committed suicide. Three months later, in May, 1923, Otto Roethke died of the illness that the doctors explained only as a "kink in the bowels."[4]

Otto's son Ted did not outwardly show his grief, but the way that he turned to the subject of his father's death in his college writing assignments and returned to it in his poetry throughout his career leaves no doubt that he suffered deeply. And part of the problem was that he did not suffer only grief, an emotion that would eventually have been replaced by happy memories of the florist working among his flowers; his father's early death—Ted was fourteen—also deprived him of a chance to resolve those feelings that were even more painful than grief—the anger and perhaps hatred he felt toward the tyrant his father had sometimes been.

In writing poems dealing with his father's death, Roethke at first kept a tight formal control on his style and, by extension, on the dangerous emotional content that lurked far below the surface. But eventually he discovered that he could write moving poems by describing the physical details of life—and death—in the greenhouse, focusing on the plants but suggesting the presence of the old florist hovering in the background. Following this discovery came another one: that he could manage his emotions well enough in a loose, expressive style if he tempered them a bit by intellectualizing them. By this I mean that Roethke gradually transformed the loss, anger, and guilt stemming from his father's death into the kind of search for God that many stricken people undertake. Roethke may or may not have consciously considered this strategy (the evidence suggests he did), but this in effect is what happened. For him, his lost father came to represent the God that he and other twentieth-century Americans had lost. (The year in which Roethke's greenhouse world was shattered (1922), is also the year T. S. Eliot published his picture of a godless, dying civilization, *The Waste Land*.) Roethke's theme became not personal grief and guilt but the broader ideas of naturalism, scientific skepticism, and the difficulties, perhaps impossibilities, of religious faith. His emotionally charged handling of this theme carried him through and beyond the difficult time of establishing his reputation as a poet.

II *Roethke's Education*

During his schooling Roethke did not show signs of poetic talent, except perhaps on one occasion in high school. For an assignment he wrote a promotional essay describing the nature and goals of the International Red Cross that was translated into twenty-six languages. After his father's death, during his sophomore year in high school, Roethke became the "man" in the family. When he graduated from high school, he decided, against his mother's wishes, that he was going away to college. In the fall of 1925 he entered the University of Michigan at Ann Arbor.

Perhaps the most important thing he learned at Ann Arbor, at least as far as his later writing is concerned, was a deeper knowledge than he had previously had of the American Transcendentalists, especially of Ralph Waldo Emerson, Henry David Thoreau, and Walt Whitman. Before college he had formed a liking for these writers and had bought his own subscription to Scofield Thayer's *The Dial*, a revived version of a magazine originally founded by Emerson. But in college he learned what they had to say on a theme that he himself continued to explore throughout his poetic career, the search for identity. Like The Transcendentalists, he saw that the growth of a true identity was jeopardized by the apparently unlimited proliferation of society's institutions—government, big business, school systems, and organized religion—and by the way American society encouraged the spread of false individuality. Most people's demands for equality and for their rights were no more than a mask for greed and laziness, and in such a society part of the poet's task was to wake people up to their true self-interest.[5] Like the Transcendentalists Roethke also came to see that American society's striving for an ever higher standard of living was simply another name for materialism, what he later called making "a fetish of 'thinghood' " (*SP*, 19). He shared Emerson's and Thoreau's view that the unending quest for more possessions took the place of the difficult true growth of a person's spirit. Another important idea that he learned from the Transcendentalists was that it was possible to have powerful religious needs that could not be met by the doctrines and forms of worship of established churches. Roethke, like Emerson, spent most of his adult life searching for an idea of God that did not offend his intellectual honesty—or skepticism— and yet that offered hope of the one possession worth having, an immortal soul, a soul that was not merely one of nature's more complex physical processes.

Roethke's discovery that he was not to be a writer but a poet came about the time he graduated from the University of Michigan in 1929. Following his graduation he spent the year taking graduate courses in English at Harvard. While there he took some of his first poems to Robert Hillyer, a member of the faculty and an established poet. Hillyer praised the poems and soon after that Roethke began publishing (*SP*, 16).

In 1931, without finishing work on a degree at Harvard, Roethke began teaching English and coaching the tennis team at Lafayette College in Easton, Pennsylvania. It was here that he became the "teaching poet" that he was to be the rest of his life. During the four years he taught at Lafayette, he met a number of publishing poets who helped him toward the mastery of his craft, the most important ones being Stanley Kunitz, Louise Bogan, and Rolfe Humphries, all of whom became his close friends. Also during this time he perfected his considerable skills as a teacher. Teaching always remained for him a vital activity, second in importance only to poetry. The knowledge of poetry he gained from writing it he attempted to pass on to his students by any means that seemed to work. He let his students know what he thought of them as individuals and he expended tremendous emotional energy showing them what poetry was. This meant that he did not encourage what he called "text-creeping," a sort of priestly analysis of arcane texts that he despised in some colleagues, but that he made the students see what kind of person and what kind of emotional situation would give inevitable rise to the words of the poem at hand. He could recite many poems from memory and could refer immediately to any one of thousands more whenever doing so would shed light on the poem being discussed. Many of his students considered him the best teacher they had ever had.

In the fall of 1935 he began teaching at Michigan State College (now University) in East Lansing. For some reason when Roethke arrived there to begin teaching, he fell into a habit of drinking great quantities of Cokes, beer, and whiskey, accompanied by large doses of aspirin. One night in November, after about one month of teaching, he went walking in the woods near town and experienced what he felt was a mystical union with nature. Roethke's friend and biographer, Allan Seager, has quoted Roethke's own brief account of what happened: "For no reason I started to feel very good. Suddenly I knew how to enter into the life of everything around me. I knew how it felt to be a tree, a blade of grass, even a rabbit. I didn't sleep much. I just walked around with this wonderful feeling."[6] The next morning he went into the dean's office and declared, "I feel too good. Get me down off this." He was then hospitalized for the first of a number of times and granted a leave of absence without pay. At the end of the academic year, Michigan State College budget arrangements forced "readjustments in the personnel," and "for his own good and the College's" Roethke's appointment was not renewed. Following his release from the hospital in January, 1936, Roethke had his graduate credits transferred from Harvard to the University of Michigan and earned his master's degree there in that same year. In the fall of 1936 he began teaching and coaching the tennis team at the Pennsylvania State College (now University) in State College. He was teaching there when his first book, *Open House*, was published in 1941 (Roethke was thirty-three) and he retained his appointment there until 1946.

The death of his father and the recurring experience of manic-depressive psychosis are the two key emotional sources for most of the themes in Roethke's poetry. Both were painful to him in the extreme, and he needed years of circling toward them before he could express his feelings with any degree of openness. The two experiences merge in complex ways and both are made more manageable by being given abstract significance beyond the personal. The loss of his father becomes the loss of God, and the uncontrollable plunges from sanity into wild elation or utter despair take on the semblance of the mystic's successes and failures in the struggle to achieve union with God. Roethke was actually not a mystic in the sense of being a person who disciplined himself with the sole aim of union with God. He did, however, experience "presences," visions, and feeling-states that were out of the ordinary and that he was unwilling to dismiss as psychotic.

III   *Roethke's First Book,* Open House

Open House (1941), like all the books Roethke was to publish, is divided into groups or sequences of poems. In this first book, the common denominator of each of the five numbered sections is sufficiently difficult to define that the poems can be more profitably discussed according to recurring themes than by the numbered groups appearing in the book. If I did want to approach the book through Roethke's grouping of the poems, I would characterize the subject matter of the five groups as follows: the sick spirit, nature, the flesh and the spirit, sex and writing, and, finally, the problems of American society. But a more useful way to approach these poems is to see how Roethke circles toward the pain that lies beneath most of his themes, here and in the later works. The order of the poems in the following discussion is not that of the book, but one set up to emphasize the wariness with which Roethke approaches his overwhelming feelings about his father's death and his own mental illness. The five themes that recur throughout *Open House* are here arranged from the most emotionally distant to the one that most closely approaches the painful center. Though the themes are separated by analysis for the sake of clarity, in the poems they are interwoven so thoroughly that one never occurs without one or more of the others also being present. The themes, designated to stress their relation to the emotional center, are: natural description that carries an implication of something more, the poet's vision of something beyond the natural, the poet's powers of "invention" as a cure for an inherited curse, the defensiveness of the "spare spirit," and the horror of death and mental illness. All these reflect what one critic has described as the source of Roethke's writing: "Roethke was to find the themes of his work in the fluctuations and intensities of his own psyche. . . ."[7] That observation provides the most useful orientation for a reader of Roethke's poetry.

The best poems in *Open House* are ones that present a natural description laden with implications of another order of experience. For instance, "The Premonition," the very title of which refers to glimpsing the ominous future, describes a lone walker in the fields remembering a walk years earlier when he kept "close to the heels" of his father and sensed what the future held. When the two came to a river, his father dipped his hand into the water, and the son noticed how "Water ran over and under / Hair on a narrow wrist bone." This image evokes, not by statement but by implication, the father's physical vulnerability. The boy's "premonition" of his father's death is brought home by the last lines of the poem: "when he stood up, that face / Was lost in a maze of water."[8] The father's reflection is diffused when he draws back from the river's surface. The poem's distance from the pain and loss keeps it from being weakly sentimental, yet the emotion is undeniably acknowledged.

"The Light Comes Brighter" describes the details of a winter scene, again viewed by a lone walker, but this time one who looks directly into the future rather than doing so by way of the past. This is the first of many poems Roethke was to write presenting the wakened awareness that comes before an anticipated moment of change. Here the "walker at the river's edge may hear / A cannon crack announce an early thaw." But right now the "guarded snow is winter-sealed," and, slowly, "At bridgeheads buckled ice begins to shift. . . ." The light that is coming brighter with the approach of spring affects not only the external world of nature but the inner world of the human spirit:

> And soon a branch, part of a hidden scene,
> The leafy mind, that long was tightly furled,
> Will turn its private substance into green,
> And young shoots spread upon our inner world.   (*CP*, 11)

In what sense does a branch unfurl inside the mind? And what is a "leafy mind"? Roethke, as a reader of the American Transcendentalists, would have no trouble answering those questions. Thoreau's *Walden*, for instance, develops at length the idea of the correspondences between the private "substance" of our inner, mental, world and the public substance of the outer, leafy, one. One sentence from the first chapter of *Walden* seems especially germane to Roethke's poem: "They were the pleasant spring days, in which the winter of man's discontent was thawing as well as the earth, and the life that had lain torpid began to stretch itself." For Roethke as well as for Thoreau, spring does not come any more certainly to the rivers and trees than it does—undetermined by the calender—to the human mind and spirit. This poem is a hopeful picture of an emotional and spiritual renewal that Roethke feels in the offing.

"Night Journey," the last and perhaps best poem in *Open House*, also presents a natural scene that carries implications of something more. In fact, the value of the poem lies particularly in the subtlety and originality with which Roethke handles the implied meanings. The speaker, on a train heading west, "stares into the night." He passes "bridges of iron lace" and a "lap of mountain mist." From these two metaphors alone ("lace" and "lap") and from the possible pun in the reference to his train coach as a "Pullman berth" (a "pull-man" is an obstetrician, and "birth" is obvious), the reader may sense that "Night Journey" resembles "The Light Comes Brighter" in evoking or implying a renewal of life. And so it does, and this time the renewal is birth, not physical but emotional and spiritual birth. This sense is heightened by a bit of night-trainride description that could easily suggest an infant's physical sensations during birth, sensations corresponding to Roethke's abstract theme: "Full on my neck I feel / The straining at a curve, / My muscles move with steel, / I wake in every nerve." The world the poet (*and* the newborn child) sees is suddenly "washed with light," and despite the harshness of the wheels shaking "the roadbed stone," Roethke ends the poem with another picture of himself as a wakened, meditative watcher: "I stay up half the night / To see the land I love" (*CP*, 34). These poems of natural description with implications are the earliest examples in Roethke's poetry of what may be called poems of "symbolic landscape," a type of writing he developed more highly in each succeeding book he published. The full meaning of the term will be taken up later.

The second theme, one that approaches more closely the underlying emotional core of *Open House*, expresses Roethke's preoccupation—sometimes obsession—with the spiritual power of vision. In "Prayer" that power is contrasted with the fleshly limitations of the other organs of perception, and Roethke prays that if he must lose all but one of his senses he be allowed to keep his sight. He holds that "the Eye's the abettor of / The holiest platonic love" because "Its rape is gentle" (*CP*, 8). The way in which the eye "fitly serves" the Lord is made clear in "The Signals," a poem about signs from somewhere beyond the natural world. Roethke wrote often about such "clues to existence" (*SP*, 38), such hints of another order of reality, but he never permanently lost his skepticism about them or permanently believed that they were more than half-hints and fleeting intuitions. In "The Signals" he says, "Often I meet, on walking from a door, / A flash of objects never seen before." Whatever these signals are, "They slip between the fingers" of his sight, a metaphor indicating that the mind sees more than the eye beholds. In other words, vision is the mode of perception most amenable to the imagination, most likely to become visionary. The senses of hearing, tasting, and touching deal more corporeally with their objects, and what they perceive is therefore determined by external things to a greater degree than is vision, which is partially determined by the inner forces of the imagination. The last lines of the poem suggest that what is revealed actually comes from deep within the poet's psyche: "Sometimes the blood is privileged to guess / The things the eye or hand cannot possess" (*CP*, 8). As with the theme of the symbolic landscape, that of sight that becomes more than sight is one that Roethke continued to develop until the end of his career.

The third theme, that invention or creativity can cure an inherited curse, is one that grew out of Roethke's personal experiences with manic-depressive psychosis but, despite his continued attacks, is not often pursued in his later poetry.[9] The experiences that gave rise to this theme do find expression in other themes, though. Many of Roethke's friends and colleagues have testified that he had to keep writing poetry or his "whole personality would lose its recognizable shape."[10] Several poems in *Open House* suggest this absolute importance of poetic expression as a cure, and several others vividly describe the inherited disease itself. "Death Piece," for instance, implies that "invention" is coterminous with life itself: "Invention sleeps within a skull / No longer quick with light. . . ." The dead person's "thought is tied, the curving prow / Of motion moored to rock . . ."(*CP*, 4). One who is in such an "insentient" state can have no thoughts or feelings about that most emotionally charged of all subjects— death. Perhaps "Death Piece" shows Roethke mimicking death. For in the poem he expresses no feeling whatsoever about the dark, quiet loss of his own powers of invention.

Most of the *Open House* poems, though, do express considerable feeling. "Feud" describes the poet as a "darling of an infected brood" who feels "disaster" climbing in his veins. The internecine struggle between the living member of the family and "the dead" who "leap at the throat" is an early portrayal of what was to become Roethke's abiding concern with the effect the dead have on the living. Roethke reported that the poet John Peale Bishop read "Feud" and objected to the antagonistic relation between the living and the dead described in the poem: " 'You're impassioned, but wrong. The dead can help us!' And he [Bishop] was right; but it took me some years to learn that" (*SP*, 23). In many of Roethke's later poems, such as "Four for Sir John Davies," the presence of the dead aids him in the writing rather than threatens him as it does in here. "Feud" ends with a reference to another tactic that Roethke used, in addition to invention, to cure or at least stave off the inherited curse: "The spirit starves / Until the dead have been subdued" (*CP*, 4). The tactic referred to here constitutes the fourth recurring theme in *Open House*.

That fourth theme may be called the defensiveness of the spare spirit. This theme is a step closer to the emotional core than is the theme of the curative powers of creativity, because it acknowledges the danger of unrestrained expression of Roethke's painful memories of his father's death and painful fears for his own sanity. " 'Long Live the Weeds' " makes a move toward generalizing Roethke's personal curse into the biblical curse on Adam and Eve or on Cain (long live "All things unholy, marred by curse, / The ugly of the universe"), but it also expresses Roethke's sense of his own oddness ("The rough, the wicked, and the wild. . . . These shape the creature that is I," *CP*, 18). Generalizing an emotion, a form of the intellectualizing discussed earlier, acts as a restraint because it takes away some of the power of the emotion. It detaches the emotion from the self and allows it to be looked at and handled. It makes possible confessions about one's infirmities. It makes possible a new approach.

"Epidermal Macabre" is an even clearer, though more humorous, expression of Roethke's feud with his own fleshly self. The fact that as an adult Roethke was six feet three inches tall, weighed two hundred and forty-five pounds, and moved clumsily may have contributed to his feeling for this theme. In any case, Roethke begins "Epidermal Macabre" by admitting that "Indelicate is he who loathes / The aspect of his fleshy clothes. . . ." And halfway through the poem he concedes, "Yet such is my unseemliness: / I hate my epidermal dress, / The savage blood's obscenity, / The rags of my anatomy . . . (*CP*, 19).[11] And he concludes by wishing he could "sleep immodestly, a most / Incarnadine and carnal ghost." This time what the blood guesses is not as spiritually desirable as it is in "The Signals," which shows Roethke glimpsing the half-hints of a divine reality beyond physical nature; in "Epidermal Macabre" what is glimpsed is more like the inherited curse of "Feud." In "'Long Live the Weeds'" and "Epidermal Macabre," Roethke suggests that his only protection from the disease or curse that is wasting him is keeping his "spirit undefiled" and dispensing with "the false accouterments of sense." That is, he must control, repress, "match his wits" against, a vague enemy he associates with his own oddness and his own physical body and its desires.

In a talk entitled "On Identity," which Roethke gave in a panel discussion at Northwestern University in 1963, he quoted another poem on the theme of the spare spirit, "Open House," the title poem of the first volume, which is largely a boast:

> I'm naked to the bone,
> With nakedness my shield.
> Myself is what I wear:
> I keep the spirit spare.

At this point early in his career as a poet, he is, as he says in his comment on the poem, following the American Transcendentalists, especially Thoreau, and attempting to strip away all the subterfuges and disguises that society has encouraged him to develop. The last of the three stanzas makes this even clearer and alludes to the violent emotions that will then find expression: "I stop the lying mouth: / Rage warps my clearest cry / To witless agony" (*CP*, 3). Roethke's comment on this poem shows how much meaning he had packed into these lines and points the way toward his future development:

I was going through, though I didn't realize it at the time, a stage that all contemplative men must go through. This poem ["Open House"] is a clumsy, innocent, desperate asseveration. I am not speaking of the empirical self, the flesh-bound ego; it's a single word: *myself*, the aggregate of the several selves, if you will. The spirit or soul—should we say the self, once perceived, *becomes* the soul?—this I was keeping "spare" in my desire for the essential. But the spirit need not be spare: it can grow gracefully and beautifully like a tendril, like a flower. I did not know this at the time.(*SP*, 21)

This comment shows several things: Roethke's early tendency toward transforming his mental illness into something akin to mystical experience, his search for identity by allowing the self to grow into soul or spirit, and the importance of perception, particularly self-awareness, to this growth. But at the time of writing the poem, Roethke thought that the way to free his essential spirit was to pare away, to repress, the various selves and their desires that he associated with his physical existence. By denying the value of the body and its appetites, he was being more otherworldly than he would ever be again until the last poems in his final book.

In a review of *Open House*, the poet W. H. Auden called attention to the feud between Roethke's spirit and his flesh and praised the way Roethke created poetry out of the conflict: "Many people have the experience of feeling physically soiled and humiliated by life; some quickly put it out of their mind, others gloat narcissistically on its unimportant details; but both to remember and to transform the humiliation into something beautiful, as Mr. Roethke does, is rare."[12] This praise indicates that despite the painfulness of the emotions toward which Roethke was circling in *Open House*, he had not stayed so far away from them that a sympathetic reader would fail to sense their presence.

The fifth theme in *Open House* is that of the explicit statement of the horrors of madness and death. In several poems Roethke does not speak of tactics for containing or detoxifying the emotions at the core; he presents the emotions directly. "The Gentle" gives a brief but honest view of life in a hospital for the mentally ill:

> The son of misfortune long, long has been waiting
> The visit of vision, luck years overdue,
> His laughter reduced to the sing-song of prating,
> A hutch by the *EXIT* his room with a view.   (*CP*, 29)

The personal meaning in these lines can be glimpsed through the reappearance of the poet in the role of the "darling of an infected brood" and in that of the visionary loner waiting for a revelation or a hallucination, both roles being accompaniments of themes discussed earlier. Seldom in his poetry did Roethke confront directly, as he does here, the unpleasantness of being imprisoned within the walls of a hospital room in the mental ward. "On the Road to Woodlawn," another unblinking look at the source of pain, is a nightmarish vision of a burial and is very likely Roethke's attempt to deal with his memories of his father's death approximately fifteen years earlier. The poem begins by portraying the funeral procession in inappropriately lively terms ("I miss the polished brass, the powerful black horses"), but quickly turns to a picture of the inauthentic trappings, the "sentimental verses" on the "floral offerings," the "stale perfume," and "the mourners' anonymous faces." The last line of the poem, though, comes as a horrifying shock as the speaker looks down at an old-fashioned coffin with a glass window over the face of the body "—And the eyes, still vivid, looking up from a sunken room." This is Roethke's most jarring image of the grave, and it belongs to a larger category of images, those of threatening enclosure, that was to become in his second book, *The Lost Son and Other Poems*, an obsessively repeated concern.

Four years after the publication of *Open House* (1941), Roethke included in a letter to Kenneth Burke a self-evaluation: "My first book was much too wary, much too gingerly in its approach to experience; rather dry in tone and constricted in rhythm."[13] Possibly the cause for that wariness and dryness lies deeper than mere inexperience as a poet. It may lie in the understandable difficulty any writer would have in confronting and publicly expressing unresolved grief and guilt caused by a father's death and by an outbreak of severe mental illness.

Open House was well received by the reviewers. Auden, in the review already quoted, declared it "completely successful."[14] Several reviewers, the established poet Louise Bogan among them, praised Roethke's gift for epithet and his craftsmanship.[15] But many of them advised the new poet to "show greater boldness" and expand his technical range.[16] And that is exactly what he did when he began work on poems for his second book.

CHAPTER 2

Sprouts of Identity: The Greenhouse Poems

I *Preparation for the Second Book*

THE years between 1936, when Roethke began teaching at
Pennsylvania State College, and 1948, when his second book,
The Lost Son and Other Poems, was published, were a time of
personal turmoil and accomplishment. The fact that World War II
occurred during these years could never be guessed from Roethke's
poetry, but the poems do record something of his private battles.
Following his first mental breakdown in Lansing in October, 1935,
he was released from Ann Arbor's Mercywood Hospital in January.
He was awarded his master's degree by the University of Michigan
at the end of the academic year and in the fall took up his teaching
and tennis coaching position in State College, Pennsylvania. In the
late 1930s he wrote book reviews and prepared for the publication
of *Open House*. It was also during this period that he met and
formed a close, lasting friendship with a poet who influenced his
early work very considerably, W. H. Auden. The year in which his
first book was published and in which the United States declared
war on Japan, Roethke was rejected by the armed services because
of his stay at Mercywood.

In 1943 he was granted a leave of absence from Pennsylvania
State University so that he could accept the honor of a visiting
professorhip at one of the best small liberal arts schools in the
country, Bennington College in Vermont. Here he met the poet
Léonie Adams, who influenced some of his early work to such an
extent that he called one of his poems a "literary love child" of
theirs (*SP*, 65-66). And even more important for Roethke's growth
as a poet, he met the critic Kenneth Burke, whom he called "Papa"
for the rest of his life. Roethke's letters show that Burke contributed
significantly, if only as a sounding board, to the poetic breakthrough

that Roethke achieved in 1945. Both 1944 and 1945 were years of gestation, in which Roethke published only one new poem. But with the apparently sudden discovery of not one but two new poetic modes (those of the Greenhouse Poems and the Lost Son Narratives), Roethke's life began to change rapidly. He won a Guggenheim Fellowship in 1945 and in the same year was asked to leave Bennington because of an affair he was conducting with a student.[1] He began writing at a furious rate, publishing nine new poems in 1946. The culmination of the turmoil was another mental breakdown, like that he suffered in 1935, and again he was hospitalized, and this time given electroshock.[2] After his release from the hospital in January, 1946, he returned to Saginaw where he spent the spring and summer writing, financed by his Guggenheim grant. He taught part of the 1946-1947 academic year at Pennsylvania State, but in February resigned his post there and in the fall began teaching at the University of Washington in Seattle, a post he retained until his death in 1963.

In March, 1948, *The Lost Son and Other Poems* was published. Since this volume includes the two sequences that represent Roethke's greatest break with his own earlier poetic practices, the present chapter will not treat the entire second book but will confine itself to the first of these sequences, the poems that Roethke called "News of the Root" while he was working on them but that have been called the Greenhouse Poems since their first publication. The longer, experimental narratives will be treated in the next chapter.

Whether it was on the advice of the reviewers of *Open House* or on the promptings of his own intuitions as a poet, between 1941 and 1948 Roethke knew with ever-growing certainty where he was headed in his development. He stated his goals for his second book many times. For instance, in 1945, when he was deep into his new work, he wrote in the letter to Kenneth Burke quoted earlier: "I am trying to loosen up, to write poems of greater intensity and symbolical depth" (*SL*, 114). He described another thing he hoped to achieve, in an application for a summer term at Yaddo writers' colony,[3] in which he wrote that he wished to pursue the direction he had embarked on in the first several Lost Son Narratives:"I wish to go beyond these poems. This means going into myself more deeply and objectifying more fully what I find, probably in a dramatic poem that could be staged" (*SL*, 126, n.). Roethke worked for many years, sometimes in collaboration with playwright Lillian Hellman, on a stageable play. But though he never achieved that goal, he did achieve a nonstageable kind of drama in the Greenhouse Poems and in the Lost Son Narratives.

What did Roethke mean by the "looseness," the "greater symbolical depth," and the "drama" that he hoped to get into his poetry after *Open House?*

By "looseness" he meant the fluctuations in rhythm and line length that accompanied the changes in his own perceptions. As a poem unfolded line after line, its rhythmic movements could reflect the alterations in the speaker's perceptions, ideas, and emotions, that is, in all the movements of his mind and spirit. Such fluctuations, which are typical of the free-verse poetry that Roethke had at first scorned, replaced the predetermined, beat-counted line lengths of *Open House.* Throughout the rest of his career he was to favor the free-verse forms that he discovered in the early 1940s, but he never ceased to use the fixed metrical line and the rhyme scheme that accompanied it whenever he found them advantageous.

By "greater symbolical depth" Roethke meant that the images in the new poems were to create a "genuine imaginative order out of what comes from the unconscious . . ."(*SL*, 129)[4]. He was now making a much more purposeful effort than previously to confront and express the painful emotions that lay behind the themes of his poetry. What some of the meanings of these symbols are will be discussed in connection with particular poems.

By "drama" Roethke meant the direct presentation of the mind of the speaker of a given poem. The "drama" of the Greenhouse Poems and the Lost Son Narratives differs from the discursive talk about emotions seen in most of the *Open House* poems. It also differs from the meditative mode that he was to move into after the narratives, most obviously in the "Meditations of an Old Woman." The drama of the speaker's mind may be said to be the drama of Roethke's mind by a legitimate extension of terminology. The speaker of the Greenhouse Poems and of the narratives is a boy who matures as each sequence develops, and his similarities to Roethke are undeniable. He, too, is the son of a greenhouse owner who loves roses and who dies. The child's mind that Roethke dramatizes is inseparable from his personal memories of his own childhood and youth. The important point is that the drama lies in his regressions into the terrifying parts of his past, regressions in which his painful emotions threaten to overwhelm him, and in his sudden progressions into a greater maturity. One of Roethke's most frequent explanations of the drama he was trying to achieve in these two sequences is this: "I believe that to go forward as a spiritual man it is necessary first to go back. . . . There is a perpetual slipping-back, then a going-forward; but there is *some* 'progress' " (*SP*, 39). Going deeper into the unconscious is going backward in time to earlier emotions that have been repressed because of their painful nature. Such unconscious emotions can disrupt a person's life, as they did Roethke's, by causing psychotic upheavals. They can also be dealt with and relieved—and relived—by someone as honest and as persistent as Roethke.

II   *The Way into the Greenhouse*

The most important means by which Roethke lets his reader know that the Greenhouse Poems have more than a literal meaning is by their arrangement in a sequence from birth to death. The first two titles are "Cuttings" and "Cuttings *later*," which refer to the common method of propagating plants by cutting a piece off an established plant and putting it in a rooting medium where it begins a new life of its own. The series then describes (in "Root Cellar," "Forcing House," "Weed Puller," and "Orchids") various ways in which during the raising of the plants some are forced to grow while others lie neglected and still others are destroyed. After five poems about the very chancy attainment of maturity ("Moss Gathering," "Big Wind," "Old Florist," "Transplanting," and "Child on Top of a Greenhouse"), the series ends with two views of death ("Flower Dump" and "Carnations"). The order of the poems does not rigidly follow the life-cycle, and it is possible to view the sequence in different ways. What is essential, however, is to see that the poet has arranged the poems and that that arrangement points toward a symbolic level of meaning.

What is this symbolic meaning? In a way, that very natural question is misleading. It implies that there is a single right answer that everyone can agree upon, and of course that is not the case. The symbols often have the meanings they have in traditional symbolism, but Roethke is also using them in the exploration of his personal past and in doing so is extending their meanings. As he himself has said, "the symbols will mean what they usually mean— and sometimes something more" (*SP*, 42). Certain difficulties in understanding arise because, when the symbols take on this personal meaning, they are expressing things that lie beyond the verge of consciousness and are expressing shadowy and shifting emotional and spiritual states.

Thus the symbolism in the Greenhouse Poems is a suggestive parallel constantly running below the surface, a vaguely felt metaphorical meaning that is never quite made explicit. Kenneth Burke, whom Roethke asked to "run interference" for this first attempt at nontraditional poetry, describes this kind of symbolism when he calls these poems "the imagistic figuring of a human situation."[5] In other words, the images metaphorically present emotional events. But when a reader looks for references to human beings, he finds that six of the fourteen poems have no such references and that two others are essentially devoid of people. Only six poems refer explicitly to the human presence in the plants' world. Clearly, the absence of human beings is more striking than their presence, and what the reader must do in order to understand how poems in which there are no human beings can be about human emotions is to look for the *implied* human presence. The following readings of particular poems will stress that implied presence.

One more general comment before turning to the poems. What the implied human presence means cannot be discovered by simply equating the life-cycle of the plants with the human life-cycle, as several commentators have mistakenly done. The key is that the quality of life the plants experience reflects the quality of the emotional and spiritual life of the poet. And the poet in these poems (the speaker of the words) is not merely a middle-aged English professor with a history of emotional disturbance, but more importantly he is the son of the greenhouse owner, a boy who is in danger of becoming a lost son. When Roethke uses memories as material for a poem, he becomes his earlier self. Since we may assume that he is in his own father's greenhouse, he is not literally but figuratively lost. The most important fact about the quality of his emotional and spiritual life is that he is cut off, alienated, from his parents, especially from his father. What the boy sees in the plants is thus a reflection of his own struggle to survive and grow.

III   *Some Individual Greenhouse Poems*

"Cuttings," the first poem in the series, is a still life, with emphasis on the *still*, in two senses of the word. The picture is one of a great stillness in which the newly planted cuttings dry off after being sprayed, the only motion seeming to be the water being coaxed upward inside their miniscule veins. But one visible movement tells the watcher that after their perilous birth there is still (i.e., continuing) life:

> One nub of growth
> Nudges a sand-crumb loose,
> Pokes through a musty sheath
> Its pale tendrilous horn.   (*CP*, 37)

"Cuttings" is one of the poems in which the human presence is only implied. The adult greenhouse workers, who are parental figures for the plants and for the boy, are present only in their effects: they have made the cuttings; in a sense, they have given birth to the new plants. Since the boy who is the observer and speaker throughout the series does not refer to himself in "Cuttings," his presence is also only implied. But what is important about his implied presence is that he watches with a strange emotional intensity.

Two of Roethke's prose statements help clarify what is going on here. Almost twenty years before the writing of this poem, Roethke wrote a piece called "Some Self-Analysis" for a college writing class, in which he described accurately a talent that contributed to the breakthrough he made in his poetic style in 1945: "I can sense the moods of nature almost instinctively . . . . A perception of nature—no matter how delicate, how subtle, how evanescent,—remains with me for ever"(*SP*, 4). And then in 1946, the year in which "Cuttings" was written, Roethke noted in a book review that images when they are intensely seen become symbols: "The visible and the invisible meet and reside in the powerfully observed"(*SP*, 122).

His sense of awe—that the tiny visible motion was caused not by an inorganic, mechanical process like evaporation but by some interior miracle that can be called life—suggests that he not only "powerfully observes" but feels a close bond with this frail, struggling bit of life. As yet he does not raise the question of whether he should curse or bless the day of his and the plants' birth. That comes in the next poem.

"Cuttings *later*" shows the boy becoming aware of the pain suffered by the plants during their birth; he sees the cruelty in the word "cuttings." In this poem the stillness of the preceding poem is broken by the sound of "sucking and sobbing," a sound not heard by the ears but felt deep within: "In my veins, in my bones I feel it." To his mind the plants are like Christian martyrs in their heroic struggle to rise to a new life. And perhaps like a Christian watching a martyrdom, he is frightened but drawn: "I quail, lean to beginnings, sheath-wet" (*CP*, 37). The emotion here owes its intensity to the boy's seeing his own inner life reflected or symbolized in the lives of the plants. They, like him, have had their separate lives thrust upon them by apparently cruel, all-powerful beings, who now leave them to survive as best they, and he, can.

One of Roethke's notebook entries, written about the time of the composition of this poem, says this about the greenhouse world: "What was the greenhouse? . . . It was order & disorder; Was it an escape? No, for it was a reality harsher than reality."[6] Part of that harshness comes from the fact that the child and later the adult poet who returns to the greenhouse in memory are both looking honestly at painful emotions, at the fear of being a lost son.

"Root Cellar," the third poem of the series, not only describes but in its grammatical structure enacts an enclosure in which the forces of life are almost evenly matched by the threat of the inanimate. The poem describes an underground room where bulbs, leaf-mold, manure, and lime are stored. The poet's memory of the root cellar is sensuous and focused, but detached. The poems before and after "Root Cellar" are in the present tense, but it is in the past tense. What the poet remembers is that even in the dark he saw how "Shoots dangled and drooped, / Lolling obscenely from mildewed crates." He smelt the "congress of stinks" and felt the "slippery planks." He even heard the very dirt "breathing a small breath."

The focal point where all these sensuous details converge is the idea that the root cellar, as well as perhaps the negligence of the greenhouse workers (the parental figures), seems inimical to life; but yet the place is crawling with growing things. The implied human presence of the adults, or at least the effect of their actions, is seen in the dark, gravelike enclosures to which they have apparently relegated the unwanted plants. And it is essential for the reader to keep in mind that the boy sees his own spiritual condition, its origin and fate, in the plants. An examination of the words in the poem that name man-made things reveals that all but "congress" refer to forms of enclosures, prisons that threaten to become graves: the *cellar* itself, "dank as a *ditch*," the *boxes* and "mildewed *crates*" in which the bulbs have been left. But despite these stifling enclosures, the living plants are triumphant. The first and last lines of the poem, which because of their similarity to each other form a kind of enclosure for the center of the poem, emphasize this ascendancy of the miraculously living over the threatening nonliving. The first line is: "Nothing would sleep in that cellar, dank as a ditch. . . ." The last two lines are grammatically and semantically similar to that line: "Nothing would give up life: / Even the dirt kept breathing a small breath" (*CP*, 38). This repetition of line beginnings is an example of what in biblical poetry is called "the envelope technique" and can also be seen in Roethke's "Elegy for Jane," discussed later. The last lines of "Root Cellar" are biblical, too, in their evocation of the Genesis description of God breathing the breath of life into a man of clay.

"Forcing House" shows the plants when they are being given almost excessive care, in contrast to the bulbs in the root cellar. The workers have put the tropical vines, "rubbery shoots," cannas, and cyclamen in the hottest, most humid part of the greenhouse to hasten their growth. These plants, along with the ever-present mildew, pulsate in rhythm with the pipes of the heating system. In fact, as in the preceding poems, the more intently the poet looks at the line between the living and the nonliving, the more that line seems to blur. In "Forcing House" the reader cannot be sure whether the heating pipes or the capillaries in the plants are "Shooting up lime and ground bones." Is that line an image of an organic or an inorganic process? This doubling of vision continues in the next two lines, which conclude the poem: "Fifty summers in motion at once, / As the live heat billows from pipes and pots"(*CP*, 38). A span of time is transformed into an object in motion, things that cannot occur simultaneously do so, and the life-giving heat begins to live itself. The intensity of the life-force sometimes seems to overwhelm everything.

"Weed Puller," the fifth of the series, is one of the few Greenhouse Poems not anthologized, yet it is a helpful guide to the meaning of the entire sequence. In this poem the boy has reached the age at which he can help his father by pulling out unwanted vines and weeds that spring up beneath the concrete benches on which the flowers grow. The boy, though, instead of feeling proud of his role, feels he has been relegated to a kind of root cellar of his own. As he works down in the muck, he is not like the cared-for flowers blooming above him, the "Lilies, pale-pink cyclamen, roses, / Whole fields lovely and inviolate. . . ." On the contrary, he is a nameless one, like the mere weeds and "fern-shapes," a piece of "perverse life," who belongs

> down in that fetor of weeds,
> Crawling on all fours,
> Alive, in a slippery grave.   (*CP*, 39)

These are the last lines of the poem, and they express the same
contraries seen in "Root Cellar"—the threatening enclosure, here
named as the grave, and the counterthrust of perverse life that, like
a defiant child, will not give up.

The importance of "Weed Puller" to the understanding of the
entire sequence lies in the clarity with which the symbolic meanings
come through. The boy unmistakably identifies with the lower
forms of plant life, especially those that must constantly fight to stay
alive. His spiritual and emotional distance from his father, the
florist, at this stage is as great as the difference between the
nameless "webs and weeds" and the fields of "lovely and inviolate"
flowers.

"Big Wind," the eighth poem of the series, describes an actual
incident that occurred when Roethke was young. During a severe
winter windstorm, the Titabawasee River was blown away from the
intake pipes for the Saginaw water supply, and the town was
without water for the night. The resulting lack of water was
especially serious for the Roethkes, who had a large greenhouse full
of roses that were kept warm and alive by steam heat. The family
struck upon the ingenious idea of circulating liquid fertilizer
through the waterless heating pipes and in this way saved their roses
and saved themselves from a heavy financial loss. In this poem the
boy has matured appreciably beyond his days as a weed puller and
has achieved a kind of rapproachment with his father. He proudly
works alongside the adults throughout the night, trying to save the
roses. The important human presence is made explicit in the word
we, and the human beings show themselves to be ingenious, perse-
vering, and selfless. Their ingeniousness can be seen in the use of
liquid fertilizer in the heating system: "So we drained the manure-
machine / For the steam plant. . . . " Their perseverance can be
seen in their staying all night, "stuffing the holes with burlap
. . . ." And their selflessness can be seen in the rose-house's being
given credit for saving the flowers, with the human beings taking
their customary place in the background:

> But she rode it out,
> That old rose-house,
> She hove into the teeth of it,

> The core and pith of that ugly storm,
> Ploughing with her stiff prow,
> Bucking into the wind-waves. . . .

This is one of the few Roethke poems in which adults are pictured with unqualified approval. They allow the boy to work with them, yet in his view their presence and their labor are displaced by the rose-house itself.

"Big Wind" uses the same kind of metaphoric description as "Forcing House," distorting the realistic picture in order to create a more vivid one. Here the stationary greenhouse is transformed into a moving ship and the storm into the ocean. This metaphoric view leads to the poem's beautiful conclusion, in which the wind-waves are "Finally veering, wearing themselves out, merely / Whistling thinly under the wind-vents. . . ." And the rose-house has at last ". . . sailed into the calm morning, / Carrying her full cargo of roses" (*CP*, 41). The metaphoric transformation of time into space—dawn being seen as a calm expanse of ocean—continues an important technique begun in "Forcing House." This distortion of time and space usually accompanies the miraculous triumph of life over the forces that would return it to inanimate existence. Many times when this poem is published, the distortion is taken out of the last lines by a misprinting that has the rose-house sailing *until* the morning, a less exciting image than that of the stationary greenhouse over which a storm has passed being seen as a ship sailing into a calm expanse of sea that is actually the dawn.[7] In any case, the achieved serenity, the closeness to Papa, is a new state for the boy, and it is one he will struggle to return to in the Lost Son Narratives.

"Frau Bauman, Frau Schmidt, and Frau Schwartze," the tenth Greenhouse Poem, is the only one that refers explicitly to the poet's present adult life and to the fact that these pictures of the greenhouse world are drawn from memory.[8] Other poems, like "Root Cellar," only imply the separation between event and poem by being in the past tense. In this poem the poet recalls to life "the three ancient ladies" who worked in the greenhouse and who gave him as a boy the attention and affection he so much needed. Like the boy's father, the old florist, they seemed to work miracles with the plants they cared for:

> Their hands twinkling with wet;
> Like witches they fl w along rows

> Keeping creation at ease;
> With a tendril for needle
> They sewed up the air with a stem;
> They teased out the seed that the cold kept asleep. . . .

But unlike the boy's father, though, they gave the boy as much attention as they gave the plants. And the effects of that attention are present in the adult poet, present in ways that are more profound even than memory. Just as they "teased out" the cold seeds, they also helped the boy in his growing, and their caring is still with him as an adult:

> Now, when I'm alone and cold in my bed,
> They still hover over me,
> . . . .
> [with] their snuff-laden breath blowing lightly over me
>   in my first sleep.   (*CP*, 44)

These concluding lines of the poem are reminiscent of the last line of "Root Cellar": "Even the dirt kept breathing a small breath." Both endings suggest that the boy and the adult poet can draw strength from the Genesis conception of life as a gift from a fatherlike God. In "Frau Bauman, Frau Schmidt, and Frau Schwartze," it is not the father who lightly breathes the breath of life over his sleeping son, but at least it is his representatives. Roethke the adult awakens into a dream in which the comforting presence of "these ancient leathery crones" replaces the cold loneliness of his ordinary waking life. In writing the poem he has recalled them to life, and their felt presence breathes new life into him.

"Flower Dump," the thirteenth poem of the series, deals with death. If most of the preceding poems focus on the boy's awareness of struggling forms of life, whether neglected or tended, "Flower Dump" reasserts the power of death and the frailty of life. It describes the pile where the "inviolate" flowers ("Carnations, verbenas, cosmos") and the weeds end up. Viewed in relation to the implied human presence, the poem suggests that the adults side with the leveler death, who indiscriminately destroys flowers and weeds. The greenhouse workers pitch them all together, and in fact become so indiscriminate that they sometimes dispose of the living along with the dead:

> Everything limp
> But one tulip on top,
> One swaggering head
> Over the dying, the newly dead.   (*CP*, 43)

These concluding lines stress the poet's sharp sense of the contraries that have informed the entire series: frail life struggling to preserve itself "in a slippery grave."

"Carnations," the last poem, is Roethke's earliest picture of an emotional and spiritual unity that transcends time and the contraries of animate and inanimate, of life and death. It describes the cool part of the greenhouse where the carnations thrive. It also evokes the stillness of "Cuttings" with which the sequence begins and the serenity that comes at the end of "Big Wind." "Carnations" in several ways suggests a state of eternal peace, not, of course, a state which the boy will occupy permanently, but one that seems somehow to be above time, to be a moment out of time. As long and as laboriously as Roethke struggled toward a perfect, unending spiritual state, which can best be described as union with God, the Father, his poetry never lays claim to such an achievement. He felt that he had many times experienced "oneness, . . . the first stage of mystical illumination," but he also said, "I can't claim that the soul, my soul, was absorbed in God" (*SP*, 26). "Carnations," then, presents not a union of the boy with his father but a state of illumination in which the boy transcends the contraries of life and death, of parental care and parental negligence, and of being a weed puller and helping to fight the big wind.

Just as the grammar of "Root Cellar" reinforces the imagery of a threatening enclosure constricting the living bulbs and shoots, so the grammar of "Carnations" reinforces the picture of timeless peace. The seven lines of the poem are punctuated as a single sentence, but it is a sentence with no main verb. The carnations do not exist in the past, or future, and are therefore in a sense timeless.

The final image employs the same kind of spatial and temporal distortion seen in "Forcing House" and "Big Wind." The peace that comes with the escape from time and its contraries is pictured in the last lines:

> A crisp hyacinthine coolness,
> Like that clear autumnal weather of eternity,
> The windless perpetual morning above a September cloud. (*CP*, 43)

Words like "autumnal," "weather," "morning," and "September" remind the reader of the changeable world of time that has been left behind. But in this unearthly realm, the weather does not change and morning does not decline into day—a beautiful and effective conclusion for the series.

CHAPTER 3

The Pain and the Loss:
The Lost Son Narratives

I "Open Letter"

A S mentioned in the preceding chapter, four poems from *The Lost Son and Other Poem*, including the title poem, were not discussed with the other poems in that volume but reserved for a chapter of their own. One reason for postponing the discussion is that those poems became, in Roethke's third book, *Praise to the End!* (1951), part of a fourteen-poem sequence divided into two sections of six and eight poems, and this sequence deserves a thorough discussion. These are the experimental narratives that Roethke wrote between 1945 and 1951, and they are different from anything he wrote before or after this time. Since they present the reader with many difficulties, it is wise to use as a guide an introduction that Roethke wrote to accompany two of the narratives.

In 1950 the poet and critic John Ciardi included eight of Roethke's poems in the anthology *Mid-Century American Poets* and introduced them with an "Open Letter" from Roethke.[1] Ignoring six of the poems, Roethke's statement discusses only the two experimental narratives, "The Lost Son" and "The Shape of the Fire," and the planned sequence of which they were to be a part.

"Open Letter" advises the reader to listen to these poems—to read them aloud, listening to the rhythms, to the music of the vowels and consonants, and to the tones of voice. "Open Letter" warns the reader not to attempt a logical analysis, because that mode of understanding, like the eyepiece of a microscope, narrows the field of vision. It prevents him from glimpsing loose associations among the images and from responding to the unconventional cues to the speaker's emotional states. Instead, the reader should keep his "whole being awake, [his] faculties loose and alert." With this "childlike" approach, the reader should find the admitted obscurities bursting into clarity and should find himself inside the mind of a child. As Roethke said: "Rhythmically, it's the spring and rush of the child I'm after. . . ." And, it must be emphasized, rhythm is the most important key to these poems, signaling as it does the speaker's change from one state of mind to another. The various rhythms, of course, are part of the overall musical qualities of the narratives, and those qualities in turn form part of the structure and themes.

The structure of each of the poems, says "Open Letter," is like that of a piece of music, the themes developing in alternation and no logical or narrative connections tying them together. Rather than following a story line or an argument, this "psychic shorthand" follows the increases and decreases in tension between emotional states. For instance, is a pond filled with algae and "bug-riddled foliage" disgusting or is it a wealth of biological miracles? The answer, of course, depends entirely on the state of mind of the person looking at the pond. And, within any person—especially in a Roethke poem—the mental set can suddenly shift from one state to an opposing one. As an extension of this fact, in these fourteen poems, the protagonist, the lost son, is cursed and blessed with an emotional life that is repeatedly placed under such great stress that it veers between euphoria and spiritual annihilation, between ecstasy and a desire for death. Such structural "incoherence" confronts the reader with an array of difficulties.

Another source of difficulty for the reader is the juxtaposing of experiences, some similar to, others contrasting with, each other. This juxtaposing is actually another form of the tensions Roethke creates between logically unconnected parts of the poems. Each of the narratives follows in "psychic shorthand" a series of problems that usually moves toward a resolution at the end of the poem. The lost son's frantic searching and his repeated temporary discoveries of peace are defined in "Open Letter" by the statement that "Disassociation often precedes a new state of clarity." The frenetic, at times incoherent, boy moves toward an understanding and acceptance of himself and his pain, the pain of the loss of his father through death and the pain of his own mental instability. The understanding and acceptance resemble the spiritual state of finding and being reconciled with his father, in memory and in felt presence if not in literal fact.

"Open Letter" says that each narrative is a "struggle out of the slime, a part of a slow spiritual progress" and that the sequence as a whole forms a "history of the psyche." Elsewhere Roethke has described the sequence as "a kind of tensed-up *Prelude*" (*SL*, 148), a reference to Wordsworth's *Prelude*, the subtitle of which is "The Growth of a Poet's Mind, An Autobiographical Poem." This subtitle could easily serve as the title of Roethke's sequence. The title of the book in which this sequence first appeared in its entirety, *Praise to the End!*, is borrowed from the first book of Wordsworth's *Prelude*, this exclamation coming at the end of a passage that could provide a capsule summary of the growth of both poets' minds. Since that summary applies so perfectly to Roethke's sequence, I will quote it at length:

> Dust as we are, the immortal spirit grows
> Like harmony in music; there is a dark
> Inscrutable workmanship that reconciles
> Discordant elements, makes them cling together
> In one society. How strange, that all
> The terrors, pains, and early miseries,
> Regrets, vexations, lassitudes interfused
> Within my mind, should e'er have borne a part,
> And that a needful part, in making up
> The calm existence that is mine when I
> Am worthy of myself! Praise to the end!   (*I*, 340-350)

The "end" that is being praised by Wordsworth is that calm unity in which all contraries, all discordant elements, are reconciled, and it is the end toward which both Wordsworth and Roethke moved. Roethke, always aware of being dust and sometimes aware of the growth of his "immortal spirit," marveled that his "early miseries" could be assimilated into the tranquillity toward which he periodically felt himself growing. Jenijoy La Belle, in a study of Roethke's use of other poets, explains how Wordsworth in *The Prelude* and Roethke in the narratives "journey" from the particulars of their private experiences toward the "huge and mighty Forms" of visionary or "trans-personal" experience.[2] Such explanations may be interesting, but easily begin to require more explaining than what it is they are trying to explain.

"Open Letter" describes the spiritual progress of the lost son as "an effort to be born, and later, to become something more." Part of that something more is that as an adult he becomes a poet who can record the growth of his own mind. "Open Letter" speaks somewhat mysteriously of the lowest point away from which he struggles and grows, calling it "the mire," "the slime," and "the Void." This low point actually is the state of "lostness," of being cut off from his father, both his earthly father and God. It is also a state of despair in which the lost son believes that his own origin and the origin of life generally is not divine creation but merely a chance happening in the chemical processes of nature. When "Open Letter" speaks of "the struggle to be born," it is referring to the boy's overcoming his naturalistic (as opposed to a supernaturalistic) vision of life and death. Furthermore, the boy's progress is "cyclic," meaning, as pointed out earlier, that "to go forward as a spiritual man [or as a lost son] it is necessary first to go back." The landmarks along this path of progress and regression are symbols that have both traditional and personal meanings. These will be discussed in connection with particular poems.

One final way in which "Open Letter" helps the reader overcome some of the difficulties of the narratives is by providing a list of literary ancestors. If the experimental character of these poems seems to make them incomprehensible, the reader would do well to view them in the light of one or more of the following: German and English folk literature, "particularly Mother Goose"; the songs and rants of Elizabethan and Jacobean drama; the Bible; and the works of the English poets Thomas Traherne and William Blake. Even a reader who has no detailed acquaintance with these literary ancestors might assume from this list that when he reads the narratives he will be entering a world that is childlike, violent, and religious.

II   *Some Particular Lost Son Narratives*

Standing like a guard at the beginning of the sequence of narratives, "Where Knock Is Open Wide" challenges the reader with lines as bizarre as any Roethke ever wrote (*CP*, 71-73).[3] But anyone who reads the poem aloud will hear the disjointed strangeness with which the poem begins give way to a beautiful description of a boy and his father fishing and that in turn give way to the pain the boy feels later when his father dies. Unlike many poems in the sequence, this one does not end with a resolution of the lost son's problem of achieving "a new state of clarity." It ends, rather, with the loss of an innocent world in which he knew nothing of death.

The title "Where Knock Is Open Wide" is a line from "A Song of David" by the eighteenth-century English poet Christopher Smart, in whose poem a state of deathless innocence is being described in the passage where the words occur. But the child in Roethke's poem is already in the process of learning that the world is not just the way he would have it. What he has not yet learned, though, is that the small pains and frustrations with which he can easily cope are only slight clues to what is in store for him. He learns that a kitten can "Bite with his feet" and that Papa and Mama can hurt by not having time to listen. But these pains, and even the grief caused by the loss of an uncle who is "gone for always" (a clear foreshadowing of his father's death), can be crooned away: "I sing a small sing / . . . I sang I sang all day." In this state of innocence, when the child begins to feel "lost," he prays to be "fished out," and his God-like father gives him "a near": "Hello happy hands." The phrase "a near," which Kenneth Burke pointed out suggests "an ear" meaning "listened to," refers to a closeness between father and son that, once lost, became a major part of Roethke's spiritual goal.

Section four is a memory of an event occurring several years later than the infantile problems and resolutions seen in the first three sections. This reminiscence is characterized by a greater coherence and momentarily at least by a maturer serenity than that of the crooning infant. The boy remembers a pleasant fishing trip with his father, one of the occasions when his father did have time to listen:

> I was sad for a fish.
> Don't hit him on the boat, I said.
> Look at him puff. He's trying to talk.
> Papa threw him back.   (*CP*, 73)

This grateful memory of his father in a sense answering his prayer (giving him "a near") leads to a glimpse of another memory, this time of the father as the miraculous gardener whose "thumb had a rainbow" as he watered the roses. The literal action behind this evocative description is his father holding his thumb over the end of a nozzleless hose to spray the roses better and a rainbow forming in the spray.

But then the poem reaches its major turning point. With the

words "I fell! I fell!" the boy alludes to his father's death without actually confronting it. Here is a pain that cannot be crooned away, and the boy "sees the cold." In the final section the boy's sadness is beautifully rendered as he futilely prays his father to awaken from death: "Kisses come back, / I said to Papa; / He was all whitey bones / And skin like paper." The sense of loss growing from the unanswered prayer becomes an even greater one—a loss of faith. There can be no fatherly God who miraculously created life, who set a rainbow as a sign of his covenant to protect life, or who receives that life back into his "happy hands" after death: "God's somewhere else, / I said to Mama. / . . . / Maybe God has a house. / But not here." And the poem ends on this note of a lost son's despair.

The second poem, "I Need, I Need," shows the young boy struggling to find his place in a lonely, fatherless world. He broods in a cellar with no one to talk to but a dripping faucet. As earlier, he still tries to explain away his sorrow, to cope with his needs (especially for his father) by denying them, unconvincingly telling himself: "There's no alas / Where I live." The child reasons that his absent father can no longer be a source of pain—after all, "Do the dead bite?" Anyone who is not physically present cannot be important: "It's a dear life I can touch" (*CP* 74-76). One he cannot touch, like his father, cannot be allowed to matter.

The title of the next poem, "Bring the Day!," suggests the ancient carpe diem theme, seize the day. Usually that theme is developed as a lover's plea to his lady to make the most of time. Human life is short and the best way to spend it is loving. However, in Roethke's poem the speaker is probably too young to be proposing lovemaking to a woman. Several lines, though, can be construed as if he is doing just that: "She asked her skin / To let me in. . . ." But on the whole the poem is as devoid of explicit human presence (*she* is mentioned only twice) as most of the Greenhouse Poems. The boy, in the stage of his growth probably represented in "Bring the Day!," instead of trying to talk to a leaky faucet, is now discovering that some of his needs, his loneliness, his lostness, can be eased by his drawing closer to nature. Whether in the greenhouse or in the wild, he hears the singing, the whispering, and the kissing of all things. The boy's sense of the interinanimation among the parts of the natural world, his sense of the world's organic wholeness, goes beyond the living "bees and lilies" to take in even the inanimate rocks, rain, and air:

> The herrings are awake.
> What's all the singing between?—
> Is it with whispers and kissing?—
> I've listened into the least waves.
> The grass says what the wind says:
> Begin with the rock;
> End with water.

As he tries to feel just how integral a part he is of this wholeness ("I'm almost a tree"), his awakening sexual feelings let him know that he cannot yet be totally absorbed into nature. "I can't marry the dirt," he reminds himself. But, despite this limitation, the wakening birds and blossoms bring him such pleasure that they bid fair to replace the "old angels" of the innocent days before his fall. The poem ends with the boy's eagerness to start a new life in something like a paradise regained—"It's time to begin! / To begin!" (*CP* 77-78).

"Give Way, Ye Gates," a title that is a variation on "Where Knock Is Open Wide," follows the boy as he matures beyond his eagerness to seize the day. His increasing sexual needs force him to turn from his desired union with nature toward a woman. He brags that he is part of nature, that he "bleeds like a tree" and could "love a duck," but through the first three out of the four sections in this poem, it is not nature he addresses but the woman. She seems so desirable that she could almost be an incarnation of nature itself: "Such music in a skin! / A bird sings in the bush of your bones." She comes for him like a cat after "milk and vasty fishes," and she takes him out of his "green sleep," his boyish union with nature. She plays to his newly aroused sexual itch. (His beaverlike tail—a phallic analogue?—"hates a flat path" because it likes to be stimulated as it is dragged across the ground.) As he and she achieve their human union, nature steps back and becomes an observer— "The sea will be there, and the great squashy shadows. . . ." The boy and girl move "closer to their own most particular [human] reality," as Roethke says in "Open Letter." He casts a wistful look back at the time of his "green sleep," when he could *be* a bird or a bear.

The final section of "Give Way, Ye Gates" suddenly switches to a view of his new state that is as different from that in the preceding sections as a negative is from a photograph. The erotic and loving pleasure when she "twiced" him nicely becomes with the blinking of an eye the depressing "Touch and arouse. Suck and sob. Curse and mourn." The sea is no longer a member of the congregation at their wedding; now, ominously, only "Shapes in the shade / Watch." He steels himself to endure this new loss and to accept the harshness of a world that is merely physical. The poem ends with an epigram that might be found in a bible of philosophical materialism: "What slides away / Provides" (*CP*, 79-80). The Bible of his innocence told him that the Lord provides, but now he sees that the only provider is the flux, the ever-changing world of physical phenomena.

"The Lost Son" is the best poem Roethke wrote before his final poems of the early 1960s. It is clearer and more powerful than the other experimental narratives that accompany it. And, conveniently for the student of Roethke's poetry, it sums up the major themes and images that occupied him during the first half of his career, roughly between 1935 and 1950. These themes, touched on in earlier poems but fully expressed in "The Lost Son," are those of alienation from one's father and from God, the philosophy of naturalism, and faith in divine creation and life after death. The main images that embody these themes are those of threatening enclosures (of which the grave is the archetype), those of protective enclosures (of which the nest and the womb are the archetypes), and those of birth.

"The Lost Son," the eighth of the fourteen narratives, begins the second of the two groups into which Roethke divided the poems. This place in the overall sequence emphasizes the parallels between "Where Knock Is Open Wide," the first poem of the first group, and "The Lost Son." "Where Knock Is Open Wide," as pointed out earlier, shows a very young child's attempts to deal with physical and emotional pain. He is able to do this somewhat satisfactorily by lulling himself with songs. Sometimes he prays and finds his prayers answered by his father's presence. But the fourth and final sections of the poem show the boy at a later age "falling" from his closeness into a world of pain and loss, a world that cannot be replaced by crooning serenity. Without explicit statement but through the rhythms and the suggestive details of the images, the poem implies that the boy's "fall" was actually his father's death. The poem ends with the son lost in a world devoid of the comforting presence of a father and of a God: "Maybe God has a house / But not here."

The structure of "The Lost Son" resembles that of "Where Knock Is Open Wide," with the important difference of ending on a note of hope rather than despair (*CP*, 53-58). Again, the first three sections depict the boy's pain, but it is not simply the pain of being scratched by a cat or of being ignored temporarily by a parent, as in the earlier poem. It is the spiritual, and therefore much deeper, pain of being lost, of feeling cut off forever from father and from God. The boy's emotional state in the first three sections of "The Lost Son" corresponds to the philosophical view known as naturalism, a view that denies the existence of anything transcending the realm of physical nature. There is no God and no immortal soul. Naturalistic theory holds that life originated in chance chemical reactions, not in the divine creation of man and woman in a beautiful garden. Furthermore, death does not lead to the soul's eternal bliss or damnation but merely to the body's decay.

Although it is accurate to call Roethke a naturalist, for he was indeed obsessed with that view, it is important to realize that he never adopted that view wholeheartedly and that he struggled continually to achieve faith in a supernatural being and in his own immortal spirit. To speak of the lost son's separation from his father and from God would appear inconsistent to a thoroughgoing naturalist, for whom there would be no God to be separated from. Roethke, though, was not interested in systematic philosophy as such, but in the emotional, the pictorial (imagistic), and even the rhythmic counterparts of philosophical ideas. That his thinking was, in fact, at times naturalistic can be seen in many of his notebook entries, two representative ones being: "If we think long enough about God, we may create Him" and "The body is the soul" (NB, 225-26). The first of these expresses skepticism about God's existence but also suggests a longing to believe; the second tells us that what we might believe is supernatural spirit, the soul, is actually only flesh and bone.

But it is the following passage in the notebooks that best conveys the association of the boy's separation from his father with the naturalist's alienation from God and also hints that attentive waiting is the solution to this problem, an important development in the themes of "The Lost Son": "Wait. Watch. Listen. Meditate. He'll come. When? No, I know He won't come. He doesn't care about me any more. No. I mean Him, the Big He, that great big three-cornered Papa" (NB, 168). The "three-cornered Papa" is probably the Christian Trinity, but it is also Papa, the greenhouse owner. In this passage, Roethke expresses the feeling of rejection coupled with a slender hope that waiting, watching, listening and meditating will reveal or perhaps create His presence.

Structurally, the most important transition in "The Lost Son" is the one between sections three and four. The boy's frantic attempts to escape from the naturalist's vision of the world as physical process culminate in another "fall," similar to the one in section four of "Where Knock Is Open Wide." In the accounts of the fall in the two poems, the boy's despair is at its most intense. The fall in "The Lost Son," though, unlike the earlier one, leads to a renewal of faith. The emotional (or is it spiritual?) mechanism by which it does so is one recognized by mystics, those men and women who seek union with God through renunciation of the personal will and desires. Like a mystic, the lost son reaches a point at which he ceases to struggle, and paradoxically—miraculously—he is given the very thing that his struggle had not brought. To use the phrase from "Where Knock Is Open Wide," he is given "a near": "Ordnung! Ordnung! / Papa is coming." The German command of "Ordnung!" ("Attention!") signals the presence of the greenhouse owner walking in his garden in the cool morning. After a difficult night, the boy feels his father's presence again.

The fourth and final sections of "The Lost Son" accomplish several things. In the fourth, the boy relives in memory the closeness of his father's presence in the greenhouse Eden that he knew as a child. He sees once again that the birth of life is a divine miracle and that death cannot separate him forever from his dead father. The boy's vision in this section is not what Roethke sometimes referred to as an "easy" Christian faith in life after death but is an understanding that the dead can affect the living, sometimes even more profoundly than other living beings do. In that sense they live on. The final section moves further toward belief in the possibility of reunion with the father's "lively understandable spirit," not just in memory but in actuality. What is needed is to achieve through discipline the same renunciation of will that was achieved once through the fall. He counsels himself to "Be still. / Wait."

Noting the structure and themes of "The Lost Son" as I have just done leaves unexplained the most challenging aspect of the poem— the images. As mentioned earlier, the images, along with the rhythms, give body and emotional coloring to these themes. Careful attention to the images reveals among them a contrastive pattern that parallels the contrastive pattern of the themes of naturalism and faith. Although not every image can be fitted into this pattern, in the three naturalistic sections (one through three), the images generally are ones of imprisonment, paralleling the boy's belief that

life is ultimately trapped in the grave. The images in the last two
sections (four and five), in which the boy's faith in the triumph of
life asserts itself, offer two kinds of contrast with the threatening
enclosure of the grave—first a protective enclosure like a womb or
nest and second an expansion of vision and emotion that betokens
spiritual freedom.

"The Flight," the first section of "The Lost Son," begins with a
series of images of threatening enclosures:

> At Woodlawn I heard the dead cry:
> I was lulled by the slamming of iron,
> A slow drip over stones,
> Toads brooding in wells.
> . . . .
> Sat in an empty house
> Watching shadows crawl. . . .   (CP, 53)

If the boy is trapped, as these images suggest, in his belief that life
is a physical process ending inevitably in decay, he is at least waiting
for something to tell him differently. As Roethke describes "The
Flight" in "Open Letter," "the protagonist is so geared-up, so over-
alive that he is hunting, like a primitive, for some animistic
suggestion, some clue to existence from the sub-human" (SP, 38).
But the only voices he hears are echoic ones that intensify his feeling
of rejection, his lostness: "Dark hollows said, lee to the wind, / The
moon said, back of an eel, / The salt said, look by the sea, / Your
tears are not enough praise. . . ." And the period of "hallucinatory
waiting," as "Open Letter" calls it, gives way to the flight proper:

> Running lightly over spongy ground
> Past the pastures of flat stones . . .
> . . . .
> Hunting along the river,
> Down among the rubbish, the bug-riddled foilage,
> By the muddy pond-edge, the bog-holes,
> By the shrunken lake, hunting, in the heat of summer.   (CP, 54)

The lost son's terrified running takes him to a stagnant pond, a
place where decay, with its "soft repose," seems to put an end to all
life, but also a place where new life seems to grow out of the dead
by spontaneous generation. An entry in the notebooks may explain
why the boy would seek "some clue to existence" in such a place:

"There is a time when the mould seems to sprout its own announcements, when the dead detritus speaks only of life" (*NB*, 151). The sought-for "clue to existence" is an answer to his questions whether the naturalistic or the supernaturalistic vision of life and death is the true one. "The Flight" ends, however, with the mysterious creatures of the slime refusing to yield an answer that will allay his fears that naturalism is truth.

"The Pit," which "Open Letter" describes as "a slowed-down section; a period of physical and psychic exhaustion" (*SP*, 38), poses a series of riddling questions about the origin of life and, by extension, the finality of death. For if the answer that the Book of Genesis gives to questions like "Who put the moss there?" and "Who stunned the dirt into noise?" is true, then the lost son has found his father and the Divine Creator. On the other hand, if the naturalist's answer to these questions is true, then the boy's lostness will never end. But in this section, as in the first, the boy discovers no clear answers, and his search continues.

"The Gibber," section three, takes the lost son through a struggle with his obsessive fears into a crooning serenity that is quickly transformed into its emotional contrary, an outburst of rage. As in "The Flight," the images of threatening enclosure symbolically express the boy's imprisonment in a natural world devoid of spirit. Mere physical nature cannot be loved and cannot give any hopeful answers to his questions:

> At the wood's mouth,
> By the cave's door,
> I listened to something
> I had heard before.

Nature viewed through the terrified eyes of the lost son teaches him one lesson—that he must die. His response to this knowledge is to lull himself with a "small song" as he did when he was a young child. But even in his crooning, the nightmare world that he feels he inhabits asserts itself: "I'm cold. I'm cold all over. Rub me in father and mother. / Fear was my father, Father Fear. / His looks drained the stones." If his father and mother, symbolically the origins of all life, are physical substance, they can offer no real comfort, and the fear of death threatens to become overwhelming. The "small song" abruptly ends as the boy's spiritual needs ("some clue to existence") become confused with his insistent sexual desires. "Open Letter" describes this phase of "The Gibber," which leads up to the poem's climax, as a "rising agitation, rendered in terms of balked sexual experience, with an accompanying 'rant,' . . . and a subsequent near-blackout" (*SP*, 38). Unable to lull himself as he once could, the lost son with increasing irrationality worries the questions that obsess him: "Is this the storm's heart? The ground is unstilling itself." "Do the bones cast out their fire?" "What's left of my life?" "Has the worm a shadow?"

The spiritual agitation underlying this outburst is plain, but what is not so plain is the reference in "Open Letter" to "balked sexual experience." An examination of the complete passage, which cannot be undertaken here, suggests that the frightening naturalistic vision of life and death gives rise not only to images of threatening enclosure but also to ones of masturbation. The "balked sexual experience" seems to mean responding to "the lash of primordial milk" (i.e., semen) by spilling one's seed on the ground ("the ditch is running white") rather than by contributing to the tragical farce of life by producing another generation of lost children. (It may be noted in connection with this point that Roethke himself never did father any children.) At the peak of his spiritual and erotic frenzy, the boy loses what little self-control he has and feels himself "falling through a dark swirl."

"The Return" describes the boy's return in memory to the greenhouse Eden of his childhood, to a time and place of innocence, before he "fell" into the knowledge of death. As mentioned earlier, that fall occurred when his father died. This section is also a return of the lost son to his father. Through memory, perhaps even through faith, the boy triumphs over death. The rhythms and images here do not suggest the forced calm of the earlier "small song" but a true serenity: "The roses kept breathing in the dark. / They had many mouths to breathe with."

If there is irony in the boy's "falling through a dark swirl" into a prelapsarian world, there is an even greater irony in his desperate onanism's giving rise to birth. Yet that is what is symbolically expressed in the middle of "The Return":

> There was always a single light
> Swinging by the fire-pit,
> Where the fireman pulled out roses,
> The big roses, the big bloody clinkers.

The pit that in section two was the all-consuming grave is now a

source of warmth and light, and it even miraculously becomes a
source of life, a kind of womb. What is pulled out of the pit is not
mere inanimate matter, clinkers, but living roses. They are "bloody"
because the red-hot clinkers are transformed in the boy's new vision
into red roses, and their bloodiness may also suggest the shedding of
blood that accompanies childbirth. In other words, these roses are
like the plants in the two Greenhouse Poems of birth, "Cuttings"
and "Cuttings *later*," in which the plants are struggling like
newborn infants. But the roses, instead of representing—as did the
cuttings—the cruel birth inflicted on them by sometimes uncaring
parents, represent a spiritual rebirth, a discovery of the divine
miracle that creates life.

The last section of "The Return" describes the felt presence of
father, though not an actual account of his appearance. The
emotional effect on the boy of this spiritual reunion is conveyed by
images of warmth and light, and more importantly, by ones of
freedom after enclosure:

> A fine haze moved off the leaves;
> Frost melted on far panes;
> The rose, the chrysanthemum turned toward the light.
> Even the hushed forms, the bent yellow weeds
> Moved in a slow up-sway. (*CP*, 57)

The details of "The Return" indicate that the setting is the
protective enclosure of a greenhouse on a winter night, but as
daylight comes the frost-covered glass grows transparent. The boy's
vision of his world expands and he is filled with a sense of freedom.

The final section, "It was beginning winter," raises the father-son
reunion in memory to a higher spiritual significance, making it into
something like the state that mystics call "Illumination." Illumination is the direct emotional and sensuous awareness of God's
closeness, and it can be worked toward through self-abnegating
discipline.[4] The boy's faith that he will be able to return to his
father's spiritual presence is reflected in the imagery of this "in-
between time":

> Light traveled over the wide field;
> Stayed.
> The weeds stopped swinging.
> The mind moved, not alone,
> Through the clear air, in the silence. (*CP*, 58)

These lines, which continue the expansive feeling of "The Return," suggest a hopeful faith. But more than that, they reveal that the earlier stagnating imprisonment and frantic searching have been replaced with a patience that becomes discipline. If the lost son did not know "who stunned the dirt into noise," after the return he feels the "Stillness becoming alive, / Yet still." In the closing lines of the poem he speaks to himself in comforting tones, reminding himself that the essence of the mystic's discipline is trying to make his own spirit match the stillness of the Father's spirit:

> A lively understandable spirit
> Once entertained you.
> It will come again.
> Be still.
> Wait.   (*CP*, 58)

"Entertained" in this context means "granted a near." Thus the poem ends with the boy believing that his deepest spiritual needs— to feel the presence of his father and God, to see that life is divinely created, and to see that death does not return the spirit to dust and ashes—have been answered and will be answered.

"The Lost Son," as pointed out earlier, introduces the second group of the fourteen narratives, and I will conclude discussion of the entire sequence by looking at three of the remaining seven poems in that second group. After the "near" the lost son was granted in "The Return," he regresses to a state of blank despair several more times before the sequence concludes with him waiting hopefully to be revisited by his father's spirit. His prevailing direction, then, is one of spiritual progress, but that is achieved only by his repeatedly "going backward." Each of the three poems to be discussed begins with him bogged down in guilt and despair but ends with him in a field of light.

Roethke described the poem that follows "The Lost Son," "The Long Alley," in a letter to the poet and translator Babette Deutsch. Roethke spoke of the poem as dramatizing the lost son's effort "to reach, to apprehend the unnamed 'Luminous one' " and as achieving Illumination at the cost of incurring sexual guilt (*SL*, 141). In other words, the lost son struggles to free himself from stifling guilt caused by something his father would have disapproved of (masturbation?) and to be reunited with his father's spirit and with God. The symbolic landscape with which the poem opens conveys the boy's unhappy state: "A river glides out of the grass. A river or a serpent. / A fish floats belly upward. . . ." Once again, his despair of finding his father and God is embodied in images of threatening enclosure. When he asks, "What does the grave say?" his own despair gives him the answer: "My gates are all caves." In order to escape, he begins what Roethke has called "a nutty sexual dance," a jittery motion, as the rhythm indicates, but still a motion. During this dance, his "last waltz with an old itch," he apparently arrives at a less repressive view of his own animalistic behavior. He is, after all, related to the cat, the fish, and the goat. This little bit of emotional freedom provides sufficient self-esteem for him (in section four) to invoke Jesus and the flowers. What follows is a beautiful "light passage" in which his spirit expands and grows with the greenhouse plants of his childhood. He invites the "littlest, tenderest" flowers to come out of

> The long alleys of string and stem;
> Bend down, small breathers, creepers and winders;
> Lean from the tiers and benches,
> Cyclamen dripping and lilies.
> . . . .
> The leaves, the leaves become me!
> The tendrils have me!   (*CP*, 61)

He has been able to apprehend the "unnamed Luminous one," possibly because he has seen himself as worthy in spite of his sexual guilt.

Roethke finished the next poem, "A Field of Light," at the end of July, 1947, when he was at the Yaddo writers' colony. Robert Lowell, who was also at Yaddo that summer, praised the poem as Roethke's best to date. Roethke himself described it as "almost an interlude," in which a period of stagnation is escaped through "conflicting action," which leads to a euphoria described in another "light passage" (*SL*, 142). Again, the opening images clearly place the speaker's spiritual state: "Came to lakes; came to dead water, / Ponds with moss and leaves floating, / Planks sunk in the sand." This time the escape is made by the heightening of tension that comes when he invokes the supernatural ("Angel within me") while still seeking something very unangelic "Under the blackened leaves, / Behind the green viscid trellis . . . ." (*CP*, 62). Roethke elsewhere has referred to this searching in the slime as "some kind

of ritualistic, even penitential act . . ." (*SP*,25-26). After kissing the
dust and stones, awakening even the inanimate to life by means of
this "mild dance," the boy achieves a minor ecstasy in which he
walks "through the light air" and moves "with the morning." He
has completed another spiral on the winding stairway his spirit is
climbing.

"The Shape of the Fire" is slightly more difficult than the
preceding two poems because of the unclear impetus that moves the
speaker from the "violent regression" in which he begins to his
tranquil maturity at the end of the poem when he contemplates a
constellation of beautiful symbols (*SL*, 142, 129). That the poem
does begin in "violent regression" can be seen in the echoes of the
first narrative, "Where Knock Is Open Wide," with which this
poem opens: "What's this? A dish for fat lips. / Who says? A
nameless stranger." Despite his praying for his mother to stir from
her "cave of sorrow" and "mother" him "out of here" (in section
one), he is almost overwhelmed (in section two) by his sense of
dirtiness: "Who, careless, slips / In coiling ooze / Is trapped to the
lips, / Leaves more than shoes. . . ." Like his kissing the dust in "A
Field of Light," these lines express his guilt and perhaps serve as
another penitential act. The imagery then (in section three) suggests
that he begins to wait attentively for that moment of change, the
pipe knock that signals the return of his father's spirit. While
waiting he reminds himself that "The journey from flesh is longest. /
A rose sways least. / The redeemer comes a dark way"—all three
lines echoing "The Return" in "The Lost Son" where "The way to
the boiler was dark." For the second time in this poem, however,
the preparation for the spirit's progress does not issue immediately
in the expected movement. In the next section (the fourth), he
delves deeper into his own unconscious or, what is the same thing,
returns in memory to earlier life: "Morning-fair, follow me further
back / Into that minnowy world of weeds and ditches. . . ." He sees
again the beauties of his childhood Eden, but as an adult he
understands more fully than he did then just why that world seemed
perfect: "Death was not. I lived in a simple drowse. . . ." He had
not yet encountered death, whose power and terror he came to feel
only after his father died. "Love sang toward" that innocent world,
and perhaps for the adult it still can. The final (fifth) section is a
beautiful "light passage" that shows the quiet, mature man, "Still
as a child in its first loneliness," seeing symbolically the innocence
that is preserved inside him:

> To stare into the after-light, the glitter left on the lake's surface,
> When the sun has fallen behind a wooded island;
> To follow the drops sliding from a lifted oar,
> Held up, while the rower breathes, and the small boat drifts quietly
>   shoreward;
> To know that light falls and fills, often without our knowing,
> As an opaque vase fills to the brim from a quick pouring,
> Fills and trembles at the edge yet does not flow over,
> Still holding and feeding the stem of the contained flower.   (*CP*, 67)

Regardless of whether the symbols taken separately convey definite meanings, this passage as a whole clearly imparts the man's tranquillity and his own preservation of something beautiful from the greenhouse Eden—"The contained flower," something of his innocence that has survived even the loss of his father.

Lines from two of the four poems left undiscussed in the second group of eight narratives will provide a final touch to the overall picture. In "Unfold! Unfold!" Roethke states in perfect archetypal terms the idea behind his extensive symbolism of protective and threatening enclosures or containers: "What the grave says, / The nest denies" (*CP*, 91). Whenever possible the images throughout the narratives should be thought of as the confrontation of birth and death. When the "I" of these poems feels the presence of his father and God, he sees the images of protective holding, such as a nest, or images of freedom, such as sunlight and fresh air. When he is a lost son, cut off from his father and from God, he sees the images of imprisonment, the archetype of which is the grave. The final poem of the sequence, "O, Thou Opening, O," does not end with either a grave or a nest. After seeing his father "Deep in the belly of a thing to be" (that is, with life still to come), the poet waits: "I see; I seek;/I'm near" (*CP*, 99).

CHAPTER 4

The Womanly Answer:
The Poems of the 1950s

I The Shorter Poems, 1951-1953

THE shorter poems of 1951-1953 were written after an unproductive period that followed the completion of the narratives. In these poems Roethke treats themes from *Open House* and *The Lost Son* but does so in a style that is distinctively new. The theme of the contrary loves of nature and woman, treated previously in the loosely flowing narratives, is now expressed in a well-organized poem, "The Visitant." The theme of the symbolic landscape, which Roethke first used in the tightly constructed poems of *Open House*, is now expressed in the looser "A Light Comes Brighter" and "Elegy for Jane." But more important than these revivals of familiar themes is the successful exploration of a more philosophically complex theme in "Four for Sir John Davies" and "Meditations of an Old Woman." This new theme might be called (somewhat clumsily) human desire and the shapeless night. I shall return to it after discussing the revival of the earlier themes.

"The Visitant" is a three-part poem enacting the well-known story of a man who lived in close communion with nature (section 1) until a beautiful girl captured his love (section 2) but left him as quickly as she had come (section 3). The final implication of this story, at least as Roethke treats it, is that even though nature cannot fulfill *all* of a man's desires it can at least be counted on to be there when he wants it. The first section suggests that the voices, the "soft replies" of watery ripples, offer the man a quiet haven, but he waits alertly for something more. And soon she comes, "her white arms reaching" toward him, "the wind in her hair." After a night of love—not described in the poem—he wakes up "staring at a tree" (another phallic analogue?). He asks where the visitant has gone, but receives no answer from his former friends "the bright day" and "the close willow" (*CP*, 101). The simple, straightforward poem wisely makes no emotional or moral comment on the experience.

"A Light Breather" explores a symbolic landscape, as do so many of Roethke's poems before it and after it. (See the discussion of "Light Comes Brighter" in chapter 1.) The poem begins with an overt statement of the poet's condition: "The spirit moves, / Yet stays. . . ." Such a movement, reminiscent of the light that "traveled over the field" yet "stayed" at the end of "The Lost Son," resembles a dance and symbolizes the poet's acceptance of his present condition. A dancer moves without trying to get to another place, and so the spirit, the breather of light, is here seen "Taking and embracing its surroundings, / Never wishing itself away. . . ." Those surroundings are a symbolic landscape, in which the light, the shadows, and the currents of a stream represent an immeasurable universe in flux surrounding the "small thing," the nascent spirit. The spirit is "a small thing," the "minimal" of an earlier poem, yet it is "unafraid of what it is," (*CP*, 101). Like all the vulnerable creatures in many of Roethke's poems, it is a living thing that must one day die. The landscape symbolizes both that fact and a more important one—that the spirit can take and embrace even such a fate.

"Elegy for Jane: *My Student, Thrown by a Horse*," another poem employing the theme of the symbolic landscape, is quite different from "A Light Breather." In it Roethke is not introspective but is intent on celebrating the loveliness of Jane's spirit; he is also writing in the form of a biblical Psalm. One of the elements of that form, what is known as the "envelope technique," is the shaping of blocks of ideas not by the familiar device of end rhyme but by grammatical and semantic parallelism at the beginning of lines, as in this passage from Roethke's poem:

> The shade sang with her;
> The leaves, their whispers turned to kissing;
> And the mold sang in the bleached valleys under the rose.

But a more significant use of the formal techniques of the Psalms is that of developing a structure out of the poet's awareness of the distance or closeness between him and his subject. In the Psalms the subject is often the Lord, and, to take a familiar example, the twenty-third Psalm has a three-part structure that grows out of the poet's speaking of the Lord in the third person ("The Lord is my shepherd" in verse one), then in the second person, emphasizing closeness ("thou art with me" in verse four), and finally in the third person again ("I will dwell in the house of the Lord forever" in verse six). "Elegy for Jane" begins with the somewhat detached view represented by the grammatical third person:

> I remember the neckcurls, limp and damp as tendrils;
> And her quick look, a sidelong pickerel smile;
> And how, once startled into talk, the light syllables leaped for her. . . .

As the details accumulate, symbolizing with increasing fullness the motions of her spirit and Roethke's attachment to her, he moves, despite her absence, to a feeling of greater closeness, represented by the grammatical second person: "My sparrow, you are not here. . . ." Then, in the last verse paragraph, he draws back, again looking at her and his relation to her from a distant viewpoint:

> If only I could nudge you from sleep,
> My maimed darling, my skittery pigeon.
> Over this damp grave I speak the words of my love:
> I, with no rights in this matter,
> Neither father nor lover.   (CP, 102)

Somehow, by denying his right to love and grief—after all, he was only a teacher and she a student—he makes the poem convincing and moving. And in accepting the irrevocability of her death, he repeats the light breather's "taking and embracing [of] its surroundings." This poem compares favorably with a similar one by Dylan Thomas, "A Refusal to Mourn the Death, by Fire, of a Child in London."

The last two of the shorter poems of 1951-1953, "Four for Sir John Davies" and "The Waking," are more philosophically complex than any poems Roethke had written previously. Both have elaborate rhyme schemes, both are abstruse, and both force the reader to make difficult leaps in associations, as did the narratives. "Four for Sir John Davies" is, however, the more difficult, and a summary of it will be helpful before detailed examination. The Sir John Davies of Roethke's dedicatory title was a contemporary of Shakespeare's who served as attorney general of Ireland and wrote two philosophically ambitious poems, *Orchestra* (1596), a metaphysical explanation of the value of dancing, and *Nosce Teipsum* (1599), an explanation of human knowledge and the soul's immortality. Roethke's poems do not develop themes from either of Davies' poems but do develop a theme that was a commonplace during Davies' time, the Neoplatonic ladder.

The first of the four, "The Dance," represents the familiar ploy of Roethke's (or the speaker's) lulling himself to relieve his spiritual pain. As usual in Roethke's poems, the pain derives from the poet's fall into a fatherless world where death waits for every living thing. This time the poet boasts that he—like a caged bear or the poet W. B. Yeats, whose relevance will be explained later—can dance even in this darkness. "The Dance" sets the philosophical stage for the succeeding three poems.

"The Partner" introduces the woman, the "visitant," who deserts him like the visitant in the earlier poem with that title. In "The Partner," however, the poet is no longer the simple lover of nature he then was but is more skeptical and intellectually demanding. Even while celebrating the beauty of his newfound dancing partner and her marvellous sexual power over him, he questions the origin of his desire: is it from the spirit, or the body, or both equally? It seems to be both.

"The Wraith" develops that answer by explaining how woman's beautiful body can become a perfect symbolic picture of what seems to be his greatest desire—immortality. Perhaps here Roethke's poem approaches most closely to Sir John Davies' *Orchestra*, for in that poem Antinous, the most courtly of Penelope's suitors during her husband Odysseus' twenty-year absence, tells Penelope that his greatest desire is to see her enhance her already unsurpassable beauty by dancing. Roethke's dancing "wraith," like Penelope, seems to unite spiritual and physical beauty exactly as his greatest desire would have her do.

But "The Vigil" concludes the set by showing the poet's drinking in of her beauty leading not to an ecstatic union but to intellectual skepticism and self-consciousness and, then, to an affirmation of his desire *anyway*. The steps of this last dance run as follows: At first, the poet, realizing that in perceiving his lady's spiritual beauty he is following in Dante's inimitable footsteps, again questions the ultimate object of his desire, for she does not lead him to a vision of God, as Dante's Beatrice did him, but only to an awareness of the "shapeless night." The last puzzling lines of the poem affirm the value of his desire even if it does fall back to earth without his ever knowing whether or not beyond his lady's spiritual beauty, somewhere hidden in the shapeless night, there lies God the Creator. Roethke suggests that Dante saw what his desire was strong enough to see. Furthermore, Roethke suggests that each person, in the end, "sees" (in the sense of "believes") what he most strongly desires to see. And of course the source of that desire is not some simple unified impulse called "faith" but is the sum of all that person's physical, intellectual, emotional, and spiritual experiences.

Before examining the four poems more closely, I would like to answer two objections that have been brought against them. Some of Roethke's reviewers, especially the reviewer in the *Times Literary Supplement*, charged Roethke with failing to move beyond his one theme, that of childhood, because he did "not possess the conceptual greatness" of Dylan Thomas. Actually, neither poet was "conceptually great" by the standards set by Yeats, Eliot, and Stevens. But a close reading of "Four for Sir John Davies" and a dozen poems that follow it should show that Roethke was capable of handling fairly complex ideas in verse. Another obstacle to true appreciation of "Four for Sir John Davies" is the mistaken belief of some readers that these poems present the mystic union of the poet with God.[2] As the preceding summary shows and the following more detailed examination will show, the poems are about the failure of such a union rather than its consummation.

Antinous, in Sir John Davies' *Orchestra*, describes all measured motion in the universe, from the movement of the heavenly bodies to the beating of a human heart, as a kind of dance. The first of Roethke's four poems, "The Dance," begins with the question "Is that dance slowing in the mind of man / That made him think the universe could hum?" Roethke's world, in other words, is not the world of Sir John and Antinous, and the reason it is not is that belief in a divinely ordered universe has been eroded for many educated people by scientific discoveries and by skepticism. In fact, by the time of Roethke's writing that erosion had been in progress for over three centuries. One stimulus to Roethke's interest in early seventeenth-century poets may have been that they were historically the first English poets to be deeply troubled by naturalistic doubts.

In *The Elizabethan World Picture*, E. M. W. Tillyard has described the effect of the "new philosophy" (i.e., the scientific method) on the traditional Elizabethan and medieval world picture of the universe as a divinely ordered hierarchy; in a chapter entitled "The Cosmic Dance," Tillyard says that *Orchestra* testifies to the preponderating faith the Elizabethans somehow maintained in their perilously poised world. Not that Davies does not know the things that imperil it:

> Only the earth doth stand for ever still,
> Her rocks remove not nor her mountains meet;
> (Although some wits enricht with learning's skill
> Say heav'n stands firm and that the earth doth fleet
> And swiftly turneth underneath their feet):
> Yet, though the earth is ever stedfast seen,
> On her broad breast hath dancing ever been.

If Davies knew (as here he shows he does) the Copernican astronomy, he must have known that this science had by then broken the fiction of the eternal and immutable heavens. But he trusts in his age and in the beliefs he has inherited, and like most of his contemporaries refuses to allow a mere inconsistency to interfere with the things he really has at heart.[3]

For Roethke, trusting in his age could not give any assurances as it had Davies: the dance had indeed "slowed in the mind of man." And in this first of the four poems, Roethke expresses his frustration and his loneliness.

His position duplicates that of the lost son in "The Flight," but now instead of frantic efforts to escape his dark naturalistic world, he reminds himself that bears even in captivity still dance.[4] Why can't he, a poet and human being? "For they are all my friends: I saw one slide / Down a steep hillside on a cake of ice,— / Or was that in a book?" His image of the bear's freedom is immediately undercut by this question and then undercut again when he remembers seeing a bear dancing in a cage, "O watch his body sway!— / This animal remembering to be gay." Like the bear swaying in his enclosure, the poet will try to dance even in his imprisoning world of doubts and fears. His lonely dancing is a bodily expression of his longings, his desires: "I tried to fling my shadow at the moon, / The while my blood danced with a wordless song." In fact, the very expressiveness of his movements makes him feel that he is not merely a piece of physical flesh. His dancing is certainly not "the joyless motion of a stone."

In the last stanza of "The Dance," Roethke says, "I take this cadence from a man named Yeats" and goes on to say that Yeats and the bears would know how he came to be "dancing mad" (*CP*, 105). Roethke has been censured for allowing his indebtedness to Yeats, especially in the poems of the 1950s, to show through too clearly. And indeed Roethke did believe he felt Yeats's presence in the room while writing "The Dance," (*SP*, 24). Actually, the style and even the cadence of the poem are not derivative from Yeats, but Roethke's attempt to dance and sing despite the apparent loss of God is very much like Yeats's.

"The Partner" introduces the woman and the perplexities of a sexual desire that illuminates the darkness. The poet feels the strength of his desire for her but does not know whether that desire is personally his or is the impersonal dictate of biological law: "That woman would set sodden straw on fire. / Was I the servant of a sovereign wish, / Or ladle rattling in an empty dish?" As with his discovery in the preceding poem that his bearlike dance was "not the joyless motion of a stone," so here he discovers that his desire, his "impulse to make someone else complete," allows him to "live beyond" his "outer skin." That is, the desire itself or its consummation is an ecstasy (from the classical Greek *ekstasein*, "stand outside oneself"), and he turns in the third and the final stanzas to a celebration of sexual desire, whether it be animalistic or spiritually "sovereign," biological or most deeply personal: "The living all assemble! What's the cue?— / Do what the clumsy partner wants to do!" The last two lines of "The Partner" repeat the bravado of "The Dance." The partners, man and woman, and in a sense flesh and spirit, dance to the measure of their desire, accepting the darkness of their world: "The body and the soul know how to play / In that dark world where gods have lost their way" (*CP*, 106). The gods who have lost their way are all those deities once believed in but now fallen into desuetude.

"The Wraith" continues the idea that "body and soul know how to play in that dark world." The title, which denotes an apparition of someone about to die or recently dead, along with the description of the surrounding darkness as "all the lonely pastures of the dead," indicates that the dark world is actually the realm (the naturalistic world view) in which nothing seems to be immortal. But the imagery of illumination also increases, and Roethke's vision of the woman he loves still bears the possibility of a new life, one beyond death. Just as the dance of the man and woman appears to be also the play of body and soul, so his erotic desire for her (like Dante's for Beatrice) blends into his desire for immortality and knowledge of God:

> The spirit and the flesh cried out for more.
> We two, together, on a darkening day
> Took arms against our own obscurity.

If it may be granted that their "obscurity" is their death, the question arises whether death is a necessary accompaniment of living in a physical body, and if so, whether that body should not be condemned. Roethke's answer to these questions, like Yeats's, refuses to accept the divorce of body and soul, refuses to consign the "evil" body to the grave and send the disembodied spirit to heaven. Rather, his answer praises the body's value and the inseparable union of the two:

> The flesh can make the spirit visible;
> We woke to find the moonlight on our toes.
> In the rich weather of a dappled wood
> We played with dark and light as children should.

As mentioned earlier, the style and cadence of Roethke's poem are not borrowed from Yeats, but some of the ideas possibly are. In "The Tower" Yeats rejects the view (of the ancient philosophers Plato and Plotinus) that the spirit can have a life separate from the flesh and describes the ambiguous reality of the object of man's greatest desire, immortality:

> And I declare my faith:
> I mock Plotinus' thought
> And cry in Plato's teeth,
> Death and life were not
> Till man made up the whole,
> Made lock, stock, and barrel
> Out of his bitter soul,
> Aye, sun and moon and star, all,
> And further add to that
> That, being dead, we rise,
> Dream and so create
> Translunar Paradise.[5]

In other words, the realm of eternal life is created by the dreams of the risen dead—a most ambiguous reality.

The beautiful final stanza of "The Wraith" depicts the similarly ambiguous reality of what the partners actually achieve by flinging their "shadow at the moon":

> What shape leaped forth at the sensual cry?—
> Sea-beast or bird flung toward the ravaged shore?
> Did space shake off an angel with a sigh?
> We rose to meet the moon, and saw no more.
> It was and was not she, a shape alone,
> Impaled on light, and whirling slowly down.   (*CP*, 106-7)

The "sensual cry" comes with the consummation of their desire, but, as with the lost son's falling through a dark swirl, the partners "see no more" at what should be the supreme moment. The loved-one's shape that comes "whirling slowly down" is a wraith; it is apparitional; its reality is ambiguous because the shape is a projection of Roethke's greatest desire and possibly has no objective existence.

The last of the four poems, "The Vigil," is an abstruse mixture of the Renaissance theme of the Neoplatonic ladder and modern skepticism. The basic idea of the Neoplatonic ladder is simple, though its appearance in particular poems can lead to difficulties for an unsuspecting reader. As many Renaissance poets developed the theme, and as Roethke does, it contributed to the reaction against an ascetic disparagement of the flesh. The world is viewed, according to this idea, as a series of steps leading man upward from the beautiful body of the woman he desires, through love of her spirit, love of all human souls, and finally to God. In a discussion of this theme, Herschel Baker has written that "love is the compulsion behind man's gradual ascent to wisdom. An object of beauty inspires love in man precisely because it evokes in him the mysterious intimations of his own immortality." This explanation of the Neoplatonic ladder may be applied without hesitation to "The Vigil." Baker's reference to ". . . man's capacity of attaining, by the ascent to ever higher objects of desire, a spiritual knowledge of his creator" [6] also may assist a reader of Roethke's poem but must be limited by an important reservation. Roethke's skepticism, his awareness of the dark, is never finally replaced by an unmediated knowledge of God.

The title "The Vigil" suggests a deathwatch, a contemplation of the dead; unfortunately, it is one without the comforts of faith that perhaps sustained Sir John Davies and certainly did sustain Dante.

The comparison of Roethke and his Beatrice with Dante and his Beatrice that begins the poem closely echoes a passage in canto 30 of Dante's *Purgatorio*. At the top of the mountain of Purgatory, Dante suddenly sees the spirit of the woman he loved before her death ten years earlier: "And my spirit, which now so long had not been overcome with awe, trembling in her presence, without having more knowledge by the eyes, through hidden virtue that came from her, felt old love's great power."[7] But Roethke's echoing of these lines is undercut by his persistent skepticism, especially in the last two lines:

> Dante attained the purgatorial hill,
> Trembled at hidden virtue without flaw,
> Shook with a mighty power beyond his will,—
> Did Beatrice deny what Dante saw?
> All lovers live by longing, and endure:
> Summon a vision and declare it pure.   (*CP*, 107)

Longing is here seen to be the essence of love, and for Roethke that longing is never extinguished by being gratified. The source of the lovers' vision is their own longing, not God, and the vision's purity is not absolute but is declared by the lovers themselves.

Roethke is aware that there are many steps in the ladder of desire and that no one, not even Dante, "leaps to heaven at a single bound." As he is led upward ("Her look was morning in the dying light") from the world of physical things, he and his guide are drawn toward what the eye cannot see: "The visible obscures. But who knows when? / Things have their thought: they are the shards of me; / I thought that once and thought comes round again; / Rapt, we leaned forth with what we could not see." As he becomes more aware of his partner's spiritual appearance, he realizes that a spiritual significance lies within all things. Every object has its thought, its spiritual meaning, and this knowledge sustains him in lieu of God's unmediated presence: "We danced to shining; mocked before the black / And shapeless night that made no answer back." It is in these lines that the revision of the Renaissance theme of the Neoplatonic ladder by skepticism is most clear and most devastating. As far upward as his desire has led him, he finds only a clean well-lighted place beyond which is the apparently unending dark. Unlike Sir John Davies and most of the other English poets of his day, Roethke feels uncertain that the ladder leads ultimately to God.

The last stanza affirms that the poet will be satisfied with what he has found even though it is less than what Dante was granted: "Alive at noon, I perished in her form. / Who rise from flesh to spirit know the fall: / The word outleaps the world, and light is all." The impression created here of the darkness finally giving way to the full light of noon may be misleading. Perishing in "her form" is certainly not the same as Dante's beatific vision of God, and of course the next-to-last line acknowledges that the weight of the flesh cannot be escaped indefinitely. The last line, which seems to suggest an escape into the realm of pure spirit and thus to contradict the preceding line, actually does not say that the poet or the lovers out-leap the world, only that "the word" does. And it should be noted that this is not "the Word," the Christian Logos, but merely the poet's and lover's very human word.

"Four for Sir John Davies" marks a new and higher level of achievement for Roethke in several ways. It allowed him to use the techniques of creating loose associations among a group of symbols, as he had done in the narratives, while at the same time working within a more demanding rhyme scheme than ever before (ababcc). In this poem, too, he treated the love between man and woman more seriously and maturely than he had previously. But the most important advance in his powers as a poet comes with the greater philosophical complexity of the themes developed in this poem.

"The Waking," one of Roethke's most frequently anthologized poems, resembles "Four for Sir John Davies" in its associational looseness within a tight form and in its thematic complexity. The form is that of a villanelle, a six-stanza poem built on two rhymes, with two lines repeated alternatingly as the final lines of each of the three-line stanzas and used together in the final stanza, which has four lines. Its brevity (nineteen lines), of course, prevents it from reaching the level of complexity of "Four for Sir John Davies," but it is certainly more complex than Kenneth Burke suggests when he says that it ". . . risks a simple post-Wordsworthian account of pure joy."[8] The theme, once again, is that of desire and the shapeless night.

The first line, which becomes the second of the two refrains, implies that if life leads only toward death, life should be savored, the *carpe diem* theme again. The other two lines of the first stanza amplify this by saying that the journey of life can be "taken and embraced," to use a phrase from "A Light Breather," even though it wends its way through and ends in the shapeless night of death:

> I wake to sleep, and take my waking slow.
> I feel my fate in what I cannot fear.
> I learn by going where I have to go.

The second stanza dismisses any comfort that might derive from the attempt of the intellect to bring order to the chaotic darkness; the poet will make do with his feelings about his awareness of himself:

> We think by feeling. What is there to know?
> I hear my being dance from ear to ear.
> I wake to sleep, and take my waking slow.

Perhaps a more remote implication here is the idea—shared by Unamuno and other twentieth-century philosophers[9]—that in the universe there is one spirit that becomes ever more conscious of itself. It does so through the medium of physical existence and in the human race through desire, especially through man's longing for immortality. Man's greatest desire—to wake eternally—enacts its drama (a tragedy?) against the setting of the shapeless night and unending sleep.

If the notion of the spirit evolving by becoming more conscious of itself is implied in stanza two, the remaining stanzas reinforce that implication. In fact, without that implication giving some continuity to the lines, the third and fourth stanzas would be all but impenetrable. The third introduces a mysterious second person and place:

> Of those so close beside me, which are you?
> God bless the Ground! I shall walk softly there,
> And learn by going where I have to go.

The speaker is once again the lost son wondering in the "lonely pastures of the dead." But now he has felt the presence of the dead, and instead of running in terror, he blesses "the Ground," which is the physical earth but also the spiritual condition, the darkness, against which he takes his slow waking. Those so close beside him are all the dead, and the "you" he addresses is probably his father.

The fourth stanza presents, in contrast to the dark background of life, the bright mysteries of growth and evolution:

> Light takes the Tree; but who can tell us how?
> The lowly worm climbs up a winding stair;
> I wake to sleep, and take my waking slow.

The Tree is a physical tree standing in the sunlight and making its life from that light, but it is also the Tree of Life in the center of the Garden of Eden and the biological tree of life that shows the evolutionary relations between all living things. Possibly it may also be the Cross of the Crucifixion, with the life-bearing meaning of that Tree. The "lowly worm" climbing "a winding stair" deepens the meaning of the allusions to the evolution of physical forms, an evolution that is a concrete, symbolic parallel to the evolution of the spirit. The verse epigraph of Ralph Waldo Emerson's essay *Nature* has an image that is remarkably similar to this strange line of Roethke's:

> The eye reads omens where it goes,
> And speaks all languages the rose;
> And, striving to be man, the worm
> Mounts through all the spires of form.

Emerson's first line, like Roethke's "I learn by going where I have to go," affirms that the human spirit can see "shards" of itself (to use a word from "Four for Sir John Davies") and of its fate in the gracefully growing tendrils in a greenhouse, in the minimal, in roses, and even in the "lowly worm." Just as life has evolved, according to evolutionary theory, from lower forms to higher, more complex forms, so the poet feels that his spirit or perhaps all spirit, what Emerson called the Oversoul, progresses to greater degrees of self-awareness. Consciousness—or "waking"—is spreading throughout the universe.

If the third and fourth stanzas of "The Waking" form a miniature dialectic, with one asserting that death is part of the Ground of all life and the other, that life is continual progress, then the fifth stanza presents a synthesis or resolution of these opposites:

> Great Nature has another thing to do
> To you and me; so take the lively air,
> And, lovely, learn by going where to go.

The other thing that nature has to do to the poet and the reader ("you") is "other" than the affirmation of life just made in stanza four; it is death. But the conjunction *so* tells the reader that he should live intensely precisely because death is the Ground of his being. The "lovely" here is not a loved woman, in which case the word would be capitalized, but is the essential quality of life when the spirit, the light breather, takes and embraces its surroundings. You can learn to regard your fate as "lovely."

The final stanza may refer to the dialectic just sketched or to the systole and diastole of a living heart:

> This shaking keeps me steady. I should know.
> What falls away is always. And is near.
> I wake to sleep, and take my waking slow.
> I learn by going where I have to go.   (*CP*, 108)

Probably the "shaking" is a variation on the image of the dance, which, as we have seen, Roethke often used to symbolize acceptance of his spiritual condition. And such an acceptance comes more easily now that he knows death does not absolutely sever the still living from the once living. The dead can still give the lost son a "near."

II   *Love Poems of the Early 1950s*

The Lost Son Narratives and "The Visitant" pictured the woman who elicits love from the poet as a disrupter of his union with nature, a disrupter who cannot be counted on to replace what she has destroyed. In the more philosophical poems, "Four for Sir John Davies" and "The Waking," the poet is able to face the darkness beyond his life without seeking comfort in an unhealthy dependence on either nature or the woman he loves. The love poems of the early 1950s return to the earlier opposition between love of nature and love of woman and resolve it into a new union—the woman and nature become one.

"The Dream" presents, in four stanzas of eight slant-rhymed, pentameter couplets, the poet's growing sense that the loved woman is an embodiment of nature and that as lovers he and she can live by immersing themselves in the world of time, the world of change. The poem begins by allying her with nature and by suggesting a life outside of time: "I met her as a blossom on a stem / Before she ever breathed. . . ." But this hinted-at preexistence or escape from time is rendered highly ambiguous by its being called a "dream," continuing the skeptical view of the translunar paradises from "Four for Sir John Davies." Indeed, the second stanza affirms that this woman, in being part of the oneness of nature, is not a "visitant" from a translunar, changeless paradise:

> She came toward me in the flowing air,
> A shape of change, encircled by its fire.
> I watched her there, between me and the moon. . . .   (*CP*, 119)

Despite her being an unpredictably changeable creature, the dream-like perfection in the union of man, woman, and nature in some sense endures: 'I turned my face away, and yet she stayed. / A bird sang from the center of a tree; / She loved the wind because the wind loved me." The wind is often, in Roethke and in other poets, an image suggesting the changeableness of all things beneath the moon, or at least of the things caught in the wind, as the mortal lovers are here. In the third stanza, the lovers' acceptance of change, particularly their mortality, is virtually elevated into doctrine: "Love is not love until love's vulnerable." Instability, doubts, pain are part of the essence of human love. In the poem's final stanza, the poet seems so rapt by the power of their love that his tone becomes one of religious celebration: "Like a wet log, I sang within a flame. / In that last while, eternity's confine, / I came to love, I came into my own." What he praises in these paradoxes is not the erotic desire of the narratives but an obviously much deeper, more personal love, one that thrives on even its own extinction.

The theme of union of the poet with the woman he loves and with nature continues in the title poem of the first collection of Roethke's works, "Words for the Wind." The poem is divided into four numbered sections, the first and last having eight-line stanzas, and the second and third, seven-line stanzas. Throughout, the lines end predominantly in slant rhymes (e.g., "tree-breathe") shading off without any apparent order into unrhyme (e.g., "earth-beyond"). The development of the theme is organized as follows. The poet first emphasizes her changeableness, then speaks of his own delight in change, hers and nature's. Yet he feels that something abides beneath nature's changing face, and perhaps his love itself is part of some enduring pattern. But in the end he realizes he cares more for the "soul's immediate joy" in the sensual embrace than for metaphysical speculation.

This poem does not follow the pattern so frequent in Roethke's poems of the speaker's beginning in a state of despair or terror and moving to a peaceful resolution. Even in the opening lines he feels that all is right with the world, and he suggests that he almost euphorically accepts his own changeableness and even his own emotional instability, his "oddness":

> Mad in the wind I wear
> Myself as I should be,
> All's even with the odd,
> My brother the vine is glad.

He compares the loved woman, who is the source of his happiness, first to a lily ("Love, love, a lily's my care"), then to a bird ("Sweet Phoebe, she's my theme"), then to a "lovely substance," and finally to a moving statue: "A shape from deep in the eye— / That woman I saw in a stone— / Keeps pace when I walk alone." She is like a statue in being a perfect embodiment of his desires and perhaps in seeming to be above the turmoil caused by change. Her ghostly perfection recalls the "wraith" in "Four for Sir John Davies."

But the poem deserves a more detailed examination. In the first section, the poet experiences an alteration of his sense perceptions, perhaps because of the intensity of his desire for the woman he loves: "light fell / Across her pulsing throat; / I stared, and a garden stone / Slowly became the moon." This is part of the transformation she undergoes in his sight as she becomes more like a statue and, simultaneously, a wraith. In the second section, he reminds himself that earth is the only proper place for love and that she is earth's inhabitant:

> She sways, half in the sun:
> Rose, easy on a stem,
> One with the sighing vine,
> One to be merry with,
> And pleased to meet the moon.

The moon, that symbol of the changing world, had earlier played its part in his altering perceptions, but now the poet denies the static ideal represented by an unaging statue and affirms love's proper place *beneath* the moon:

> A fair thing grows more fair;
> The green, the springing green
> Makes an intenser day
> Under the rising moon;

> I smile, no mineral man;
> I bear, but not alone,
> The burden of this joy.

A "mineral man," of course, would be the proper mate for the statue the woman had almost become in his idealizing sight. Now she walks beside him as they bear their joy, which is a "burden" because it has the vulnerability of any living thing.

In the third section, the poet again acknowledges the lure of the ideal, especially as it seems to exist in the apparently unchanging cosmic dance. The earth abides forever and so do its patterns: "Under a southern wind, / The birds and fishes move / North, in a single stream; / The sharp stars swing around. . . ." He wonders whether wisdom is the ability to see, with altered perception, the unchanging pattern beneath the surface of things. His love seems to lead him to a faith that "Whatever was, still is." But his love also teaches him, if I may allude to Yeats, that he cannot love the idealized dance without loving the aging dancer:

> What time's my heart? I care.
> I cherish what I have
> Had of the temporal:
> I am no longer young
> But the wind and waters are;
> What falls away will fall;
> All things bring me to love.

His heart is a timepiece, and it shows the hour of caring. He cherishes his physical life even though it is moving toward its own end. All that he knows of change only serves to deepen his love.

In the beautiful concluding section, he sees her once more as inseparable from the ever-changing face of nature:

> The breath of a long root,
> The shy perimeter
> Of the unfolding rose,
> The green, the altered leaf,
> The oyster's weeping foot,
> And the incipient star—
> Are part of what she is.
> She wakes the ends of life.   (*CP*, 123-26)

A Renaissance poet would have said she was a little world made cunningly. Everything, from the root underground to the star being formed in the depths of space, is manifested in this one beautiful being. And the poet himself is inseparable from her as he joins her in the very earthly dance of love. His soul sings the "immediate joy" it takes in her skin and in his own quickened breath ("She breaks my breath in half"), not the remote joy of the unchanging cosmic dance. And yet even the physical dance of bodies has a spiritual effect. His perception is altered once again, this time revealing his self in the woman he loves.

"I Knew a Woman," one of the most frequently anthologized of Roethke's poems, explores more deeply than "Words for the Wind" the poet's "immediate joy" in the woman's physical beauty and in her erotic power over him. Its four seven-line stanzas do state the theme of the union of man, woman, and nature, but in a comic way and with emphasis being placed on her enticing movements. The woman-nature theme, which is introduced in the second line, quickly gives way to the praise of her mobility:

> I knew a woman, lovely in her bones,
> When small birds sighed, she would sigh back at them;
> Ah, when she moved, she moved more ways than one. . . .

He feels the almost overwhelming force of what Whitman called "sheath'd hooded sharp-tooth'd touch" and gladly becomes her pet poet. "She taught me Touch, that undulant white skin; / I nibbled meekly from her proffered hand. . . ." Only the final stanza raises any hint that his intellectual or spiritual needs might go beyond his animalistic pleasures. He even hints, very gently to be sure, that he has been forced to make the ultimate sacrifice for her: "I'm martyr to a motion not my own; / What's freedom for? To know eternity. / I swear she cast a shadow white as stone." In his slavish love of her, he is not free, and consequently he has forsaken any knowledge he might have gained of eternity. For him, even her shadow dismisses whatever desire he has for something unchanging. Eternity is for other martyrs; he will be her slave in time: "But who would count eternity in days? / These old bones live to learn her wanton ways: / (I measure time by how a body sways)" (*CP*, 127). The comic vein in which Roethke here handles one of his favorite themes has probably contributed to this poem's popularity.

In some of the love poems, such as "The Voice," the woman, in her close association with nature, transcendentally "exults" the poet. He does not celebrate his "soul's immediate joy" in the sensual but feels intimations of a world beyond the mortal, an airier world filled with birdsong. "The Voice" begins with a statement of the poet's readiness to be beyond: "One feather is a bird, / I claim; one tree a wood; / In her low voice I heard / More than a mortal should. . . ." These lines illustrate synecdoche, a using of a part to imply a whole. But here the movement that the mind takes in synecdoche carries the poet beyond the borders of normal existence. The poet's ability to be lifted up by the "voice" of the woman he loves is at one with his ability to identify imaginatively with a bird in flight: "I roamed out where / Those notes went, like the bird, / . . . I lived with open sound, / Aloft, and on the ground." The remainder of the poem, the third and fourth stanzas, is obscure. Roethke seems to be saying that his forming a trinity with the woman and bird is an expression of his "choice," his greatest desire. The bird, like Shelley's skylark, sings unseen in the world above, its voice identical with that of the woman, and only the poet is aware of the hint of something beyond the normal.

The final stanza, though, returns him to the temporal world, in which a long summer noon is slowly pulsing away its life:

> Desire exults the ear:
> Bird, girl, and ghostly tree,
> The earth, the solid air—
> Their slow song sang in me;
> The long noon pulsed away,
> Like any summer day.   (*CP*, 128)

The specialness of the moment, the supernatural heightening of his perception—these could not be maintained indefinitely, and he returns to a day that is like "any" other. Interestingly, this subsidence occurs immediately after he skeptically notes that it is his desire that leads him to hear exactly what he wants to hear, the implication being that his glimpse of a higher world is not credible.

The love poems of the early 1950s generally present a theme that was new for Roethke, the theme of the union of man, woman, and nature. In previous poems, especially the narratives, the poet's (or lost son's) terrifying view of his world as a fatherless and Godless realm ruled by death had been relieved by his intense love of flowers, birds, sunlight, and air. This love was actually a union of human being and nature. But this union was disturbed, sometimes even destroyed, when the boy's incipient sexual desires led him away from nature in search of the satisfactions only a woman could give. The erotic passages in the narratives are usually tinged with guilt, and the woman turns out to be a much less trustworthy soul mate than the flowers and sunlight. However, in the love poems, the series of impersonal erotic satisfiers is replaced by one woman, and she is not only desired but loved. Something about her allies her with nature, and in the union of man, woman, and nature, Roethke finds a greater happiness than he had ever known.

III   *"Voices and Creatures"*

Whether the poems of "Voices and Creatures" were written after the love poems or simultaneously with them, they are emotionally more mature works. The new and more intense joy accompanying the poet's discovery of the one woman who shares in the wholeness of nature, the theme of the love poems, is now replaced by a grimmer but stronger feeling. The new theme running through "Voices and Creatures," and in fact continuing to the end of Roethke's career, is that of self-reliance. In the love poems Roethke had discovered that the woman did not necessarily destroy his union with his first love, nature, as it had seemed to him in the narratives. She could share it and offer an emotional stability, a permanence, that matched nature's own. It is true that sometimes she seemed to teach him such pleasure in the senses that he forgot his longing for knowledge of a perfect spiritual world. And it is apparently this limitation of hers that leads him to continue seeking for solace against the enduring pain of being mortal. The solace that he now finds is self-reliance.

"The Song," a poem of three brief, irregular sections, shows the poet—not, this time, the loved woman— "waking the ends of life," to use a phrase from "Words from the Wind." The "ends" of life that he here calls into active presence are his own youth and old age. The poem begins with the poet encountering "a ragged man," who is most likely a mirror-image of himself as he now is or a projection of what he will be when the aging process is through. The resistance to painful self-knowledge and the bite of remorse is suggested in the opening lines:

> I met a ragged man;
> He looked beyond me when
> I tried to meet his eyes.
> What have I done to you?
> I cried, and backed away.

Possibly what the poet is really asking is "What have I done to myself?" True to the pattern for lost sons, he responds by fleeing, and once again the scene of his flight is the "lonely pastures of the dead": "I went running down a road, / In a country of bleak stone, / . . . I lay/ With the saxifrage and fern / At the edge of a raw field." His obsession with death leads him to a gravelike hole, which he stares into as if hypnotized or seeking some "clue to existence from the sub-human," while he croons to himself for comfort: "I stared at a fissue of ground / Ringed round with crumbled clay: / The old house of a crab; / Stared, and began to sing." The final section shows him regaining the other end of his life, that of the child innocent of the knowledge of death, with whom he now sings in unison. But whatever comfort there is in such singing is cold and hard, for his "lips [are] pressed upon stone."

> I sang to whatever had been
> Down in that watery hole:
> I wooed with a low tune;
> You could say I was mad.
> And a wind woke in my hair,
> And the sweat poured from my face,
> When I heard, or thought I heard,
> Another join my song
> With the small voice of a child,
> Close, and yet far away.
>
> Mouth upon mouth, we sang,
> My lips pressed upon stone.   (*CP*, 146)

He has not returned to the greenhouse of his father; he has not joined himself with nature or a loved woman; he has found a most difficult way to sing, with a voice that is "close" inside him but "far away" in the past—his own voice as a child, which provides the best answer he can make to himself as a ragged old man.

In "The Exorcism," a poem of two unmatching sections, the poet's grim, strong self-reliance is even more pronounced than it is in "The Song." Once again he does not turn to any of his former sources of comfort—memory of his childhood happiness or of his father, or union with a woman and nature. He seems at first to be back in the role of a lost son in terrified flight, but at the end he has successfully asserted, or achieved, a significant maturity.

As in the poems of *Open House*, he places the cause for his pain within himself, in his own unspecified guilts, rather than in the darkness that surrounds mortal life. Like a lost son the poet asks plaintively, "Father of flowers, who / Dares face the thing he is?" And the spirit of the father-florist seems to reply. In one of the Greenhouse Poems, "Old Florist," the boy sees that his father can "make the dust buzz with a light spray." Here the answer from the "Father of flowers" comes in a similar though even more miraculous image: "As if pure being woke, / The dust rose and spoke. . . ." But the poet does not hear the answer given because he is lost inside the corridors of his own fleshly and guilty self:

> And yet I was not there,
> But down long corridors,
> My own, my secret lips
> Babbling in urinals.

After this image of utter self-disgust, the poem moves, in the second section, to an allegorical picture of the poet destroying whatever it is within him that causes his guilt: "I saw my several selves / Come running from the leaves, / Lewd, tiny careless lives / That scuttled under stones. . . ." Whatever these capabilities for evil are, these possible persons he could become, he manages to defeat them, apparently by a spiritual struggle (wrestling with his angel?) in which he rages against God:

> I turned upon my spine,
> I turned and turned again,
> A cold God-furious man
> Writhing until the last
> Forms of his secret life
> Lay with the dross of death.   (*CP*, 147)

Being a "cold God-furious man"—a man furious with God for allowing suffering and death or for keeping Himself hidden—is quite different from being a lost son. The personal triumph that Roethke expresses here, after achieving his own wholeness ("I was

myself, alone"), is effectively underscored in the last words, referring to the dried perspiration after the internal battle: "Cold, in my
own dead salt." The pride in his self-reliance is obvious.

"The Small," a poem of four six-line stanzas, also expresses the
theme of self-reliance, though not as clearly as "The Exorcism" or
"The Song." The title names a concern that begins early in
Roethke's work (in a poem such as "The Minimal") and lasts until
the end (see the discussion of "The Meadow Mouse" in chapter
5)—a concern for those creatures who seem particularly vulnerable
to death, the victims not the victors. Roethke exhibits his self-
reliance by uniting himself specifically with these unlikely friends,
another act of defiance on the part of a "cold God-furious man."
Being with "the small" even in the presence of death enables his
heart to hold "to its joy." He now seems to possess the "clues to
existence" that he, earlier, as the lost son, sought from the subhuman. In his newfound pride and strength, he almost casts himself in
the role of creator of "the small": "What rustles in the fern? / I feel
my flesh divide. / Things lost in sleep return / As if out of my
side...." If not the creator, the poet at least resembles Adam's having
his flesh divided for the creation of Eve. Or perhaps it would be
more accurate to say that the "small birds" and other creatures are
"shards" of him as he said in "Four for Sir John Davies." Their joys
and their fears and especially their fates are all encompassed by this
imaginative and self-reliant man. In the final stanza his perception
undergoes a change, as it has in other poems, and he feels the living
presence of the dead: "The small shapes drowse: I live / To woo the
fearful small; / What moves in grass I love— / The dead will not lie
still . . ." (CP, 148). What is especially interesting here is that even
though he is "wooing" these vulnerable creatures, he is not seeking
them because of his own fear but because of his strength. He wants
to be with them to share their fate and to comfort them. The lost
son has become a father.

All the poems of "Voices and Creatures" in one way or another
express the theme of the poet's self-reliance. In some of them, such
as "The Song" and "The Beast," Roethke passively undergoes a
change in his perception. But even in these poems where he himself
claims the least credit, he does not follow his former pattern of
giving credit for his survival to God, to nature, or to a woman. In
other poems, such as "The Small" and "The Exorcism," he asserts
his self-reliance more strongly, even to the point of bragging about
his own triumph over madness and "the dross of death." This grim,

lonely strength represents a new level of maturity in Roethke's poetry.

IV   *"Meditations of an Old Woman"*

The poems of "Voices and Creatures" express a new level of maturity, but their style lacks the power that should accompany such an emotional advance. Roethke achieved that more powerful style in the last group of poems in *Words for the Wind.* "Meditations of an Old Woman," a group of five substantial pieces, flows with the looseness of the best narratives while keeping the toughness and the epigrammatic jabs of Roethke's best traditional poetry. The alternating between rhymed metrical passages and free-verse passages is enhanced by Roethke's weaving together of themes from all of his earlier work. But the meditations are not merely a compendium of previous material. When the old woman, who is the speaker of these poems, expresses her self-reliance, she does so without the grimness seen in "Voices and Creatures." The most important new element brought into Roethke's poetry by "Meditations of an Old Woman" may not, however, be the stylistic one or the new happiness in the speaker's self-reliance, but the less tentative, more secure, expression of religious belief that concludes the final poem.

Several things may explain the new achievement made in these poems. When Roethke's mother died in February, 1954, he was thrown into a depression and for some time was unable to write. In 1956, while on a Fulbright lectureship in Italy, he began work on these poems as an homage to his mother's memory. When the finished poems were published as a selection by the Poetry Book Society of London, Roethke obligingly supplied an introduction, pointing out that although his mother had finished only the third grade, her "favorite reading was the Bible, Jane Austen, and Dostoyevsky." He went on to describe her as "a gentle, highly articulate old lady believing in the glories of the world, yet fully conscious of its evils" (*SP*, 58). In composing these poems, then, Roethke set himself the task of capturing not the mind of a child, as he had done in the narratives, but the mind of an intelligent, well-read woman facing death. To capture her personality, he turned to a form of poetry he had once characterized scornfully as "the Whitmanesque, meditative thing." For Roethke, this form could easily be a lure into the wrong kind of looseness, into slackness. In a letter written in 1959, he showed that while composing the poems he had been well aware of this danger:

—As for the old lady poems, I wanted to create a character for whom such rhythms are indigenous; that she be a dramatic character, not just me. Christ, Eliot in the Quartets is tired, spiritually tired, old man. Rhythm, Tiresome Tom. Is my old lady tired? The hell she is: she's tough, she's brave, she's aware of life and she would take a congeries of eels over a hassle of bishops any day. (SL, 231)

The old woman's intelligence and knowledge are not the pedantic kind that Roethke hated and that he saw in the Eliot of the *Four Quartets*; rather, her mind has the irreverent gaiety and the toughness of Yeats's Crazy Jane or even more precisely that of the speaker in Yeats's "A Woman Young and Old." (The relation of Roethke's group of poems to Yeats's and to the *Four Quartets* will be looked at in the discussions of individual poems.)

Like all of Roethke's poetry, "Meditations of an Old Woman" shows the poet's search for identity, and here more than in his shorter poems that search takes the form of a dialectical progress, an interaction of opposites that arrives at a conclusion more secure than either of the competing contraries. A brief summary of each of the five poems, before a more detailed reading, will show that dialectic at work. The opposites that form the basis of the old woman's meditations are, on the one hand, her feeling of satisfaction with her life and her fate (once again the spirit "taking and embracing its surroundings") and, on the other hand, a recurring dissatisfaction, her spirit's longing for something more, for "another condition." Part of the working out of this conflict involves her attempts to understand exactly what satisfies her and what she detests. By the end of the fifth meditation, she knows who she is, what she is drawn to, what she is repelled by, and that there is some well of spiritual strength outside herself that she can draw on.

The "First Meditation" places the old woman in a harsh spiritual landscape composed of natural and societal images that express her discontent. She is comforted briefly by memory of her childhood happiness, symbolized by a greenhouse and birdsong, but she immediately realizes with frustration that in all the years separating the present from that greenhouse her spirit has not journeyed forward appreciably. The poem ends with her accepting this failure.

The second meditation, "I'm Here," asks whether her spirit can be fully satisfied if it does not journey to "another life." She bitterly recognizes the loss of her youthful body with its attendant pleasures, but age has its pleasures too, tranquillity being preeminent among them, and even the closeness of death cannot disturb her calm.

"Her Becoming" confirms her satisfaction with her lonely self-reliance in the face of death, but it goes beyond that to suggest acceptance also of her lifelong aberrant perceptions, perhaps even her mental instability.

The "Fourth Meditation" expresses again her spirit's apparently insatiable longing for something more, something outside herself. Even if her desire is unfulfilled, she cherishes it because it sets her apart from her "self-involved" contemporaries, who complacently make-do with their tawdry lives. Besides, there is some fulfillment of her desire in the closeness she feels to "the great dead" (among them, as mentioned earlier, biblical writers, Jane Austen, and Dostoevsky). These are spirits outside her own who, either through her personal memory or through words they left behind, communicate with her as if they were living presences.

The final meditation, "What Can I Tell My Bones?" begins with a high degree of frustration: many times in her life she has arrived at the same level of satisfaction expressed in the preceding poem, but she still longs "for absolutes that never come." Her life seems to have gotten her nowhere, with its cycles of discontent and satisfaction and discontent. She accepts herself for what she is and accepts her imminent death, but *still* she cannot tell her bones that their deepest desire—to live again—will be satisfied. With resignation she begins to enumerate the qualities that compose her spirit. But gradually the resignation gives way to joy, and the poem ends with her sudden awareness of some spiritual power outside herself communicating with her. Whatever it is is not merely a projection of her own desire, and in that sense it is the "absolute" she has always longed for. It, not she, makes the final wordless answer to her bones.

The "First Meditation" opens "On love's worst ugly day," undoubtedly a time of loneliness and of sensing the pervasive decay of the world. "The small winds make their chilly indictments," and even the flesh ("the rind") of one's own body rebels against the spirit ("the life within"). She thinks of her spirit's failure to have arrived at a better destination than its present state. The symbolic landscape of a bus trip "through western country," an unlikely but effective picture of the thousand shocks the spirit is heir to, eventually lulls the old woman into a revery of pleasanter times when she was a child: "Two song sparrows, one within a green-house, / Shuttling its throat while perched on a wind-vent. . . ." But this "journey within a journey" leads only to a renewed sense of frustration: "The ticket mislaid or lost, the gate / Inaccessible, the boat always pulling out. . . ."

After a break and the beginning of a new numbered section (the third), the imagery abruptly shifts to an underwater landscape, reminiscent of that in the early poem "The Minimal." Here there is some "tentative" progress as the woman's spirit is first likened to a crab, "Grotesque, awkward," "sliding slowly backward," then to a "salmon, tired, moving up a shallow stream." In the last section, the woman's awareness of the sterility and tedium of much of life returns. That emptiness is internal as well as external: "I have gone into the waste lonely places / Behind the eye; the lost acres at the edge of smoky cities." Contemplating this vacuous world, she realizes it is not change per se that fills her with discontent but change that is merely the sterile passing of time; what she wants more than anything is the change that is a sign from another world. As she looks past the "lonely places behind the eyes" and the "lost acres," she sees that

> There are no pursuing forms, faces on walls:
> Only the motes of dust in the immaculate hallways,
> The darkness of falling hair, the warnings from lint and spiders,
> The vines graying into a fine powder.
> There is no riven tree, or lamb dropped by an eagle.

Here she is in the spirit's waste land, first described in Roethke's poetry in the early poem "Dolor." In this passage the biblical quality of the details in the last line is reinforced by the envelope technique (see the discussion of "Elegy for Jane"), which appears in the parallelism of line beginnings and in the structural development that moves from what is lacking, to what is present, and back to what is lacking.

The poem's final seventeen lines, though, assert the other side of the dialectic. Despite the absence of supernatural signs, "There are still times, morning and evening" when even on "the smoky ridges" outside the cities she hears the birdsong that meant so much to her as a girl. There are moments when her spirit, as suggested by the imagery of the symbolic landscape, flames into being, into some heightened state that seems like a gift from beyond nature but is not:

> A flame, intense, visible,
> Plays over the dry pods,
> Runs fitfully along the stubble,
> Moves over the field,
> Without burning.
>> In such times, lacking a god,
>> I am still happy.   (*CP*, 157-60)

Thus the dialectic in this meditation ends with a true synthesis of the opposing attitudes, the naturalist's lack of a God and a feeling of satisfaction. That this resolution comes as light moves over a field in early winter shows the similarity between the old woman's spiritual struggle and the lost son's. He found peace through patient watchfulness in a setting like this at the end of "The Lost Son." Perhaps this imagery and the accompanying emotion were rooted in a moment of closeness between Roethke and his father in some wintry Michigan field.

"I'm Here" begins by disturbing the equilibrium reached at the end of the "First Meditation." The old woman asks herself whether the purely natural "flaming" she has experienced is enough. The images of her joy now are less dramatic than the flame that does not burn: frost leaving a window pane, dew in the morning sun, and the sound of children's voices and sleighbells on a snowy evening. (The attention called to morning and evening in both meditations subtly reminds the reader of times of change.) But immediately the countermovement occurs, the birdsong ceasing to please and becoming just another inane noise. "The same sparrows bicker in the eves," the vireo is insistent, and even "the prattle of the young no longer pleases." In this renewal of her testiness, the old woman feels herself shrinking into a hag.

Her bitterness leads her into thinking of what she used to be, in her "heart's summer," but no longer is. The pleasures of "flesh-awkward" adolesence, suggested in a series of evocative images, are long ago outgrown, but her spirit still seems to tally point for point with what it was then: "So much of adolescence is an ill-defined dying, / An intolerable waiting, / A longing for another place and time, / Another condition." She still faces an "ill-defined dying," though now it is more ominous than the adolescent's movement from youth into maturity. At times she still finds the waiting "intolerable," and, most importantly, one of the basic themes of her meditations is her recurrent "longing . . . for another condition," an escape from spiritual sterility and perhaps from naturalism.

In the next section (the third) she recalls moments in her earlier years when she glimpsed something beyond the ordinary borders of the seen: "In the slow coming-out of sleep, / On the sill of the eyes, something flutters, / A thing we feel at evening, and by doors. . . . " Even her youthful body, not just her desirous spirit, was drawn toward inexplicable ecstasies, rocking "in and out of itself." But the excitement and the sensuous aliveness have left her body, and she now (in section four) takes pleasure contemplating her roses so lovingly that their afterimage remains in her mind when she looks away. She even prefers this "still joy," this tranquillity, to her earlier, more violent, raptures. The final section (the fifth) extends the old woman's present feeling of security and self-reliance to the point where she boasts that if the wind, that image of change bringing death, "means her," she is ready. Her needs, temporarily at least, seem easily satisfied: "I need a pond with small eels. And a windy orchard." She has outgrown the adolescent attachment to tangible things, especially possessions: "I'm no midge of that and this." And she assures herself that the death she is now approaching is not totally different from changes she has already endured: "It's not my first dying" (CP, 161-64). The title of the poem, "I'm Here," is repeated in the last lines in which she almost dares the change of death to come: "I'm here! / Here."

The third meditation, "Her Becoming," is the most difficult of the group because it does not explicitly develop the dialectic that unifies each of the other four. In the first section the old woman thinks of her serenity and patience ("I have learned to sit quietly"), but a note of self-doubt intrudes. Perhaps she is really most like "A mad hen in a far corner of the dark." Is that all her pleasure in nature is—a crazy old woman wasting her last days on comforting delusions? No. She knows there is some spiritual presence in nature, and that same presence speaks to her in dreams:

> What's a seed?
> A face floats in the ferns. Do maimed gods walk?
> A voice keeps rising in my early sleep,
> A muffled voice, a low sweet watery noise.

It is dangerous to pin too many hopes on such hints and guesses. To do so is actually to return to one's own beginning, to "embrace" again the spirit of one's childish innocence when death was an unknown thing. She says to herself, "I'm where I always was."

In the second section she begins to speak with the "wild disordered language of the natural heart," and that language expresses the same dissatisfaction and longing as did the "low sweet watery noise" in her dream. The dissatisfaction, which is here only implied, not stated, is with the unlikelihood of ordinary human life ever bringing one the kind of fulfillment pictured in Dante's nearness to God at the end of the *Paradiso*. Roethke's old woman asks, "Dare I speak, once more, in the monotony of great praise?" She wishes to echo Dante but feels she cannot: it seems to her that life is a hellish education that begins with the ineffectual teaching of pain ("I can't laugh from a crater of burning pitch"), proceeds through the learning of human and personal limitations ("I can't . . . live the dangerous life of an insect"), and usually concludes not in heaven but with the dolorous addiction to thinghood, or what is generally known as "being an adult":

> Is there a wisdom in objects? Few objects praise the Lord.
> . . . .
> I know the cold fleshless kiss of contraries,
> The nerveless constriction of surfaces—
> Machines, machines, loveless, temporal,
> Mutilated souls in cold morgues of obligation.

She, herself, as the dialectical progression of these meditations shows, is moved by the "kiss of contraries." But even though she has learned the lessons of sterility, perhaps her spirit is not yet ready for the morgue.

In the third section the old woman meditates on her at least occasional escape from the mechanical, "loveless, temporal" world that human society has constructed as a tomb for the spirits of its citizens. Most of the section is a memory of times when she was a "raw tumultuous girl" and reality came closer. Her ecstatic spirit escapes her body (I "ran ahead of myself"), and her perception of things alters ("All natural shapes became symbolical"). Here she does not pause to wonder whether this alteration is a sympton of insanity. She accepts it as a revelation of reality, the spiritual meanings underlying the surface of things. She is at least temporarily following in the tradition of mystics, perhaps again like Dante: "Did my will die? Did I? / I said farewell to sighs. . . ." Dante often referred to Hell as a place of sighs. One of the most important steps, moreover, in the mystic's path toward union with God is the death of the will, the leaving behind of all personal and therefore egotistical or selfish hopes and fears, what Dante expressed in the line repeated throughout *The Divine Comedy*—"In His will is our peace." She remembers the revelation as an image of flaming: "I have seen! I have seen!— / The line! The holy line! / A small place all in flame." Her thoughts, after this climactic reexperience of spiritual satisfaction, return to the present. Impulsively she dismisses the possibility of union with mere physical nature ("Out, out, you secret beasts") in favor of the condition of fire ("One follows fire. One does."), because her human breath (meaning "spirit"?) is more than that of beasts. She knows that dissatisfaction, longing, must precede satisfaction: "I sigh before I sing. / I love because I am / A rapt thing with a name." She is not a mere "secret beast."

But in the final section she draws back from the old mistake that she was about to commit—that of seeking her satisfaction in a changeless, supernatural ideal, symbolized by the flame. (Flame, of course, is always changing, but the old woman—Roethke—is referring to the spiritual state of flaming into being; a supernatural condition that resembles Yeats's condition of fire and the mystic's illumination.) She rejects thinghood as it is seen in society's "loveless, temporal" machines (commodities and even institutions that have no spiritual meaning other than their immaculate hallways and their paper clips), but she does not reject the "natural shapes" that "become symbolical" for the visionary spirit. She boasts of her hermitlike self-reliance and her closeness to nature: "I am benign in my own company. . . . / The grandeur of a crazy one alone!— / By swoops of bird, by leaps of fish, I live." And she is fully aware that, in her spirit's finding its ultimate desire fulfilled here rather than in a changeless ideal, it is joining its own fate to that of all the transitory "natural shapes":

> My shadow steadies in a shifting stream;
> I live in air; the long light is my home;
> I dare caress the stones, the field my friend;
> A light wind rises: I become the wind.   (*CP*, 165-67)

This concluding passage of the third meditation provides an opportunity to contrast Roethke's group of poems with Eliot's *Four*

Quartets. "Meditations of an Old Woman" has sometimes been accused of being too derivative from the *Quartets*, but passages like this one, embodying the synthesis of opposing attitudes and therefore serving as the central impulse in Roethke's poems, express a belief that is diametrically opposed to the central theme of the *Quartets.* Whereas Roethke's old woman "becomes the wind," the narrative voice of Eliot's poem unswervingly condemns the realm of time, of change, as a suitable home for the human spirit. Here is one of several possible passages from the *Quartets* for contrast with Roethke's central theme:

> Here is a place of disaffection
> Time before and time after
> In a dim light: neither daylight
> . . . .
> Nor darkness. . . .
>   Only a flicker
> Over the strained time-ridden faces
> . . . .
> Men and bits of paper, whirled by the cold wind
> That blows before and after time. . . .[10]

The images used by the two poets are similar in these passages, but the intent of one set is the exact contrary of that of the other. Rather than leaning too heavily on Eliot, Roethke is actually answering him in a spirit of contradiction. For Eliot, time itself is the ultimate source of disaffection, but for Roethke the shifting stream and the wind, symbols of time and change, evoke affection.

The "Fourth Meditation" returns to the explicit development of the dialectical opposites of satisfaction and longing, once again ending in a higher level of acceptance of herself and of her fate than the old woman's meditations began with. The poem opens with the old woman looking with satisfaction over her past, self-reliant life: "I was always one for being alone, / Seeking in my own way, eternal purpose; / At the edge of the field waiting for the pure moment. . . ." But slowly the tone modulates into the longing for something more. "Yesterday" her growth was stretching "out the bones of [her] innocence," an image that may suggest giving birth, but what can her growth be today? "Yesterday" she "hid" her songs by singing only to herself, and, hermitlike, she then could be happy touching her own shadow, not needing anyone else. "But a time comes when the vague life of the [self-communing] mouth no longer

suffices. . . ." She then cites the cause of her present need for
something beyond her self-involved happiness: "The dead make
more impossible demands from their silence. . . ." The dead, whom
she will soon join, apparently make several undefined demands on
the living, one of which demands seems to be that the living speak
anew for the dead.

In the second section the old woman reviews the inadequacies
that might keep her from being an effective spokesman for the
dead: "What is it to be a woman? / To be contained, to be a
vessel?" This review culminates in the infuriating picture of a
woman as a human being who can only "gaze at a face with the
fixed eyes of a spaniel." Being unable to accept this view of herself,
she launches into an attack on the weak, emotionally sterile, women
whose lives have given that unacceptable stereotype some plausibil-
ity. These are the words the dead demand that she speak, and speak
in the fresh terms of her own time and place:

> I think of the self-involved:
> The ritualists of the mirror, the lonely drinkers,
> The minions of benzedrine and paraldehyde,
> And those who submerge themselves deliberately in trivia,
> Women who become their possessions,
> Shapes stiffening into metal,
> Match-makers, arrangers of picnics—
> What do their lives mean,
> And the lives of their children?

This invective, the essence of which has been spoken by many of
the great dead, is directed at those who have made their spirits'
home in the morguelike world of "thing-hood," those who, while
they have a chance during mortal life, have never known "the soul's
authentic hunger." Like a prophet, whether an ancient Cassandra
or a modern Germain Greer, the old woman "wishes them awake."
She prays for them: "May they be taken by the true burning; / May
they flame into being!" Then, with a difficult transition, she
envisions these embryonic spirits as beginners about to embark on
the natural path of evolution and growth, not on the perverted path
offered by society.

This last verse paragraph of section two is the sort that will
intrigue but frustrate many readers. The old woman envisions these
"still-to-be-born" souls "as figures walking in a greeny garden"
somewhere in the supernatural realm. But when they enter human,

mortal life they must recapitulate the whole progress of the race, beginning as "descendants of the playful tree-shrew that survived the archaic killers, / The fang and the claw. . . ." Along the route these evolving humanoid souls are transformed into predators, wielding "the club and the knout, the irrational edict, / The fury of the hate-driven zealot, the meanness of the human weasel; / Who turned a corner in time, when at last he grew a thumb. . . ." As the childish souls (each one "a prince of small beginnings") slowly progress, they speak "first in the coarse short-hand of the subliminal depths," primitive men uttering feelings that civilized men would repress. Eventually, with the beginning of literate history, they make from their "terror and dismay a grave philosophical language." If this racial evolution is translated into growth of the individual soul, it traces the progress of true education and maturation and stands in contrast to the false system sketched in the second section of "Her Becoming."

In the final section of the "Fourth Meditation" the old woman arrives at a synthesis that allows for her love of nature, with which the meditation began, and for the demands of the dead. For her a lake is a beautiful living thing that "breathes like a rose." She says what she has said in effect at the end of each of the earlier meditations—"Beguile me, change." Her tears, shed perhaps because of the "soul's authentic hunger," she drinks "in a place where all light comes," that is, in a place where she may flame into being. But she has not shirked her responsibilities: "I'm in love with the dead!" What this superficially strange line means is that she feels the bonds between her and the dead who have taught her how to live. They have taught her to waken the "self-involved" and to listen to her own "body speaking." They have also taught her the Elizabethan notion that a human being is "The first and last of all things," a little world, a microcosm, that encompasses something of all inanimate objects, plants, and animals. "Near the graves of the great dead" (the people who did not ignore the body's or the soul's authentic hunger when alive) "Even the stones speak" (*CP*. 168-70). The power of the dead to awaken even inanimate objects to life gives some measure of their ability to teach the living and of their worthiness to be loved.

The final mediatation, "What Can I Tell my Bones?" brings the group to a suitable close by showing the old woman arriving at a more stable equilibrium, a more secure sense of identity, than she has previously known. Like the beginning of the "First Meditation,"

"On love's worst ugly day," this one begins with the old woman dissatisfied, but now the dissatisfaction is deeper than it was then. On that "ugly day" she felt her spirit was not moving upward and that her body hated "the life within." Soon she realized that the journey of the spirit is something like a spiral and that on one side of the spiral the spirit seems to be moving contrary to its motion when on the opposite side. But in the final meditation she sickens of the whole circular, back-and-forth process. Each time she moves, for instance, from satisfaction to longing, she begins a new cycle:

> Beginner,
> Perpetual beginner,
> The soul knows not what to believe,
> In its small folds, stirring sluggishly,
> In the least place of its life,
> A pulse beyond nothingness,
> A fearful ignorance.

This is one of the passages in which Roethke echoes Yeats fairly closely, and since the Yeats lines are relevant to an idea in Roethke's poem they should be noted. In Yeats's "Sailing to Byzantium" the poet prays for the "sages standing in God's holy fire" to "consume [his] heart away; sick with desire / And fastened to a dying animal / It knows not what it is. . . ." The heart in Yeats's poem and the soul in Roethke's do not know what they are. Their sense of identity is troubled. In addition, both are joined to a physical body from which they will soon be freed. But there is a more intricate bond between the bones of Roethke's old woman and her perpetually beginning soul than between Yeats's heart and the "dying animal." The old woman warns: "O my bones, / Beware those perpetual beginnings, / Thinning the soul's substance. . . ." The bones symbolize the deepest part of her, and it may be impossible to separate their life from the soul's. In this state of "fearful ignorance" and the soul's attenuation, she is tired of "Longing for absolutes that never come." The "dance of natural objects in the mind" that once became "symbolical" and spoke to her of her own identity now has ceased. She has tired of "The songs from a spiral tree." Frustration and despair reign.

In the second section she holds a dialogue with herself. The first voice, speaking from her despair, answers the hopeful conclusion of Eliot's *Four Quartets*. Eliot affirms that "All shall be well and / All manner of thing shall be well. . . ." But Roethke's old woman feels that such a belief that all one's desires shall be fulfilled—particularly the bones' desire for immortality—is a "fatal" self-indulgence: "It is difficult to say all things are well, / When the worst [death] is about to arrive. . . ." But the answering voice within her reminds her that she is recognized by her fruits; her present feeling that she is nothing is a sign that she has matured from self into spirit: "The self says, I am; / The heart says, I am less; / The spirit says, you are nothing." The voice of despair, though, is not finished, and it asks, "What can I tell my bones?" Is not the bones' desire merely "a wind trapped in a cave?" This image of threatening enclosure has the same meaning that similar images have in the narratives— the poet cannot believe and therefore cannot see anything beyond the solid face of nature, which surrounds the spirit like a rocky wall. Echoing Ezekiel she asks, "Can these bones live?" and in her confused despair prays to her dead mother (and perhaps to Mother Earth) "tell me where I am!" She then wishes to be lulled ("delivered from the rational into the realm of pure song") as she had been when she was a "learned nimble girl" who was "sweetly daft." And then the answering voice within her tells her that it is the unending struggle *toward* God that matters; it does not matter that one never arrives there. Again, with images similar to those in the narratives, the threatening cave is transformed into a place of birth: "I rock in my own dark, / Thinking, God has need of me. / The dead love the unborn." The implication here is that death will not seal her eternally in the dark but will be a second birth. She will have the kind of life she knows the dead have.

In the third and final section, after the expression of faith with which the preceding section ends, she feels rescued from her despair, she takes stock of her new sense of identity, and she is granted a new kind of religious experience. This section, from beginning to end, resembles the last section of "The Lost Son," "It was beginning winter." As in that earlier poem, she sees the weed-skeletons in the wind as a sign of new life and she hears "The barest speech of light among the stones." She no longer fears death. As she thinks of whom she has become, she notes that the conventional images, comforts, and duties of organized religion are not part of the faith she has found: "Instead of a devil with horns, I prefer a serpent with scales; / In temptation, I rarely seek counsel; / A prisoner of smells, I would rather eat than pray." In other words, her faith is not an ascetic or otherworldly one that will insist she renounce physical nature. But her faith has indeed brought her somewhere she has never been. She is now "released from the dreary dance of opposites." She will never again be a beginner on a new round of the spiral that the spirit travels. This spiritual stocktaking is followed by a rapturous flight. Perhaps she has been "delivered into the realm of pure song." In any case, what follows is difficult to explain logically. She leaves her "father's eye" and shakes the secrets from "her deepest bones." By midnight, she "loves everything alive," and someone has taken "the darkness from the air." All of this suggests that she has been freed from every desire and fear that was weighted her down. Her longing for another condition, for "the absolutes that never come," has either been satisfied or ceased to matter. She proclaims, "I'm wet with another life."

The last lines of the poem record what has just occurred. Whereas the lost son finally arrived at a point of waiting for the return of the "lively understandable spirit," the old woman has grasped something that will never leave:

> What came to me vaguely is now clear,
> As if released by a spirit,
> Or agency outside me.
> Unprayed-for,
> And final.   (*CP* 171-73)

What occurred "*is* clear," not clear only during an ecstatic, flaming moment. It was "unprayed-for" because it goes beyond what she knew enough to pray for, such as "pure song." Perhaps most important is the strange comment on the giver of the gift—an "agency outside me." She knows now that she is not merely projecting her desires on the shapeless dark. The old suspicion that belief in the fulfillment of one's desires is a fatal form of self-indulgence has been overcome. She is at last free to believe that death will not absolutely end life.

The poems Roethke wrote in the 1950s build on the lessons he learned in writing his earlier rhymed-and-metered poems and free-verse narratives. The advances he made, though, in philosophical complexity and emotional maturity are even more important than his increased skills in prosody. The narratives written in the late 1940s do not develop any theme that has the ramifications that the principle theme of the 1950s has. That theme I have called "human desire and the shapeless night." Put simply, it means that the human spirit finds itself in a void where God and the spirit's own immortality seem to be nonexistent. The delusion that they actually do exist is created by the overpowering desire for them. "Four for Sir John Davies" expresses the skeptical force of this theme, but "Meditations of an Old Woman" shows the poet eventually breaking the hold of this skepticism. The narratives of the 1940s do not even develop the subsidiary themes that come with the emotional maturity seen in the poems of the next decade—the stable love of one woman and, following that, self-reliance. The best summary of the overall advance made in the poems of the 1950s may be to say that the lost son has become a man.

CHAPTER 5

His True Place: The Far Field

I *The "North American Sequence"*

T HE six poems of the "North American Sequence" restate most of the themes of "Meditations of an Old Woman" but in several ways go beyond those themes. As in the earlier group, here Roethke again explores the longing to know God and the untrustworthiness of paradisiacal visions; the comforting presence of the past, of childhood happiness, in memories; the "demands" the dead make on the living; the exasperation with people who make a "fetish of thing-hood"; and, finally, the attainment of spiritual equilibrium and maturity through a symbolic, finely felt union with nature. But in the present sequence Roethke trusts more readily than did the old woman in visions of fulfilled longings. And he relies less on memories of childhood happiness and awareness of the dead than she did. In lieu of these latter two spiritual supports, he explores the symbolic landscape in which he finds himself, seeking his "true place" as an adult who lives in a harsh world. The symbol that finally comes to express his tough endurance is a wild rose growing on a seaside cliff, significantly not growing in a greenhouse and not cared for by an old florist.

An understanding of the organization of the "North American Sequence" can be gained from an overview that focuses attention on just how Roethke comes to this culminating symbol, the "rose in the sea wind." Like the old woman of the earlier group, the "I" of this sequence is pushed into movement by a longing to see God but more particularly and more importantly by a longing to discover exactly what he can be united with in nature, especially in his "true place," which encompasses the North American landscape from southern New Hampshire (Oyster River) through Saginaw to Seattle.

The first poem, "The Longing," expresses his longing for "imperishable quiet" and establishes this northern strip of the United States as the land he will explore. "Meditation at Oyster River" shows Roethke uniting himself, as he has done in earlier poems, with the plucky and graceful creatures who are most vulnerable to death. In a sense, he finds that death's face cannot terrify him, that its dark depths are covered by light ("In the first of the moon, / All's a scattering, / A shining"). "Journey to the Interior" shows, through exploration of the symbolic landscape, the poet achieving a deeper self-awareness. He comes to understand that just because the perceiving mind shapes what it sees rather than passively accepting "objective" impressions, he does not need, therefore, to deny his intuitions of blessing. In other words, this skeptical poet comes to trust the landscape of his life, even though his eye altering alters all and even though he knows that he sees what he wishes to see. "The Long Waters," set on the Pacific coast where the sequence will end, deepens the poet's humility by showing his increasing sensitivity to the changes in his inner and outer landscapes, changes he has in the past taken too lightly. He does not fully understand the changes he sees, especially the change called death, but as he watches them more subtly and quietly the lack of understanding ceases to matter, and he is filled with love ("I embrace the world"). "The Far Field" shows the poet returning in memory to his earliest, though not most painful, encounter with death. He thinks of how he has arrived at his present mature state ("the end of things, the final man") and at his serene acceptance of his isolated, rugged world. "The Rose" brings the sequence to a beautiful close by showing the poet coming to an even deeper understanding of his present survival in a particular point in the territory he has explored, a point that is harsh but truly his. An important part of this understanding has to do with exactly what his memories of the greenhouse Eden and his father mean to him now. The sequence as a whole, then, is an account by means of detailed images of one man's difficult struggle into maturity and of his close union with his own particular world.

"The Longing" describes the poet, saintlike, turning away from his lust-fatigued society and entering the wilderness. In the "sensual emptiness" of "the raw cities," the "agony of crucifixion" is reenacted on barstools and replayed instantly, with analysis, over warm saliva-drenched microphones. The soul of each inhabitant of these cities, instead of growing happily ("Hands active, eyes cherished"), has been stunted and, "ready for any crevice," become an "eyeless starer." It is from "these nothings" that the "I" of the poem must begin his growth. From this "dark dream," his longing ("I'd be beyond; I'd be beyond the moon," echoic of Blake's drawing "I want, I want" in *The Gates of Paradise*) has led him on his lonely path so that when "the light cries out" he is "there to hear." He wishes to "unlearn the lingo of exasperation, all the distortions of malice and hatred" that infect the people of the raw cities. Then he turns in the direction of his longing:

> I would believe my pain: the eye quiet on the growing rose;
> I would delight in my hands, the branch singing, altering the
>   excessive bird;
> I long for the imperishable quiet at the heart of form. . . .

His pain is not someone else's crucifixion but his own slow growth, and the quiet he longs for is not that of a static perfection but that of something active and changing. The quiet will prove to be "imperishable" if it can absorb the disquieting fact of death and the invasion of "American sounds." The American sounds, which are heard later, are ones symptomatic of the raw cities pushing their blight ever further into the countryside. Roethke knows there is no place undisturbed by these sounds, but the place he is seeking will subdue them with its greater quiet. That happens in the final poem of the sequence.

He envisions the nature of his soul and its growth in its own true place in other images: "I would be a stream, winding between great striated rocks in late summer; / A leaf, I would love the leaves, delighting in the redolent disorder of this mortal life. . . ." Although the image of the stream winding between rocks is not the final image that objectifies his soul, it is one that, in several variations, leads toward the culminating symbolic rose. In the line just quoted, it suggests the lonely, rugged quality of his chosen world, and therefore of his soul. (It is a soul that prefers the silence of "great striated rocks" to the noise of the "warm microphones.") But that quality is balanced in the next line by an image which suggests that there is a sensuous richness he will not forsake. Discovering the unified meaning behind this paradox is one of the poet's motivations throughout the sequence. How can his soul find its home if it longs for a place that is both timelessly perfect and cluttered with the ever-changing things of this world?

Another paradox, also to be resolved, occurs as the quoted passage continues with images that further define "the imperishable quiet at the heart of form" and "the redolent disorder of this mortal life":

> This ambush, this silence,
> Where shadows can change into flame,
> And the dark be forgotten.
> I have left the body of the whale, but the mouth of the night is still wide;
> On the Bullhead, in the Dakotas, where the eagles eat well,
> In the country of few lakes, in the tall buffalo grass at the base of the clay buttes,
> In summer heat, I can smell the dead buffalo. . . .   (*CP*, 187-89)

Despite the comical anti-climax, these lines express a serious meaning. The apparent contradiction is that he wants to love the "redolent disorder of mortal life" where he can forget or escape the "shadow" of death, yet he is setting out to explore a world of predators and prey ("the eagles eat well") in which the stench of death is inescapable. Actually, this paradox is resolved by his saying that he has "left the body of the whale, but the mouth of the night is still wide." He has found a way of looking at life and death so that they are bearable, but he has not been able to convince his eyes that the great surrounding darkness will permanently flame into light. The last lines of the poem answer a passage in Eliot's *Four Quartets*. They do not weakly echo Eliot, as some critics have complained, but emphasize, like the concluding lines of the third "Meditations of an Old Woman," the difference between Eliot's desire to move away from a particular time and place into the timeless and Roethke's longing to find and understand his true place amid "the redolent disorder of mortal life." Eliot writes at the end of "East Coker": "Old men ought to be explorers / Here and there does not matter. . . ." Roethke's poem ends derisively but with a point deeper than mere derision: "Old men should be explorers? / I'll be an Indian. / Ogalala? / Iroquois." The point is that he will explore a particular place and not be driven to the comforts of organized religion by his awareness of death, as he felt Eliot had been.

"Meditation at Oyster River," a poem in four parts, begins the poet's active search for the place that will reveal to him what he is, his identity. The setting is the New Hampshire coast where Oyster River empties into the Atlantic, a place that seems right because it is filled with imperishable quiet: "No sound from the bay. No violence." The poet is alone watching the twilight fall. But, as the second section reveals, he himself is not as quiet as the scene because he is troubled by his old pain—his awareness of death: "The self persists like a dying star, / In sleep, afraid. Death's face rises afresh, / Among the shy beasts. . . ." His self is only beginning to perceive itself clearly and thereby become soul. It fears death but bravely joins itself to the "shy beasts" and their fate. Like them the poet knows himself to be an easy prey of death: "The doe with its sloped shoulders loping across the highway." While still in this early stage of psychic growth, he also feels himself to be like the water here in this place where the fresh water of the river mingles with the ocean—"Topped by cross-winds, tugged at by sinuous under-currents"— an image suggesting confusion rather than direction. His inner quiet is disturbed by various impulses.

The third and the final sections show his self's discovery of its proper direction and show its beginning motions. Just as the poet, in "this first heaven of knowing," feels himself united through imagi-nation (or empathy) with the shy beasts, so "the flesh takes on the pure poise of spirit." That is, the fear of the body's mortality recedes, and he seeks in memory a sound, even a violence, that will jolt him out of his present inaction. He first thinks of what his self needs to become like: "the first trembling of a Michigan brook in April". Then, by a process that several critics have referred to as sympathetic magic,[1] he pictures what is needed to get him from where he is to where he wants to be. He thinks of the Tittebawasee, the river flowing through his childhood hometown of Saginaw, Michigan, and sees it still frozen at the end of winter: "the midchannel begins cracking and heaving from the pressure be-neath." And he longs "for the blast of dynamite." In his meditation he then sees and hears "The sudden sucking roar as the culvert loosens its debris / . . . And the whole river begins to move forward, its bridges shaking." The details of this picture, many of which are left out here, suggest the smaller elements of the change in the poet's inner state. In the final brief section he feels that the threat, the mouth of the night, has withdrawn: "Now, in the waning of light, / I rock with the motion of morning." Still like the plucky and graceful sandpiper, his spirit runs in the waves on the shore of eternity. And the darkness is covered with light: "All's a scattering, / A shining" (CP, 190-92).

If "Meditation at Oyster River" shows Roethke using memory to set his self in motion toward becoming spirit, "Journey to the Interior" explores the changes in perception that accompany that motion, for these changes call into question what is real and what is delusion. The "long journey out of the self" is not a brief, comfortable ride. "There are many detours, washed-out interrupted raw places," and, as the details suggest, the frustrations to be suffered can be intense, even bringing the journey to a halt, "The way blocked at last by a fallen fir-tree."

In section two Roethke once again turns to memories of his Michigan boyhood, when as an adolescent learning to drive he raced "spitting and roaring" along the gravelly back roads. But the euphoria he felt then blends gradually into the lulling drive he is now making between Saginaw and Seattle. He is rocking with the motion of the distant sea and is dreamily aware of death's presence in the landscape: "And all flows past!— / The cemetery with two scrubby trees in the middle of the prairie, / The dead snakes and muskrats, the turtles gasping in the rubble. . . ." Being "lulled and half-asleep," just as he was at the end of "Meditation at Oyster River," he experiences another dreamlike alteration in his perception: "I rise and fall, and time folds / Into a long moment; / And I hear the lichen speak. . . ." His flesh being rocked almost to sleep, he becomes preternaturally observant.

The final section of the poem shows Roethke exploring the depths of this moment of change, not using his intellect to analyze it but his heightened sensitivity and intuition to feel its meanings. In his journey across the northern states he sees (in section two) "the sun come out of a blue cloud over the Tetons." With his altered perception (in section three) he sees the cloud as a prefiguration of his goal, the rose in the sea wind: "I see the flower of all water, above and below me, the never receding, / Moving, unmoving in a parched land, white in the moonlight: / The soul at a stand-still. . . ." The "stand-still" that he experiences here is not a static one; rather it is one in which his "thinking body" glimpses the "imperishable quiet at the heart of form." He is in a state of mind in which death is not forgotten but like the darkness is assimilated and transformed: "In the moment of time when the small drop forms, but does not fall, / I have known the heart of the sun,— / In the dark and light of a dry place, / In a flicker of fire brisked by a dusty wind." He is waiting, intensely aware, for the moment of change, for the drop to fall. This intensification of life takes place in "the stretch in the face of death," and he is pleased to be in a place that

closely resembles his spiritual home, the place where his soul will
stay, "a place leading nowhere."

The last lines of the poem harken back to the old woman in
"Meditations of an Old Woman." She, like the poet in "Journey to
the Interior," "delighted in surface change" and heard the stones
near the graves of the great dead speaking. In the present poem the
poet's "thinking body" sees synesthetically the grim silence of death
changing from darkness into song:

> As a blind man, lifting a curtain, knows it is morning,
> I know this change:
> On one side of silence there is no smile;
> But when I breathe with the birds,
> The spirit of wrath becomes the spirit of blessing,
> And the dead begin from their dark to sing in my sleep.
>
> (CP, 193-95)

That this change occurs in a dreamlike state may suggest that
Roethke is not intellectually convinced of its authenticity.

"The Long Waters," a difficult poem in five parts, shows Roethke
relinquishing his need to understand the details of a place that
closely resembles his spiritual destination. (His "true place" is to be,
as already pointed out, a seaside cliff on the Washington coast; here
he is on a "landlocked bay" near the Pacific.) The present poem
continues the movement set up in "Journey to the Interior" by
following the poet's increasing awareness of change, both inside his
mind and in the corresponding landscape, though this time the
change is not induced by a journey backward through time.

The poem begins with a review of what he knows and does not
know. The poet then broaches the crucial mystery of death, about
which he confesses to having been glib:

> And I acknowledge my foolishness with God,
> My desire for the peaks, the black ravines, the rolling mists
> Changing with every twist of wind,
> The unsinging fields where no lungs breathe,
> Where light is stone.

These lines are an expression of humility from a man who, until he
spoke them, was in danger of appearing to be an athlete of the
spirit, one for whom death had lost its terrifying power.

In the second section he prays to Mnetha, a false divinity in

William Blake's *Tiriel*, asking her to protect him from change, the shadow of death, that is always ultimately a form of the "dubious sea-change." He has temporarily ceased delighting in change and has once more begun envisioning a static paradise that can be entered only by those in whom pleasure has died. He blames himself for not having reached this perfection, a perfection which he will soon realize is false ("Feeling, I delight in my last fall").

In the third section he is rummaging like the lost son in the bug-riddled foliage of "this landlocked bay." The silence ("I have come here without courting silence") suggests the deadly visions of a translunar paradise, not the "imperishable quiet at the heart of form." Once again, as in "Meditation at Oyster River," the spirit's confused standstill is accompanied by images of salt and fresh water mingling. That imagery is amplified in the fourth section, which describes a recollection of "the eddying current. . . in the dead middle way, / Where impulse no longer dictates. . . ." In this "vulnerable place," where progress, a meaningful change, is not even hoped for, desire is suddenly awakened by a sea wind that flares up like "a fire, seemingly long dead. . . ." The spirit desires to move forward, out of this standstill, and immediately the poet's perception alters and he sees "in the advancing and retreating waters" a vision of his own childlike spirit. He had been on the verge of becoming lost in the deep waters of death's mystery, but unexpectedly he finds himself and becomes "another thing." He is also probably saved from becoming a conventionally religious man (like T. S. Eliot?) who humbly "acknowledges his foolishness with God" and prays to be carried into the timeless realm where he will escape all change. He has, instead, rediscovered his true nature: "I am gathered together once more; / I embrace the world" (*CP*, 196-98).

"The Far Field," the four-part title poem of the book, reexplores the meaning of death, with the poet again beginning his spirit's journey forward by going backward in time. The first section repeats the imagery of "Journey to the Interior," a frustrating attempt to travel when the spirit's way has been lost: "The road changing from glazed tarface to a rubble of stone, / Ending at last in a hopeless sand-rut, / Where the car stalls. . . ."

The second section begins, without explicit transition, in the poet's memories of his early days in and around a greenhouse. The focus of this memory is that in the far field one "learns of the eternal," meaning the terrifying, undeniable fact of death: "the

shrunken face of a dead rat, eaten by rain and ground-beetles . . . /
And the tom-cat, caught near the pheasant-run, / Its entrails strewn
over the half-grown flowers, / Blasted to death by the night watch-
man." But the child's "not excessive" grief is relieved by the song
of warblers, and his sight is "blurred from the bird shapes. . . ." His
self, which has not yet encountered death in a personal way, toys
with a soothing love of nature ("Fingering a shell, / Thinking: /
Once I was something like this, mindless") and with fanciful dreams
of escaping death through reincarnation ("Believing: / I'll return
again, / As a snake or a raucous bird, / Or, with luck, as a lion").
The second section ends with the poet boasting of his child-spirit's
bravery in the face of death, a bravery based, as mentioned, on
rather remote acquaintanceship:

> I learned not to fear infinity,
> The far field, the windy cliffs of forever,
> The dying of time in the white light of tomorrow,
> The wheel turning away from itself,
> The sprawl of the wave,
> The on-coming water.

If this is the beginning of his learning not to fear death, it is a
beginning that contributes to the growth and maturing of his spirit.
"The windy cliffs of forever" are part of his preparation for
discovering his true place near the rose in the sea wind.

The third section, like the preceding one, begins without a
transition. Abruptly, the poet is back in the present and experiences
an unprepared-for change. Perhaps the journey back to the far field
is actually the self exploring its own interior, the kind of self-
perception that, according to Roethke's scheme, transforms self into
soul. Now "The river turns on itself, / The tree retreats into its own
shadow. / I feel a weightless change, a moving forward / As of
water quickening before a narrowing channel. . . ." The moving
water with which he identifies his once-again-advancing self (or
spirit?) is flowing in the "stretch in the face of death," for it soon
plunges to "the alluvial plain." The degree of acceptance, of self-
discovery, of maturity, that he has achieved here he himself assesses:
"I have come to a still, but not a deep center. . . ." As he looks
inward—not in memory this time—his self-awareness deepens: "My
eyes stare at the bottom of a river. . . . I am renewed by death,
thought of my death. . . ." This self-awareness is a more mature

form of the union with nature he had experienced as a boy. "What I love is near at hand, / Always, in earth and air." Only a very narrow-minded reader indeed would condemn Roethke at this point for not being adequately "social" or "historical."

The final section is prepared for by what has preceded: it explores his feeling that he can embrace the world. In "The Long Waters" Roethke had prayed to be protected from "the dubious sea-change," but now, with a deeper awareness of his self and of death, he looks with serenity on his fleeting life: "The lost self changes, / Turning toward the sea, / A sea-shape turning around— / An old man with his feet before the fire, / In robes of green, in garments of adieu." The long waters of the mysterious sea, which he had retreated from, he now faces. He cannot comprehend what he faces, but he can recognize that it must be part of his true place. "A man faced with his own immensity / Wakes all the waves. . . ." The big questions that the mind frames lose their importance: "The murmur of the absolute, the why, / Of being born fails on his naked ears." With this accepting of the incomprehensible as a necessary part of his symbolic landscape, his spirit moves, not like water but "like monumental wind. . . . He is the end of things, the final man." He has achieved a maturity similar to that pictured in "Meditations of an Old Woman." For him, too, "All finite things reveal infinitude," and, after this very Blakean line, the poem ends with his experiencing an oceanic feeling of oneness with "memory," with the present, and with "the waters of the world" (*CP*, 199-201). He embraces it all.

"The Rose," another four-part poem, concludes the sequence by describing the particular point in the symbolic landscape where the poet's spirit is most fully expressed in the details of the time and place. All of these details appear earlier in the sequence, perhaps in a slightly different form from their final appearance, but in "The Rose" they are brought together in a unified picture. In the first section the poet identifies the place as one "where sea and fresh water meet," a place leading nowhere, an image that earlier suggested a failure to move forward but that now suggests the poet has arrived at his destination. Like the clay buttes of "The Longing," it is a place where the eagles feed well, "Where the hawks sway out into the wind, / . . . / And the eagles sail low over the fir trees. . . ." More importantly, it is a place where there are many birds but not the overwhelming birdsong he delighted in when younger: "The morning birds [are] gone, the twittering finches, /

But still the flash of the kingfisher, the wingbeat of the scoter / . . .
/ The moon retreating into a vague cloud-shape / To the cries of
the owl, the eerie whooper. / . . . / And there is silence." This
silence is, as the succeeding sections make clear, the "imperishable
quiet at the heart of form," and the coming darkness is not the
threatening mouth of the night but a prompter of minor ecstasy: "I
sway outside myself / Into the darkening currents. . . ." The influence of his memories of morning, a variation on his rocking with
"the motion of morning" in the waning light in "Meditation at
Oyster River," is suggested by the lines: "Was it here I wore a
crown of birds for a moment / While on a far point of rocks / The
light heightened. . . ?"

In the second section the poet describes the focal point of his
landscape—"The rose in the sea-wind." The section begins with an
image of the forward motion that the spirit's longing for growth
sometimes leads to: "As when a ship sails with a light wind . . . /
Our motion continues." But the rose, which represents the present
growth of this final man, does not move:

> But this rose, this rose in the sea-wind,
> Stays,
> Stays in its true place,
> Flowering out of the dark,
> Widening at high noon, face upward,
> A single wild rose, struggling out of the white embrace
>   of the morning-glory
> . . . .
> Beyond the sea pine, the oak, the wind-tipped madrona,
> Moving with the waves. . . .

The rose not only survives in its harsh surroundings, it seems even
to unify the opposing elements, such as the dark and high noon. He
then realizes how different this rose is from those of his childhood:

> And I think of roses, roses,
> White and red, in the wide six-hundred-foot greenhouses,
> And my father standing astride the cement benches,
> Lifting me high over the four-foot stems,
>   the Mrs. Russells, and his own elaborate hybrids,
> And how those flowerheads seemed to flow toward me,
>   to beckon me, only a child, out of myself.
> What need for heaven, then,
> With that man, and those roses?

The most striking single quality of the rose in the sea wind is its lonely toughness, not a quality found in the "elaborate hybrids" in their protective greenhouses, cared for by the old florist. The greenhouses and father were all the boy needed of heaven, but the final man the poet has become finds in this very different rose something of what he has lost. Again, memory is seen to be an essential part of his completed soul, but more important than memory trying to recapture the past as it was is his finding his own "true place."

In the third section the poet tests his feeling that he has come to the right place and in a physical, perhaps physiological, way proves that he has. He begins by thinking of "American sounds," and these gradually change from birdsong to the harsh sounds of the raw cities expanding and rebuilding. But his mind then turns back from "the hiss of the sandblaster, / And the deep chorus of horns . . ." to the imperishable quiet at the heart of form:

> I return to the twittering of swallows above water,
> And that sound, that single sound,
> When the mind remembers all,
> And gently the light enters the sleeping soul,
> A sound so thin it could not woo a bird,
>
> Beautiful my desire, and the place of my desire.

Roethke's use of the word "twittering" to describe the physical sound closest to the most satisfying spiritual condition he knew of contrasts perfectly with Eliot's use of the word in the *Four Quartets* to describe the vacuous world of time and place that he felt must be transcended: "Not here the darkness, in this twittering world."

The last verse paragraph of section three shows the poet at that peak moment of awareness when he awaits a change: "I think of . . . that lonely time before the breaking of morning" when "a drop of rain water hangs at the tip of a leaf / Shifting in the wakening sunlight / Like the eye of a new-caught fish." The section ends here with no suggestion of change. Usually such moments in Roethke's poetry precede a movement forward of the spirit, but this time his spirit is at home, as he says in the isolated line preceding the last verse paragraph: "Beautiful my desire, and the place of my desire."

In the final section Roethke reveals the full meaning of the rose. He himself lives in this quiet place, "far from the crash / Of the long swell" because being near this rose he has "come upon the true ease" of himself. And that "ease" he describes as an ecstasy: "As if another man appeared out of the depths of my being, / And I stood outside myself, / Beyond becoming and perishing / A something wholly other . . ." (*CP*, 202-5). Previously he had seen his own innocence, his own undeveloped spirit, running before him like a child on the windy headlands. Now it is an adult, a fully formed soul, with an accomplished identity, who appears. And this final form of self-awareness is like the dance the rose does in the wind: "As if I swayed out on the wildest wave alive, / And yet was still." He rejoices in being what he is, and the essence of that is change, no longer change of movement forward and backward but the change of natural rhythms, the tides, the day, and the seasons. These changes, like dancing, are a movement in place rather than an attempt to get somewhere else. He has arrived at "a place leading nowhere"—home. As the waves darken with approaching night, the rose keeps "the whole of light, / Gathering to itself sound and silence— / Mine and the sea-wind's." This final image suggests that the most important meaning of the rose is that it symbolizes the reconciliation of opposites he feels in his spirit now that it no longer needs to journey.

II   *The "Love Poems"*

The love poems should be considered as a sequence like the other three groups of poems constituting *The Far Field*, because these thirteen poems are more meaningful when read together than when read individually. The organization of this sequence is as follows: six poems are spoken by the woman, six by the man, and the middle poem, "Song," has a speaker whose gender is not identified. The attitudes of the woman and the man differ markedly. Neither celebrates his or her union with the other, the way the love poems of *Words for the Wind* do. Her poems are lonely, expressing more interest in the relation between body and soul than in that between her and the man. When a consummation of sorts is suggested, it is not sexual but meteorological, the woman seeing herself flying ecstatically into an approaching storm. The poems for male voice are equally lonely, but at least the man seems to feel the pain of separation more than the woman does. He is, moreover, darkly and vaguely pessimistic about aging and death. Despite, or perhaps because of, this unhappiness, his attitude toward love is sensual in contrast to her more platonic attitude.

Another point that needs to be considered in an introduction to the love poems is that several readers have complained—and I think rightly—that these poems lack the passion of the love poems of the early 1950s and are too obviously derived from Yeats. The different attitudes of the "lovers" resemble the attitudes of female and male speakers in several of Yeats's last poems. Because of that and because the style (especially rhythm, line length, diction, and images) of about half of Roethke's poems is borrowed from Yeats, these thirteen pieces are weaker than Roethke's earlier love poems and show less growth than the other sequences in *The Far Field*.

The first six poems, spoken by the woman, say hardly a word about the man but speak repeatedly of the body and soul and of the woman's true place being the heart of a storm. Two poems in particular deal with the relation between body and soul and do so in a Yeatsean way. "The Young Girl" asks, "What can the spirit believe?" and answers that "It takes the whole body." The spirit and body seem to be inextricably bound together. As she skips, apparently alone, on the shore, she waves her thin arms and tries to feel ethereal, her "bird-blood ready." Yeats's "The Lady's Second Song" concludes an exploration of the difference between the body's and the soul's ways of loving by asking, "If soul may look and body touch, / Which is the more blest?" Roethke's lady answers that question in favor of soul. In "Her Reticence" she imagines sending her lover only her "Disembodied, unbloody" hand and holding back everything—flesh or spirit—that he might grow passionate over:

> But never the full look of my eyes,
> Nor the whole heart of my thought,
> Nor the soul haunting my body,
> Nor my lips, my breast, my thigh. . . .

This "reticence," which is a love not expressed through the bodies of the lovers, is similar to that described in Yeats's "The Lady's Third Song," in which she warns a more sensual rival for the man to "Speak no evil of the soul." The lady's spirituality is such that she wishes to hear "the labouring heavens sigh" whenever a hand explores a thigh. Both Roethke's and Yeats's poems mentioned here attempt to treat highly abstract themes in too brief a space and are consequently unsatisfying.

Roethke's love poems in which the woman allies herself with a storm are more effective because they do not attempt to be profound in ten lines. "Her Longing" and "Her Time" are twice the length of the other poems for female voice, and they employ more concrete detail. "Her Longing," in two verse paragraphs, contrasts her vulnerable, "quiescent" days when she was "At one with the plants in the pond" with the present, of which she says, "The wild stream, the sea itself cannot contain me. . . ." Presumably, since this is a series of love poems, it is love that has wrought this change. She compares herself to several powerful birds and then, perhaps with a touch of reticent spirituality, to "A phoenix, sure of my body, / Perpetually rising out of myself, / My wings hovering over the shorebirds, / Or beating against the black clouds of the storm, / Protecting the sea-cliffs." This euphoria does not actually show her allying herself with the storm so much as conquering it. "Her Time," a twenty-six line poem in one sentence, is less euphoric in suggesting that her true place is flying in the storm. After the poem sinuously winds through a description of that waiting before the moment of change (a form of suspense Roethke used in the "North American Sequence"), the last lines arrive at the point

> When everything—birds, men, dogs—
> Runs for cover:
> I'm one to follow,
> To follow.   (CP, 210)

What this means is not that she is going to follow the other birds, the men, and the dogs, but that you, the reader, should follow her into the storm—if you dare.

Why should love poems deal with the pleasures of flying into storms? The answer to that very legitimate question is given in the last lines of "Her Words": "What weather of heaven is this? / The storm, the storm of a kiss." The woman's mentioning a kiss here is no real proof of the physicality of her love. It is the storm in each of her poems that metaphorically suggests the true quality of her love—a tumultuous kind of love that proves its strength in the heavens rather than in the bed.

The interlude poem, "Song," in which the speaker is unidentified, prepares for the darker male voice of the poems that follow by expressing a disillusioned questioning of love. The speaker—or speakers, if the poem is viewed as a duet—asks whether his, or her, youthful strength of emotion and sharpness of thought have gone. As he feels life being consumed, he asks of love: "What's to come? What's to come?" This anxiety about the possible pointlessness of everything is similar to that seen in another of Yeats's last poems, "What Then?" Each stanza of Yeats's poem cites an accomplishment that should make the poet's life seem satisfyingly complete but then repeats the nagging refrain, " 'What then?' sang Plato's ghost. 'What then?' " The similar uneasy questioning in Roethke's "Song" forms a transition between the female and male voices.

The love poems for male voice express his painful sense of separation from the woman and his bleak assessment of the future. "Light Listened" devotes two of its four stanzas to the pleasures of love that he and she shared but turns in the last two stanzas to the "deep shade" that "gathers night" and to the fact that "She changed with changing light." As the "cold air" brings rain, she sings "a final song"—a conclusion that does not bode well. "The Happy Three" dramatizes a marital quarrel in which Roethke decides to ignore his wife's scolding and get drunk. While he sits in the yard drinking, his pet goose, Marianne [Moore], comes up and begins pecking his toe. Immediately his rage disappears and he picks up the goose and runs into the house to get his wife. "Then we romped out again, / Out again . . . / Three in the sun." This lighthearted poem may not express the bleakness of several of the husband's other poems, but it clearly shows his pain at being angry with his wife. "His Foreboding," a poem in four stanzas, begins by expressing his "incommensurate dread / Of being, of being away / From one comely head." He wonders "who knows the end" of the separation that is hinted at when he hears himself "return / To nothingness alone." The woman seems to him a creature "all of light" who left him, and he can only "sniff the darkening air." Her desertion of him resembles the spirit's rejection of the body described in several of the woman's poems. The last poem of the sequence, "Wish for a Young Wife," continues in a muted way his feeling of separation from her. He is apparently much older than she, and he prays, without self-pity, that her limbs will "never wither" and that her hair will "ever blaze" when he has ceased to be—an effective conclusion to the sequence.

III   *The "Mixed Sequence"*

The "Mixed Sequence" acquires its title from its inclusion of poems on several unrelated themes treated in different styles. "The Abyss" is an ambitious philosophical poem in the style of "Meditations of an Old Woman," mingling concrete and abstract. Three poems, like "Otto," an elegy for Roethke's father, treat people known or loved years earlier. These poems describe in concrete detail ordinary incidents that "educated" Roethke when he was young or ones that capture the personality of the subject. Finally, several loose, descriptive poems treat "the small," the flora and fauna whose survival is least assured, as Roethke felt his to be.

"The Abyss" treats once again the dialectic, the back-and-forth movement, within Roethke's mind as it moves between intellectual analysis and intuition. These alternative ways of knowing once again fight for dominance. Conceptual knowledge, his reasoning faculty, tells him that death is inescapable and that life is swallowed up in the shapeless night. It tells him that any clue that he might have about his soul's immortality is merely wishful thinking, a delusion. But then intuition, immediate knowledge that has not been abstracted from physical sensation and emotion, sweeps away the arguments of reason: he cannot deny the visions and voices. Where will these cycles of thought and feeling end? Which will give him the final truth? "The Abyss," like the "North American Sequence," answers by showing Roethke discovering his true place.

Several interpreters have disagreed over the central theme of "The Abyss," and the interpretation offered here differs from the others. Actually, however, the conflict is more apparent than real. One interpretation views the poem as a dramatization of "a bout with madness," one of the recurring times when Roethke suffered a mental breakdown. Another interpretation views the poem as a dramatization of a mystical experience in which Roethke felt his oneness with God.[2] As stated in the preceding paragraph, the interpretation offered here is that Roethke is dramatizing an epistemological conflict between different ways of answering questions about the soul's immortality and God's existence.

It is an easy matter to reconcile these three views, for they say much the same thing in different words. One path that mystics follow toward union with God is the "negative way," a path that leads through the "dark night of the soul" in which the seeker finds himself deserted by God in an unbearable waste land. In psychological terms, the patient lost in the nightmare of a psychotic state is like the mystic in the dark night of the soul. Recovery, return to the relative serenity of the normal state, may be comparable with a feeling that one's life has become meaningful again, that one has rediscovered God and drawn near. The present interpretation accepts the validity of the religious and psychological views of "The Abyss" but uses different terms for several reasons: to avoid technical difficulties, to emphasize the vacillations in Roethke's intellectual and emotional beliefs, and to show the poem's use of symbolic landscape.

The first section of "The Abyss" reveals Roethke at the "Noon of failure," struggling to climb a (purgatorial?) stairway that "goes nowhere"—*not* to be confused with his true place, which is "a place leading nowhere." A voice warns him that the inescapable abyss is with him every step of the way. The exact nature of the abyss is unclear, but the dangerous height is like that of the cliff on which the rose in the sea wind blooms. Perhaps the edge of the abyss is once again going to prove to be one aspect of Roethke's true place, a part of his soul presented in terms of a symbolic landscape.

The second section shows the depths that Roethke's self-doubts sometimes reached. He acknowledges the voices, such as those in the preceding section, that have advised him, but he soon dismisses them as self-communings of his own "unguarded mouth." He acknowledges, again, his foolishness with God: "I have taken, too often, the dangerous path, / The vague, the arid. . . ." He is clearly on the mystic's "negative way." But then his nagging intellect asks, "Who is holy?" What other voice can he trust? Surely not those "who despise the dove," for they will never lead to peace, the "imperishable quiet at the heart of form." Then he thinks of the voice of one of the great dead who has passed through his same waste land and looked at it in a similar way:

> Be with me, Whitman, maker of catalogues:
> For the world invades me again,
> And once more the tongues begin babbling.
> The terrible hunger for objects quails me:
> The sill trembles.

He calls upon Whitman because Whitman was a poet who saw the trashiness that surrounded him but did not turn away from it. Whitman immersed himself in the "objects" of his world and through the force of his vision transformed them. Of course Eliot also saw the clutter that can so easily "invade" the soul, but his response was to discipline the "terrible hungers" right out of himself. Roethke, in "The Abyss" as much as anywhere, reveals his admiration for Eliot's descriptions of the nightmarish ugliness of modern urban life, but he does not join Eliot in renouncing it any more than he joins him in accepting the doctrines of an established church.

In the final lines of section two, Roethke, in disgust, sees the symbol of himself as a "furred caterpillar" crawling down the drawstring of a blind. The self-disgust suggested by this image and by the subsequent ones of a "mole winding through earth" and of "A night-fishing otter" is the self-disgust of one who has "lived with death." He has felt its presence and fears its return. Meanwhile, there seems little chance that the blind on which he is crawling will be raised and that he will look past the sill and see God.

The third section states its point conceptually but then restates it in the concrete language of the senses and the emotions. The first two lines explain abstractly why Roethke feels the "terrible hunger for objects." Immersing or lulling oneself in "thing-hood" is a form of relief from the vision of death and of the abyss. "Too much reality can be a dazzle, a surfeit; / Too close immediacy an exhaustion. . . ." Physically and emotionally, such a vision resembles the chastening "cold fire" one feels when opening a florist's refrigerator on a hot August day. It is like climbing a mountain above the abyss where one misstep will plunge the climber from "The slippery cold heights." But the vision of reality Roethke is trying to convey cannot be simply equated with the terror that death holds. Although the "burning heart" of this reality is "abominable," like death, it is also a volcanic core in which there is "A terrible violence of creation." The abyss, then, may be a manifestation of God, the creator who can make even galaxies spew their fire into the void. Section three ends with a sudden swing away from this blinding vision back toward the serene and the normal: "The burning lake turns into a forest pool, / The fire subsides into rings of water, / A sunlit silence." The part of the mind that wants conceptual clarity, that wants to know "what speech abides" because it is true, would ask what the vision revealed: a glimpse of the divine? a manic hallucination? or an inspired poet's imaginings?

Section four shows Roethke at first questioning the validity of his vision, then trying to renounce his reasoning faculty as a guide to the speech that abides, and finally being granted (by whom?) the "not-knowing" that he seeks. He supposes that whatever he sees of the Beyond, of the soul's eternal life, must be a figment of his dreaming mind. He asks himself, "How can I dream except beyond this life?" He wishes he could unanalytically and unskeptically accept the dream as truth: "I envy the tendrils, their eyeless seeking. . . ." And no sooner is this wish expressed then he feels an inner response: "In this, my half-rest, / Knowing slows for a moment, / And not-knowing enters, silent, / Bearing being itself. . . ." Perhaps the "half-rest" blurs the distiction between waking and sleeping, between believable fact and probable delusion. In any case, the demand for conceptual conviction diminishes, and a change occurs.

But the reader needs some background to understand the change. "Not-knowing" is a recognized stretch on the mystic's negative way toward union with God. And "being" is a venerable alternative to the dispiriting dialectical process of becoming, the constant shuttling between contraries. In Roethke's poem, the skeptical intellect intrudes once more for a single line: "Do we move toward God, or merely another condition?" But the change toward which the poem has been moving begins to occur when the intellect is answered immediately and emphatically by intuition, physical and emotional: "By the salt waves I hear a river's undersong. . . . / I rock between dark and dark. . . . / And I embrace this calm—. . . / A luminous stillness." Only an intuitive, sympathetic listener can hear the undersong of the flux, the flowing stream. Whitman heard it and helps Roethke. The blinding vision on the "slippery cold heights" was too intense to be sustained, but the luminous afterglow will last. A voice, from whatever source, invites him to draw near.

The fifth section is Roethke's confirmation of the Whitmanesque union he has achieved with his true place; unfortunately Roethke, in this final section, does not return to the central image of the abyss. Perhaps the presence of the abyss is implied in the climactic image, which I will discuss in a moment. The section begins, surprisingly, with the dialectic still in progress: "I thirst by day. I watch by night." Roethke's sense of separation from the Absolute is suggested by the distinction between him as the receiver who is also received and the ultimate receptacle: "I receive! I have been received!" But whatever, whoever, has received him has brought him closer to his place: "I hear the flowers drinking in their light. . . ." He does not experience, as mystics do, union with God, but he has accepted the abyss as an enlivening rather than terrifying part of his spiritual home:

> I am most immoderately married:
> The Lord God has taken my heaviness away;

> I have merged, like the bird, with the bright air,
> . . . .
> Being, not doing, is my first joy.   (*CP*, 219-22)

His "heaviness," which is his attachment to "thing-hood" and, perhaps, his "bout with madness," has been taken away, and he, "like a bird," has found his "first joy." He soars—in the "bright air," all that remains of the abyss—above the limited and limiting process of "doing."

Bringing the reader abruptly back to earth after the spiritual flight of "The Abyss," the next three poems in the "Mixed Sequence" ("Elegy," "Otto," and "The Chums") deal with family and friends from Roethke's boyhood. The "Elegy" for Aunt Tilly describes her acts of charity (she "fed and tended the infirm, the mad, the epileptic") and courage ("with a harsh rasp of a laugh at herself, / Faced up to the worst"). But despite these she "died in agony." The poem ends with Roethke picturing her in "some celestial supermarket . . . bearing down . . . on the quaking butcher" —a conclusion that almost frivolously suggests death has not triumphed after all (*CP*, 223).

"Otto," on the other hand, shows that, although the past can return with beautiful clarity in memory, it is irrevocably lost. Roethke celebrates his father's love of his work ("When flowers grew, their bloom extended him"), his skill as a woodsman, and his bravery in dealing with a couple of poachers. The final judgment, however, is that Otto was "both saint and boor," the latter because, among other things, he killed a neighbor's cat and "took it to her, by the tail." The last of the four stanzas turns from Otto to Roethke's memory of himself as a boy watching the sun rise over the greenhouses. The final line is a cry for everything he has lost: "O world so far away! O my lost world!" (*CP*, 224-25).

Of the remaining thirteen poems in the "Mixed Sequence," all deal in one way or another with death, especially with death's easy prey—sick houseplants, meadow mice, birds, mad poets, and "our small souls." "The Meadow Mouse," a poem in two sections, describes Roethke taking care of a baby mouse and feeling a growing fondness for it until one morning he finds it gone. The second section shows Roethke worrying about the way in which his friend will meet death:

> Where has he gone, my meadow mouse,
> My thumb of a child that nuzzled in my palm?

> To run under the hawk's wing,
> Under the eye of the great owl watching from the elm-tree,
> To live by courtesy of the shrike, the snake, the tom-cat. (*CP*, 227)

Of course, the point is that those predators have no "courtesy," and the meadow mouse will not even make it past the elm tree. The final lines constitute a kind of Neoplatonic ladder (see the discussion of "Four for Sir John Davies"), Roethke's compassion ascending from the one mouse to "All things innocent, hapless, forsaken."

"The Geranium," like "The Meadow Mouse," expresses Roethke's feeling of closeness to some helpless living thing, but this poem does not approach so closely the dangers of sentimentality. For one thing, the son of the old florist is himself responsible for the geranium's sad condition since he had, before beginning a "new routine" of vitamins and water, been feeding the plant "gin, bobbie pins, half-smoked cigars, [and] dead beer. . . ." But the therapy did not have a chance to take effect before "that snuffling cretin of a maid / Threw her, pot and all, into the trash-can. . . ." The poem ends with poetic justice when Roethke "sacked the presumptuous hag the next week . . ." (*CP*, 228-29). This is one of the unfortunately rare poems in which Roethke displays his sense of humor.

"The Pike" is set in the apparently peaceful underwater world of "The Minimal" and, like a number of other poems and passages, suggests the quiescent state of the spirit before it begins to move forward: "The crabs tilt and eat, leisurely / And the small fish lie, without shadow, motionless. . . ." In fact, Roethke even reminds himself that this is one of those symbolic landscapes in which the self undergoes a moment of change and begins the transformation into soul:

> A scene for the self to abjure!—
> And I lean, almost into the water,
> My eye always beyond the surface reflection;
> I lean, and love these manifold shapes. . . .

But this time the change is not the expected one but the sudden striking of death: "With one sinuous ripple, then a rush, / A thrashing-up of the whole pool, / The pike strikes" (*CP*, 233). The poem is more effective for ending here, without comment, than it would be if Roethke had intruded a comment on the nature of death.

The "Mixed Sequence" exhibits a more thorough separation between abstract commentary and concrete presentation than any of the other sequences in *The Far Field*. As mentioned earlier, the majority of poems in this sequence deal with the theme of death's victimization of "the small." "All Morning," like about half of the poems, describes its subject, "a delirium of birds," in very detailed terms. The idea of death enters the concrete poems without comment, as in "The Pike," or enters only obliquely, as when "all morning" becomes a "perpetual Sunday" with the presence among the living birds of "those birds forever dead, / The passenger pigeon, the great auk, the Carolina paraquet, / All birds remembered, O never forgotten!" (*CP*, 234-35). The abstract, discursive poems deal with the theme of death in a different way. "Song," for instance, asks, "Whence, death?" and answers, "From dire hell's mouth, / From the ghost without breath, / The wind shifting south" (*CP*, 236). "The Tranced," to choose another example, follows a very abstract argument to the conclusion that when "Our small souls" ceased hiding "from their small agonies," "what died with us was the will to die" (*CP*, 237-38). In the last sequence of *The Far Field*, Roethke returns to the mode of "The Abyss," the "North American Sequence," and the "Meditation of an Old Woman," in which the development of relatively complex philosophical ideas is carried on inseparably from the unfolding of the concrete details of the images.

IV   *The "Sequence, Sometimes Metaphysical"*

The final sequence of *The Far Field*, the "Sequence, Sometimes Metaphysical," is one in which Roethke again fuses ideas and images, as he had done in "The Abyss" and "North American Sequence." That fusion in itself would justify the title "metaphysical," but a further justification is that the sequence is "a drive toward God: an effort to break through the barrier of rational experience" into the supernatural.[3] The success of this effort is perhaps even more ambiguous than was the success of similar efforts in Roethke's other "metaphysical" meditations. The present sequence is only "sometimes metaphysical" because several of the poems do not participate in this drive toward God and do not fuse images and ideas. The majority of the poems, though, are metaphysical (for both reasons); and these poems develop, with an exception noted later, themes already explored in Roethke's poetry.

Roethke develops four main themes in the metaphysical poems of this sequence. He again uses the idea of a symbolic landscape, though this time in a much sketchier way than he had in the "North American Sequence." He also pursues, more deeply than he had before, the theme that I have called "desire and the shapeless night." He continues with the theme that is practically never absent from his poetry—the search for identity, the growth of the self into spirit or soul. Finally, he develops a theme closely related to the search for identity—the "barrier of rational experience." This idea is actually a variation on the theme treated earlier that focuses on a moment of change, a sudden swing from despair to joy. These four themes, while they do not begin to exhaust the meanings of the poems, are the central "thought-work," as Roethke once called it, that lies behind the sometimes obscure surfaces of the metaphysical poems of this last sequence. There are, in addition, several new concerns in these poems, so undeveloped they are difficult to detect, but if Roethke had lived to write more they might have become his new central themes. These will be introduced after discussion of the first poem in the sequence.

"In a Dark Time," the first and most difficult poem of this last group, is possibly the best and most difficult poem Roethke ever wrote (*CP*, 239). It is in four six-line stanzas with a slant-rhyme scheme of *a b b a c c*. It is metaphysical in the two senses employed here: it is a drive toward God and it fuses the ideas it treats with the images of what seems to be the poet's landscape. Roughly speaking, the first stanza shows Roethke searching for his identity as a mortal being; the second shows him invoking the aid of simpler, subhuman life forms and beginning to move toward what he is seeking; the third shows the change in perception that occurs when self becomes spirit; and the fourth shows the spirit crying out when it achieves an intense but ambiguous vision. Readers of Roethke's poetry are fortunate that "In A Dark Time" was the subject of a symposium in which it was discussed by three other poets and then commented on by Roethke himself. The following interpretation is basically a paraphrase of Roethke's comments.[4]

In the first stanza Roethke sketches his self-portrait against the background of a symbolic landscape (that is, a landscape that projects or objectifies his own spiritual states) which is pervaded by the awareness of death. Whether this is the depressive phase of the manic-depressive cycle or the mystic's "dark night of the soul" does not matter. The flesh-bound self finds itself "In a dark time" and begins to see, begins to become self-aware. Already in the second and third lines, there is a feeling of detachment as the self steps outside and looks at itself: "I met my shadow in the deepening shade; / I hear my echo in the echoing wood. . . ." The self's recourse, like the lost son's, is to look to creatures it feels close to: "I live between the heron and the wren, / Beasts of the hill and serpents of the den." As Roethke says in his discussion of the poem, these creatures give him clues to his identity (he is wise and tough like a heron; he is courageous and lecherous like a wren), but they do not prevent his "vacillating between identities."

In the second stanza Roethke turns to a second aid in his "spiritual ascent or assault," this time one that the old woman in "Meditations of an Old Woman" and the lost son both had recourse to—the dead. The "high-falutin' rhetoric," as Roetke calls it, of the first two lines is an apparently successful attempt to summon the spirit of Yeats: "What's madness but nobility of soul / At odds with circumstance?" This invocation, which vaguely echoes several passages in Yeats, is immediately followed by the "burning of revelation," as Roethke says in his prose comment. The self is moving on its journey, and the dark time is no longer dark: "The day's on fire!" However, the "true self" is perhaps moving into a cave or, as the image symbolizing the unknown shifts, along the edge of an abyss. Roethke seems to be stressing for his reader that the journey is not undertaken lightly.

In the third stanza the alteration in perception (the self becoming spirit) signaled in the preceding stanza is confirmed. The self—which, as "Meditations of an Old Woman" makes clear, operates by dialectic, understanding and manipulating its world by means of contraries—now has transcended that mode of perception and action. No longer does the self—now spirit— see the difference between day and night: "in broad day the midnight [has] come again!" The spirit reads the hinted messages of the supernatural everywhere, "All natural shapes blazing unnatural light."

But in the fourth stanza, Roethke does not move to the easy affirmation of God's concern for man and of the soul's immortality that would seem to be in store. Instead, he gives way to self-doubts again; or, to put a better construction on this magnificent, difficult stanza, his intellectual honesty makes a final effort to test the validity of what he sees with this blinding sight: "Dark, dark my light, and darker my desire. / My soul, like some heat-maddened summer fly, / Keeps buzzing at the sill. Which I is *I*?" According to

Roethke's prose paraphrase of these lines, he is crying out to himself, "Not only [is] my 'sense-ridden' self an 'intolerable' creature waiting to die, but my soul is too". This uncertain identity and self-loathing repeat, but with much greater emotional intensity, the earlier pain associated with seeking the "Beasts of the hill and serpents of the den." Then, something inexplicable happens. As he begins once more to climb out of the pit of his fear, he feels his "mind enter itself, and God the mind." Roethke's comment on this line attempts to explain the inexplicable by pointing out that the usual Christian accounts have God entering the heart. The fact that here He is entering the mind indicates that Roethke is presenting a change in belief or understanding, perhaps in the way he sees himself and his world; he is not undergoing a typical Christian conversion. His new "knowledge" is not the mystic's complete union with God but is a sudden ascent in which he "knows" that he has become "the Godhead itself, not only the veritable creator of the universe but the creator of the revealed God," as he says in his prose comment. This "cry from the mire," as Roethke calls it, may mean that he continues to be aware that his own desire for God may create God. The idea is similar to Voltaire's aphorism that if God did not exist it would be necessary to invent him. The last phrase of the poem, "free in the tearing wind," means that the wind is weeping in sympathy with the distraught seeker and that the wind is "buffeting" man and God together. This second meaning further unites the man and God because both suffer from the rebelliousness of their creations.

The remaining poems in the "Sequence, Sometimes Metaphysical" continue the "drive toward God" with less intensity but greater clarity. In addition to the four themes already mentioned (breaking the barrier of rational experience, altering perception, the search for identity, and the symbolic landscape), these poems express new concerns—bodily decrepitude or aging and, closely associated, the horror of being hospitalized. They are also distinguished by the use of a refrain ("dance on") embedded in several poems, linking them together. Finally, they record not a death-bed conversion by any means, but a detectable Christianizing of Roethke's spiritual longings. Each of these new directions will be discussed in connection with the poems that express it.

"In Evening Air," a four-stanza poem immediately following "In a Dark Time," shows Roethke calmly reflecting on the furious "ascent or assault" of the preceding poem, so calmly in fact that he seems quite at home inside the barrier of rational experience. As the title indicates, he is once again in or about to enter a dark time. He tells himself that his creative powers, his ability to write poetry however dark his theme, will sustain him: "I'll make a broken music, or I'll die." With much more humility than displayed in "In a Dark Time," he prays, "Make me, O Lord, at last, a simple thing / Time cannot overwhelm." Looking back on that preceding poem ("Once I transcended time"), he seems now content with quiet reflection rather than making another assault. Even the alteration in his perception, seeing a sunlit tree lose its light as night comes on, does not have the intensity or the agonizing significance it has in those poems where it is part of the manic-depressive cycle. His acceptance comes quietly: "Night I embrace, a dear proximity." The final stanza does not introduce a turn in the unfolding of the poem's theme like the final stanza of "In a Dark Time," but underscores the quiet acceptance: "I bid stillness be still. / I see, in evening air, / How slowly dark comes down on what we do" (*CP*, 240).

"The Sequel," a poem of four eight-line stanzas, introduces the new concerns in this sequence (bodily decrepitude and the "dance-on" refrain) and develops its themes more complexly than "In Evening Air." The poem begins with self-doubts ("Was I too glib about eternal things") and, like Roethke's love poems of the 1950s, suggests he has hoped to find solace for his immortal longings in love of a woman and has found only grief: "Whom do we love? I thought I knew the truth; / Of grief I died, but no one knew my death." No one knew his death, because it was emotional and hidden inside him. The small creatures, though, do not disappoint him; he is with them in a dark time, and they bring him to light: "We danced, we danced, under a dancing moon; / And on the coming of the outrageous dawn, / We danced together, we danced on and on." In the third stanza, his thoughts return to the woman, this time the thoughts being illuminated by morning light. But the inescapable truth is that she left him, "she swayed away / To the dark beginning of another day." Where, or rather, who does that leave him? He answers that question for himself in the last lines of the final stanza:

> I am a man, a man at intervals
> Pacing a room, a room with dead-white walls;
> I feel the autumn fail—all that slow fire
> Denied in me, who has denied desire.   (*CP*, 241-42)

He is an adult human being, not a lost son and not one of the small, loved creatures. More than that, he is a man who does not always have the "morning motion of a happy mind." Periodically, he is hospitalized for a mental disorder, a fact effectively represented in the compulsive redundancy of the lines quoted. And still more he is a man who feels the aging of his body and yet feels also the frustration of the "wild longings of the insatiate blood." It is unusual for a Roethke poem to end with an expression of personal failure. Almost always for him a sense of inadequacy or a longing, for a woman or for God, leads to movement of the self. "The Sequel" reserves that expected turn for the next poem.

"The Motion," a poem of four six-line stanzas, describes ("shows" or "dramatizes" would be the wrong words) the self's growing out of lust and into love and ends with an expression of vague hope. It is not nearly as good a poem as the less saccharin and platitudinous "Sequel." The first stanza describes the motions of the soul (butterflylike) and points the moral: "By lust alone we keep the mind alive, / And grieve into the certainty of love." The second stanza asserts that Roethke's love, like Whitman's, dares to embrace everything in the world. The third stanza, the most preachy of the four, acknowledges that "love's a faring-forth" and declares that the only "things of earth" old enough to live are those who know this "final certitude, / This reach beyond this death, this act of love / In which all creatures share, and thereby live. . . ." The final stanza returns to the butterfly image of stanza one and praises the childlike vision that sees God smiling "down this space. . . ." The last two lines bring the religious affirmation to a fitting end, in a time of brightness: "Hope has its hush: we move through its broad day,— / O who would take the vision from the child?—/ O, motion O, our chance is still to be!" (*CP*, 243). Again, Roethke ends a poem in a way unusual for him. A reader of his poetry would expect an affirmation mixed with awareness of imperfections, like that at the end of "The Rose," or an ambiguous one, like that at the end of "In a Dark Time." The next poem is an adequately dark foil for "The Motion."

"Infirmity," a poem of six six-line stanzas, develops the theme of bodily decrepitude and does so by means of concrete details, bringing the sequence back to the "metaphysical" mode temporarily abandoned in the discursive poem "The Motion." In the first stanza Roethke tries unsuccessfully to convince himself that his "image cannot die." Even though the outward image that he stares

at in a "deepening pool" shows no change, his internal infirmity,
physical not spiritual this time, is developing almost unchecked. He
tries to see this mortification of the flesh as a means of bringing his
soul closer to God:

> Sweet Christ, rejoice in my infirmity;
> There's little left I care to call my own.
> Today they drained the fluid from a knee
> And pumped a shoulder full of cortisone. . . .

His soul "delights in that extremity" because it makes it easier for
him to die to himself, that is, to "move beyond" the pleasure and
pain calculus, the dialectic, by which the self operates. In the fifth
stanza Roethke makes his usual obeisance to the "small" that have
brought him to love and then makes the only specifically Christian
affirmation anywhere in his poetry: "My soul is still my soul, and
still the Son, / And knowing this, I am not yet undone." These lines
seem to say both that he feels his soul is at one with the Son of God
and that he does not fear death. The final stanza does not take
anything away from that affirmation. When the dialectic of the self
is overcome, "When opposites come suddenly in place," he experiences that change in perception that always indicates his spirit's
health:

> I teach my eyes to hear, my ears to see
> How body from spirit slowly does unwind
> Until we are pure spirit at the end.   (CP, 244)

Thus "Infirmity," like "The Sequel," ends with an unqualified
expression of faith, and this time that faith is most likely Christian.

The earlier Roethke would have fought against the otherworldli-
ness expressed in the last lines of "Infirmity" and would have
insisted on reminding his spirit that it could not know, with "final
certitude," whether it would even exist once it was unwound from
the body. Roethke does not do that here, and on the basis of that
and of the last two poems to be discussed, it may be fair to speculate
that had Roethke lived longer his poetry would have developed in
this new direction. I would also speculate that his judgment of T. S.
Eliot would have moderated.

"The Marrow," a poem in four six-line stanzas, is a sequel to
"Infirmity," developing the themes of bodily decrepitude and the

turn to Christianity. The title refers to the innermost part of himself that Roethke with saintlike humility wishes to offer to God. In the first stanza Roethke seems to be in his true place by the rose in the seawind, but he is afflicted by self-doubts— not the usual ones about his identity but ones about his accumulated sins: "The wind from off the sea says nothing new." "The sharp speech of a crow" tells him his "drinking breeds a will to die." And the last lines of the stanza suggest that Roethke has left far behind him the comfort he once took in loving one woman: "What's the worst portion in this mortal life? / A pensive mistress, and a yelping wife." This is an unlikely beginning for another of the spirit's ascents toward God, but that is exactly what it turns out to be. In the second stanza, without any preparation, he speaks of contemplating the face of God (Christ?), apparently losing his soul in the dazzling vision. As in "The Sequel" he comes to realize his own humanity and maturity through this "brooding on God." His body with its infirmities reminds him that it is still interwound with his spirit: "Pain wanders through my bones like a lost fire; / What burns in me now? Desire, desire, desire." In the third stanza he does not turn on his desire in disgust, as he does in "In a Dark Time" and elsewhere, but with a determination suiting his maturity he struggles to waken from his mortal slumbers into a fuller, closer knowledge of God:

> In sleep's half-death,
> My body alters, altering the soul
> That once could melt the dark with its small breath.
> Lord, hear me out, and hear me out this day:
> From me to Thee's a long and terrible way.

The body's decrepitude cannot but affect the soul, and this new humility, in place of the spiritual athleticism of "In a Dark Time," leads to a quiet longing that Roethke realizes cannot be satisfied by anything inside him. In the final stanza his humility is even more pronouncedly Christian. He speaks of being driven by suffering and love "When light divided on a storm-tossed tree," a probable reference to the Agony and Crucifixion of Christ. If it is true that Roethke has come to see the Crucifixion not as an emotionally and temporally distant event but as part of his own experience, he asks to draw near and in his own way participate: "I would be near; I shut my eyes to see; / I bleed my bones, their marrow to bestow / Upon that God who knows what I would know" (*CP*, 246). It is a new thing for Roethke to speak of God as if He had an existence and a knowledge independent of what the mortal with all his desires invested Him with. The relevant desire, the knowledge Roethke wishes God would share, is undoubtedly the old one of what becomes of the spirit when it is unwound from the body.

"Once More, the Round," the last poem of the sequence, happily expresses Roethke's conviction that he shall share that knowledge: "What can be known? The Unknown." As he learns more of what there is to be known, things in the dark become more visible. He adores his life with the "abiding" small: they endure. He also adores his life because, as William Blake taught him, his "Eye altering all" does not reveal the hallucinations of a madman but the deepest truth: "And I dance with William Blake / For love, for Love's sake. . . ." Like the abiding small, a love may be vulnerable but Love endures. The poem and sequence end with the affirmation that dancing, which is not meant to get the dancer anywhere, gets him to the only place there is to Be: "And everything comes to One, / As we dance on, dance on, dance on" (CP, 251). Roethke's spirit at last enjoys its "long and terrible" journey toward God, a journey in which finally for Roethke every step is a homecoming.

CHAPTER 6

The Final Man

I N "The Far Field" Roethke speaks of "the final man" and says of
him, "The murmur of the absolute, the why / Of being born fails
on his naked ears" (*CP*, 201). As Roethke recedes into history, a
number of questions about his place and importance in American
poetry must be answered. The living must draw some conclusions
about what he accomplished with his life. It is always difficult, in
any century, to measure the achievement of a poet who has not yet
receded comfortably into history, and now, in the last quarter of the
twentieth century, such judgments are harder to make than ever.
To make them, one must have some idea about who will be reading
poetry in fifty or a hundred years and why they will be reading it.
The following remarks are conjectures about why Roethke's stature
has not yet been accurately estimated, about what he contributed to
American poetry, and finally about his appeal to succeeding generations of poets and readers. The murmur of the absolute cannot be
heard in this attempt to guage the final man that Roethke will be.

Why has Roethke's stature not yet been accurately assessed? The
answer seems to be that Roethke's closest readers are still engaged
in finding the best way of talking about what he is doing in various
poems. The present study, for instance, is an introduction to
Roethke's major sequences and as such has not been able to judge
closely the merits of separate poems. It has seemed more important
here to offer some relatively new ideas about what Roethke was "up
to." To date, no book or article on Roethke has begun the by now
overdue process of evaluating the poems in light of each other and
in light of the work of Roethke's contemporaries. How well, for
instance, does Roethke's "Fourth Meditation" stand up beside
Auden's "In Praise of Limestone" or beside Lowell's "The Public
Garden"? Instead of trying to arrive at judgments of such questions,
many of Roethke's interpreters seem to have bogged down in
needlessly complex terminology. Even so recent a book as Harry

Williams' *"The Edge Is What I Have"* (1977), which in its preface
claims to be a "critical assessment," does not pass judgment on the
poems examined. Undoubtedly, before the necessary process of
judgment can get fairly underway, the critics' overreliance on the
terminology of mysticism, Jungian psychoanalytic theory, and an-
thropology will have to be outgrown.

Just as the critics have neglected to begin the serious evaluation
of Roethke's poems, so the editors of anthologies, whose business it
is to select the best and the most representative of a poet's works,
have not made a good start either. The collections of modern
American poetry usually print several of a small group of Roethke's
poems—poems that are not examples of his best work. Before
Roethke's stature can be securely established, a critical winnowing
process must be carried out. In my opinion, the frequently anthologized pieces, like "Dolor," "My Papa's Waltz," and "The Geranium," must be replaced in future anthologies by "The Lost Son,"
"In a Dark Time," and poems from "Meditations of an Old
Woman" and from "The North American Sequence." These afford
a true sampling of his best and most representative work.

The question concerning Roethke's contribution to American
poetry is even harder to answer than the question of why his stature
has not yet been accurately assessed. There is one important way in
which Roethke failed to contribute what might have been expected
of him. He did not join in the immense dialogue that the best of his
peers, such as Eliot, Auden, and Lowell, carried on with the past.
These poets openly addressed many of their poems to writers of
earlier centuries, while Roethke rarely did so. A glance through the
titles of Auden's and Lowell's poems turns up many names of
writers that they are speaking to or for. The only poet actually
named in a Roethke title is Sir John Davies. Although Roethke
studied and formed deep attachments to earlier poets, he did not
seem to make his soul out of them or to bring them as openly into
the thoughts in his poems as did the others. This lack of a full and
explicit communication with the traditions of American, English,
and European poetry is the most serious limitation in Roethke's
work.[1] Exactly what he derived from his poetic ancestors has been
discussed in earlier chapters and will be briefly returned to in a
moment.

But what did he contribute? What are the essential qualities of
Roethke's best poems? What is it that makes them specially his? He
described in the most loving yet honest detail the beauty and
ugliness of the world he knew best—his father's greenhouse and

portions of the northern United States landscape. In his role as lonely, meditative observer, he found other cares than those pressed on him by society and history. The passing of World War II does not make a ripple in his poetry. More importantly, his taste in poetry was the widest possible: he learned from everybody. And in doing so, he demonstrated that a poet does not have to commit himself to one kind of poetry. He can pass freely across the defense perimeters of the warring camps, whether the traditionalists or experimentalists of Roethke's early career or the "university poets," the writers of "open poetry," or the poets of "the deep image" of a later day. Associated with this nondogmatic receptiveness of Roethke's was his lack of pretension. In most of his poetry and in all of his prose, be it notebooks, letters, reviews, or essays, he expresses himself with exuberant frankness. Finally, and most importantly, he never ceased living out the search for his father. As Auden pointed out at the beginning of Roethke's career, he transformed his personal pain, his loneliness, his grief over the loss of his father, into an emotional and spiritual journey with which others could identify.

The most difficult question raised in this conclusion is "What will Roethke's appeal to succeeding generations of readers and poets be?" The answer to this question must be approached by a roundabout path. In the preceding chapters Roethke's dislike of T.S. Eliot has been mentioned more than once. It is now and perhaps always has been a fact of poetic life that one writer reacts most strongly against another with whom he shares much and from whom he differs little. Eliot's "The Waste Land," published in 1922—Roethke's fifteenth year and the year of his father's death—is widely recognized as a watershed in modern American poetry. The reactions to that poem were intense and initiated a division among American poets that is still with us today. An early stage of that division can be glimpsed in the difference between the complaint of the obstetrician-poet William Carlos Williams that Eliot's poem, with its accompanying recondite notes, returned poetry to the classroom and the praise it received from Ezra Pound and others. That division was fixed almost irreparably in the famous "war of the anthologies," in which one anthology of younger American poets published the "classroom" or "cooked" writers and another published the "raw" ones. No poet was included in both anthologies.[2]

Roethke liked the "raw" poet William Carlos Williams more than he did the "cooked" T. S. Eliot, but as a poet Roethke resembles Eliot much more than he does Williams. And the special point of the resemblance lies in their sense of tradition, their caring about the past. Eliot and Roethke cared more than did Williams for their American, English, and European poetic ancestors. It is not so important whether Eliot or Roethke was, at a given point in his career, attacking or praising a seventeenth-century poet as that he cared about that poet. Eliot's and Roethke's caring was often an inseparable mixture of liking and disliking, as in Roethke's ambivalent feelings about Eliot himself and in Eliot's even more complicated feelings about a poet with whom he shared so much, John Milton. Eliot almost turned a generation of readers against Milton, despite the fact that Eliot resembled the earlier poet in many ways. Only a "classroom" poet, like Roethke, would care to ponder such a sentence as this one of Eliot's: "There is more of Milton's influence in the badness of the bad verse of the eighteenth century than of anybody's else: he certainly did more harm than Dryden and Pope, and perhaps a good deal of the obloquy which has fallen on these two poets, especially the latter, because of their influence, ought to be transferred to Milton."[3] Who cares? Williams did not care, and neither do his poetic descendants, like Allen Ginsberg. But Roethke did care, and the kind of poetry he wrote reflects that caring. What most needs to be said in defense of this kind of caring is that "classroom" need not be a dirty word. Until the level of general education has raised enormously, and perhaps desirably not even then, anything worthy of the name "poetry" will not begin to be able to compete with other forms of entertainment and pleasure. As long as poetry cannot easily compete, it will live almost exclusively in the lives of people who make at least occasional visits to the classroom. Aside from the fact that the classroom is not necessarily a tomb at the top of an ivory tower, some of the chill of the preceding statement is removed by an observation and judgment made by one of the most astute commentators on modern American poetry, Hugh Kenner, who writes: "For one Englishman who in 1671 could have identified Andrew Marvell (known from manuscript copies, privately circulated), a thousand young Americans can identify Robert Creeley: this thanks to the seminar and the paperback. That is how verse exists in the 1970s; it thrusts itself straight into the classroom. There are worse places for a phoenix to perform its fiery rite."[4] Roethke's knowledge and his disliking as well as his liking of earlier poets helped him write poems that would grant him an eternal place in the phoenix's fiery rite in the classrooms of the future.

Notes and References

Chapter One

1. Allan Seager, *The Glass House* (New York: McGraw-Hill, 1968), p. 9. Much of the material in this section is taken from chapters 2-4.
2. Ibid., p. 23.
3. Ibid., p. 24.
4. Ibid., pp. 40-41.
5. *On the Poet and His Craft: Selected Prose of Theodore Roethke*, ed. Ralph J. Mills, Jr. (Seattle: University of Washington Press, 1965), p. 20; hereafter cited in the text as *SP*.
6. Seager, pp. 90-91.
7. Rosemary Sullivan, *Theodore Roethke: The Garden Master* (Seattle: University of Washington Press, 1975), p. 4.
8. *The Collected Poems of Theodore Roethke* (Garden City, N.Y.: Doubleday, 1966), p. 6; hereafter cited in the text as *CP*.
9. I can find no evidence that Roethke thought his mental illness was hereditary. In speaking of it as "inherited," he could have been referring to his father's demanding and punitive nature as a contributing factor, or he may have been merely echoing the "inherited curse" theme treated by poets he admired at the time, such as Allen Tate, Yvor Winters, and Louise Bogan.
10. Arnold Stein, ed., "Introduction," in *Theodore Roethke: Essays on the Poetry* (Seattle: University of Washington Press, 1965), p. xiii.
11. The topic of Roethke's use of other poets deserves fuller discussion than the scope of the present study can allow. Some measure of his early attention to his ancestors, though, can be gained from noticing that the title " 'Long Live the Weeds' " is a line from a poem by Gerard Manly Hopkins and that Roethke's line "The rags of my anatomy" is taken from Henry Vaughan's "The Charnel-House." In fact, an entire book has been devoted to Roethke's echoing of other poets: Jenijoy La Belle, *The Echoing Wood of Theodore Roethke* (Princeton: Princeton University Press, 1975).
12. "Verse and the Times," *Saturday Review of Literature*, April 5, 1941, p. 31.
13. *Selected Letters of Theodore Roethke*, ed. Ralph J. Mills, Jr. (Seattle: University of Washington Press, 1968), p. 114; hereafter cited in the text as *SL*.
14. "Verse and the Times," p. 31.

15. "Stitched on Bone," in *Trail Balances*, edited by Ann Winslow [a pseudonym for Verna Elizabeth Grubbs], (New York, 1935), pp. 138-39..

16. Louis Foster, Jr., "A Lyric Realist," *Poetry*, 58 (1941), 224.

Chapter Two

1. Seager, p. 142.

2. Ibid., pp. 146-47.

3. Roethke did spend the summer of 1947 at Yaddo, where he met Robert Lowell, whom he frequently spoke of as his chief rival for prominence among their generation of American poets. After Roethke's death, Lowell referred to their time together at Yaddo in an elegy for Roethke.

4. This comment refers to "The Shape of the Fire," but it is applicable to the Greenhouse Poems and to the other narratives.

5. "The Vegetal Radicalism of Theodore Roethke," *Sewanee Review*, 58 (January, 1950), 69.

6. *Straw for the Fire: From the Notebooks of Theodore Roethke, 1943-1963*, ed. David Wagoner (Garden City, N.Y.: Doubleday, 1972), p. 150; hereafter cited in the text as *NB*.

7. J. C. Maxwell, "Notes on Theodore Roethke," *Notes and Queries*, n.s. 16 (1969), 265-66.

8. This poem is not in the first printing of the *Collected Poems*. It can be found in later printings, out of order, at the end of the sequence, on page 44.

Chapter Three

1. Reprinted in *On the Poet and His Craft*, pp. 36-43.

2. *The Echoing Wood of Theodore Roethke* (Princeton: Princeton University Press, 1976), pp. 43-50.

3. In *The Collected Poems* the narratives are printed in the order of their publication, not in the order Roethke finally intended. The discussion in this study will treat the poems in the order of their appearance in *Praise to the End!* and *Words for the Wind*, but will cite page numbers from *The Collected Poems*.

4. *Illumination* is discussed in a book that Roethke speaks of having read—Evelyn Underhill, *Mysticism* (Cleveland: Meridian Books, The World Publishing Company, 1955), pt. 2, chap. 4, esp. pp. 260, 264.

Chapter Four

1. February 7, 1958, p. 72.
2. This overly mystical emphasis is well represented by James G. Southworth, "The Poetry of Theodore Roethke," *College English*, 21 (1960), 330.
3. (New York: Vintage Books, Random House, n.d.), p. 106.
4. Davies's *Orchestra* associates bears with dancing by referring to the constellation Ursa Major, the big bear or big dipper, which dances around the pole star.
5. *The Collected Poems of W. B. Yeats* (New York: Macmillan, 1956), p. 196. "Four for Sir John Davies" does resemble some of Yeats's poems in style and cadence but not so closely that a sympathetic reader is distracted, and the differences certainly overshadow the similarities. Yeats's poems almost always develop their ideas in larger blocks than do Roethke's, use fewer end-stopped lines, and do not shift as abruptly from image to high-level abstraction. Moreover, Yeats wrote no poems in the stanzaic pattern of "Four for Sir John Davies."
6. *The Image of Man* (New York: Harper Torchbooks, Harper & Brothers, 1961), pp. 250-51.
7. *The Divine Comedy of Dante Alighieri, The Purgatorio*, trans. John D. Sinclair (New York: Galaxy Books, Oxford University Press, 1961), p. 395.
8. "The Vegetal Radicalism of Theodore Roethke," *Sewanee Review*, 58 (1950), 86.
9. Miguel de Unamuno, *The Tragic Sense of Life*, trans. J.E. Crawford Flitch (New York: Dover Publications, 1954), pp. 211-12.
10. T. S. Eliot, *The Complete Poems and Plays, 1909-1905* (New York: Harcourt, Brace, 1952). "Burnt Norton," lines 90-105, p. 120.
11. Eliot, "Little Gidding," lines 255-56, p. 145.

Chapter Five

1. Hugh B. Staples, "The Rose in the Sea-Wind: A Reading of Theodore Roethke's 'North American Sequence,' " *American Literature*, 26 (1964), 197, and *New Republic*, January 23, 1965, pp. 24, 29.
2. For a discussion of both views, see William Heyen, "The Divine Abyss: Theodore Roethke's Mysticism," *Texas Studies in Literature and Language*, 11 (1969), 1051-68.
3. *The Contemporary Poet as Artist and Critic*, ed. Anthony Ostroff (Boston: Little, Brown, 1964), p. 49.
4. Ibid., pp. 51-53.

Chapter Six

1. The complaint that Roethke's poetry shows no awareness of social problems or history—the most frequent charge brought against his work—is answered in an overly ingenious and ineffective way by Harry Williams (*"The Edge Is What I Have"* [1977], pp. 164-65), who repeats Robert Bly's notion that the "deep images" from the poet's unconscious are automatically an expression of the "national psyche" and are therefore truly political. In my opinion, no defense is a better defense than this.

2. Robert Lowell used the term "cooked" in referring to *The New Poets of England and America*, edited by Donald Hall, Robert Pack, and Louis Simpson (New York: Meridian Books, 1957) and "raw" in referring to *The New American Poetry, 1945-1960*, edited by Donald M. Allen (New York: Grove Press, 1960).

3. T. S. Eliot, "Milton I" in *On Poetry and Poets* (New York: Noonday Press, 1961), pp. 156-57.

4. Hugh Kenner, *A Homemade World* (New York: Alfred A. Knopf, 1975), p. 162.

Selected Bibliography

PRIMARY SOURCES

1. Collections
The Collected Poems of Theodore Roethke. Garden City, N.Y.: Doubleday, 1966.
The Selected Letters of Theodore Roethke. Edited by Ralph J. Mills, Jr. Seattle: University of Washington Press, 1968.
Selected Poems of Theodore Roethke. Edited by Beatrice Roethke. London: Faber and Faber, 1969.

2. Poetry
The Far Field. Garden City, N.Y.: Doubleday, 1964.
I Am! Says the Lamb. Garden City, N.Y.: Doubleday, 1961. With drawings by Robert Leydenfrost.
The Lost Son and Other Poems. Garden City, N.Y. Doubleday, 1948.
Open House. New York: Knopf, 1941.
Praise to the End! Garden City, N.Y.: Doubleday, 1951.
Sequence, Sometimes Metaphysical. Iowa City: Stone Wall Press, 1963. Limited edition of 330 copies with wood engravings by John Roy.
The Waking: Poems 1933-1953. Garden City, N.Y.: Doubleday, 1954.
Words for the Wind. London: Secker & Warburg, 1957; Garden City, N.Y.: Doubleday, 1958; Bloomington: Indiana University Press, 1961.

3. Prose
"On 'In a Dark Time.'" In *The Contemporary Poet as Artist and Critic,* edited by Anthony Ostroff, pp. 49-53. Boston: Little, Brown, 1964.
On the Poet and his Craft: Selected Prose of Theodore Roethke. Edited by Ralph J. Mills, Jr. Seattle: University of Washington Press, 1965.
Straw for the Fire: From the Notebooks of Theodore Roethke, 1943-1963. Edited by David Wagoner. New York: Doubleday, 1972.

4. Film and Recordings
In a Dark Time. Edited by David Myers. Contemporary Films, 1963.
Theodore Roethke Reading his Poetry. Caedmon CDL 51351. New York: Caedmon Records, 1972. *Nine Pulitzer Prize Poets Read Their Own Poems.* Phonodisc. The Library of Congress: Washington, D.C., 1963.

SECONDARY SOURCES

1. Books

BLESSING, RICHARD ALLEN. *Theodore Roethke's Dynamic Vision.* Bloomington, Indiana: Indiana University Press, 1974. Traces the circuit through
which energy and motion flow from the world, especially living things,
into the poet's psyche, and from there into the language of the poem,
and ultimately into the reader. This study does not offer explications of
entire poems but analyzes the ways in which energy is conveyed by
rhythms, puns, paradoxes, ambiguities, and juxtapositions of images.
Blessing is best on the sexual nuances in the Lost Son Narratives.

LA BELLE, JENIJOY. *The Echoing Wood of Theodore Roethke.* Princeton:
Princeton University Press, 1976. Compares Roethke passages that
echo other poets with the originals, demonstrating that Roethke's
imitating, far from representing an unhealthy dependency, was a
source of his most original writing. La Belle traces in detail the
sustaining tradition that Roethke discovered and created, giving special
attention to Blake, Wordsworth, Yeats, and Eliot.

LANE, GARY. *A Concordance to the Poems of Theodore Roethke.* Metuchen,
N.J.: Scarecrow Press, 1972.

McLEOD, JAMES RICHARD. *Theodore Roethke: A Bibliography.* Cleveland:
Kent State University Press, 1973. The introduction sketches the
growth of Roethke's reputation as a poet, as a reader of poetry, and as
a teacher. The bibliography lists writings, recordings, and films by and
about Roethke, published before April, 1972.

MALKOFF, KARL. *Theodore Roethke: An Introduction to the Poetry.* New
York: Columbia University Press, 1966. Generalized discussion of
sections and stanzas from Roethke's poems in relation to Jung's
psychoanalytic theory, Underhill's *Mysticism*, and Buber's and Tillich's
theology. Malkoff follows Roethke's search for identity as it is recorded
particularly in the metaphors and images presenting the interactions of
"subjective and objective, inner and outer, spirit and flesh."

MARTZ, WILLIAM J. *The Achievement of Theodore Roethke: A Comprehensive Selection of his Poems with a Critical Introduction.* Glenview, Ill.:
Scott, Foresman, 1966. An introductory essay, "A Major American
Poet" (pp. 1-18), develops the case for considering Roethke a major
poet, by reading sample poems and passages that illustrate his work as
a love poet, a nature poet, and a meditative poet.

MILLS, RALPH J., JR. *Theodore Roethke.* University of Minnesota Pamphlets
on American Writers, no. 30. Minneapolis: University of Minnesota
Press, 1963. Establishes the main lines that discussion of Roethke has
followed since 1963. Mills traces, in the poems from *Open House*
through "Meditations of an Old Woman," the self's difficult evolution

toward spiritual completeness. Mills discusses Roethke's indebtedness to Yeats but not to Eliot.

MOUL, KEITH R. *Theodore Roethke's Career: An Annotated Bibliography.* Boston: G. K. Hall, 1977. A bibliography of writings by Roethke and a comprehensive, fully annotated bibliography of writings about him, with a cut-off date of December 1973. Moul's introduction examines the help Roethke got from his best critics, his supposed "careerism," and the division in his "poetic consciousness" between anarchy and organization.

SEAGER, ALLAN. *The Glass House: The Life of Theodore Roethke.* New York: McGraw-Hill, 1968. Presents a wealth of details about Roethke's friendships, his mental illness, his university career, and his ambitions, successes, and failures as a writer. Seager does not disguise the less enticing aspects of Roethke's personality.

STEIN, ARNOLD, ed., *Theodore Roethke: Essays on the Poetry.* Seattle: University of Washington Press, 1965. In his introduction, the editor develops the idea that at each stage in Roethke's career, explorations in poetic techniques and increasing power as a poet were necessary to his survival as a person. See also articles below by Denis Donoghue, Louis L. Martz, William Meredith, Roy Harvey Pearce, W.D. Snodgrass, Stephen Spender, and John Wain.

SULLIVAN, ROSEMARY. *Theodore Roethke: The Garden Master.* Seattle: University of Washington Press, 1975. A thorough examination of the theological, philosophical, and psychological components of Roethke's search for identity. Sullivan's use of outside ideas to illuminate Roethke's work is both more extensive and more sensible than similar attempts by other critics. She does not provide line-by-line exegeses but constructs each of her chapters around one or two larger concerns, such as Roethke's sensitivity to the "minimal" creatures, his feelings about his dead father, his mental illness, his pursuit of mystical experience, and his uses of other poets.

WILLIAMS, HARRY. *"The Edge Is What I Have."* Lewisburg, Pa.: Bucknell University Press, 1977. Discusses the Lost Son Narratives, "Meditations of an Old Woman," and the "North American Sequence"—all of which show Roethke struggling to cross the "edge" between his false self and his true identity. In each sequence, Roethke's struggle is successful when he achieves a "visionary animism." Williams reviews Roethke criticism up to 1974 and looks at Roethke's influence on several later poets.

2. Articles and Parts of Books

ARNETT, CARROLL. "Minimal to Maximal: Theodore Roethke's Dialectic." *College English*, 28 (1957), 414-17. Explains how the dialectical unfolding of growth and decay—both in living things and in poetry— suggests to Roethke the existence of a higher realm.

AUDEN, W. H. "Verse and the Times." *Saturday Review*, April 5, 1941, pp. 30-31. A laudatory review of *Open House* pointing out Roethke's ability to transform self-loathing into poetry.

BERRYMAN, JOHN. "From the Middle and Senior Generations." *American Scholar*, 28 (1959), 384, 386, 388, 390. A review of *Words for the Wind* praising the long narratives but noting the damage in other poems caused by Roethke's literary borrowing, especially from Yeats and Eliot.

BOYD, JOHN D. "Texture and Form in Theodore Roethke's Greenhouse Poems." *Modern Language Quarterly*, 32 (1971), 409-24. Examines the formal and structural properties, especially the progression of metaphors, as the source of the new and distinctive voice in these poems; detailed discussion of "Big Wind," "Orchids," and "Cuttings *later*".

BOYERS, ROBERT. "A Very Separate Peace." In *The Young American Writers*, edited by Richard Kostelanetz, pp. 27-34. New York: Funk and Wagnalls, 1967. A review of *Collected Poems* that emphasizes the constant emotional vacillations in Roethke's poetry and the limiting domination of physical sensation over ideas.

BURKE, KENNETH. "The Vegetal Radicalism of Theodore Roethke." *Southern Review*, 58 (1950), 68-108. Reprinted in *Language as Symbolic Action* (Berkeley: University of California Press, 1966), pp. 254-81. Explains Roethke's *ars poetica*, seen mainly in the Greenhouse Poems, as the presentation of dynamic images of plants and animals hinting at some Ultimate Revelation.

CARRUTH, HAYDEN. "Requiem for God's Gardener." *The Nation*, September 28, 1964, pp. 168-69. A review of *The Far Field* that finds half the poems brilliant and half failing because of their sententious effort to transcend poetry.

CIARDI, JOHN, STANLEY, KUNITZ, and ALLAN SEAGER, "An Evening with Ted Roethke." *Michigan Quarterly Review*, 6 (1967), 227-45. Reprinted in *Profile of Theodore Roethke*, ed. William Heyen (Columbus, Ohio: Charles E. Merrill, 1971). Three of Roethke's friends reminisce after his death.

DEUTSCH, BABETTE. "On Theodore Roethke's 'In a Dark Time.'" In *The Contemporary Poet as Artist and Critic*, edited by Anthony Ostroff, pp. 36-40. Boston: Little, Brown, 1964. Reads the poem as the story of a purgation of madness.

————. *Poetry in Our Time*. Garden City: Anchor, 1963. Pp. 195-200. Uses T. S. Eliot's idea of the auditory imagination to explain the effectiveness of Roethke's explorations of psychic depths in the Lost Son Narratives.

DONOGHUE, DENIS. "Roethke's Broken Music." In *Theodore Roethke: Essays on the Poetry*, edited by Arnld Stein, pp. 136-66. Seattle: University of Washington Press, 1965. Traces through a series of antitheses Roethke's attempt to find a harmony uniting man, nature, and God.

EBERHART, RICHARD. "On Theodore Roethke's Poetry." *Southern Review*, n.s. 1 (1965), 612-20. Looks at the relationships between the works and the lives of three writers of Eliotic "impersonal" poetry who were not "totally engrossed" in their art and then contrasts to them Roethke's commitment to poetry and his use of his own personality in his works.

EVERETTE, OLIVER. "Theodore Roethke: The Poet as Teacher." *West Coast Review*, 3 (196), 5-11. Describes Roethke in the classroom, including an episode of psychotic breakdown.

FOSTER, LOUIS, JR. "A Lyric Realist." *Poetry*, 58 (1941), 222-25. Praises *Open House* for its realistic natural descriptions, which elicit emotions through their "exactness of epithet" and simplicity of diction; but Foster, like Auden who follows him, calls for "experimentation with metrical irregularity," for greater boldness.

FREER, COBURN. "Theodore Roethke's Love Poetry." *Northwest Review: Theodore Roethke Special Issue*, 11 (1971), 42-66. Explores "the genesis of the love poems, the dominant pattern that informs them, and the end toward which they move"—all three of which are explained by Roethke's adherence to traditional values and religion. "Four for Sir John Davies" is discussed more fully than any other poem.

GALVIN, BRENDAN. "Theodore Roethke's Proverbs." *Concerning Poetry*, 5 (1972), 35-47. Considers the epigrammatic lines scattered throughout the Roethke canon as necessary aids in the protagonist's struggle to live and grow.

———. "Kenneth Burke and Theodore Roethke's 'Lost Son' Poems." *Northwest Review: Theodore Roethke Special Issue*, 11 (1971), 67-96. Uses passages of Burke's psychoanalytic theory to shed light on lines in "The Lost Son," proving Burke was instrumental in "the loosening up of patterns of Roethke's thought and feeling."

GROSS, HARVEY. *Sound and Form in Modern Poetry*. Ann Arbor: University of Michigan Press, 1964. Pp. 282-90. Examines the relation between Roethke's statements about prosody and his practice, both of which Gross finds indebted to Auden and Eliot.

GUSTAFSON, RICHARD. "In Roethkeland." *Midwest Quarterly*, 7 (1966), 167-74. Emphasizes the physicality and simplicity of Roethke's images and themes.

HAYDEN, MARY. "Open House: Poetry of the Constricted Self." *Northwest Review: Theodore Roethke Special Issue*, 11 (1971), 116-38. Examines "positive" and "negative" spatial imagery in *Open House* as the ground from which Roethke's later growth of the self springs as it seeks to escape from constriction into larger "psychic territory."

HEILMAN, ROBERT B. "Theodore Roethke: Personal Notes." *Shenandoah*, 16 (1964), 55-84. A glimpse of Roethke as a social being and colleague, including a defense of his nonconformity, written by the chairman of the department in which Roethke taught for a number of years.

HEYEN, WILLIAM. "The Divine Abyss: Theodore Roethke's Mysticism."

Texas Studies in Literature and Language, 11 (1969), 1051-68. Reprinted in *Profile of Theodore Roethke* ed. William Heyen (Columbus, Ohio: Charles E. Merrill, 1971). Points out the similarities between Roethke's "The Abyss" and Evelyn Underhill's *Mysticism*, arguing that the poem follows her five stages of mystical development.

_____ "Theodore Roethke's Minimals." *Minnesota Review*, 8 (1968), 359-75. Focuses on "The Lost Son" and "Meditations of an Old Woman" as illustrations of Roethke's attempt to achieve psychic wholeness through identification with small forms of life, the "minimals."

HOBBS, JOHN. "The Poet as His Own Interpreter: Roethke on 'In a Dark Time.'" *College English*, 33 (1971), 55-66. Examines the weaknesses and distortions of Roethke's comments on one of his own best poems.

HOFFMAN, FREDERICK J. "Theodore Roethke: The Poetic Shape of Death." In *Theodore Roethke: Essays on the Poetry*, ed. Arnold Stein (Seattle: University of Washington Press, 1965), pp. 94-114. Examines poems that mark each of the four stages of Roethke's growth as a person and as a poet: the struggle to be born, childhood's closeness to nature, the struggle toward independence after his father's death, and, in greatest detail, the "poetic shape" of his own impending death.

HOLMES, JOHN. "Theodore Roethke." *American Poetry Journal*, 17 (1934), 2. Emphasizes Roethke's careful control of rhythm and diction while exploring the "conflict between flesh and mind." This is the earliest assessment of one of the essentials of Roethke's art.

JAFFE, DAN. "Theodore Roethke: 'In a Slow Up-Sway.'" In *The Fifties: Fiction, Poetry, Drama*, ed. Warren French, pp. 199-207. Deland, Fla.: Everett Edwards, 1970. Documents the slow development of Roethke's reputation, but argues that the poet gives a new generation of readers what it needs—"a sense of self; a willingness to share rather than to confess."

KRAMER, HILTON. "The Poetry of Theodore Roethke." *Western Review*, 18 (1954), 131-46. Focuses on the Lost Son Narratives as descriptions of the poet's movement from the dark night of the soul to a nonrational vision of the triumph of life.

KUNITZ, STANLEY. "Roethke: Poet of Transformations." *New Republic*, January 23, 1965, pp. 23-29. Reprinted in *Profile of Theodore Roethke*, ed. William Heyen (Columbus, Ohio: Charles E. Merrill, 1971). Describes the protagonists in Roethke's poems (who share something of the poet's own being) as Protean figures whose "shapes" change in accord with their highly ambivalent desires—to find the self and escape it, to find oblivion and escape it, to rise to a higher form of life and to sink to a lower.

_____ . "The Taste of Self: On Theodore Roethke's 'In a Dark Time.'" In *The Contemporary Poet as Artist and Critic, Eight Symposia*, ed. Anthony Ostroff (Boston: Little, Brown, 1964), pp. 41-48. Interprets "In a Dark Time" as the presentation of a momentary release from the confines of selfhood ("Hell is the trap where one is forever tasting oneself") and the flesh.

La Belle, Jenijoy. "Theodore Roethke and Tradition: 'The Pure Serene of Memory in One Man.'" *Northwest Review: Theodore Roethke Special Issue*, 11 (1971), 1-18. Considers some of the ways in which Roethke in his poetry discovered and defined his own cultural tradition, emphasizing the importance for Roethke of T. S. Eliot.

Libby, Anthony. "Roethke, Water Father." *American Literature*, 46 (1974), 267-88. Examines the poetic landscapes that Roethke and the other "new surrealist romantics" (Bly, Dickey, and Plath) explore in creating their "poetry of revelation"—all four seeking union with God through immersion in the flow of experience rather than through escape from it.

Lucas, John. "The Poetry of Theodore Roethke." *Oxford Review*, 8 (1968), 39-64. An evaluation of Roethke's best poems (especially "The Lost Son") discussing Roethke's borrowings from other poets and pointing out weaknesses in much of the early commentary on Roethke's work. The basis for many of Roethke's poems is found to be his fear of involvement with another person.

McLatchy, J. D. "Sweating Light from a Stone, Identifying Theodore Roethke." *Modern Poetry Studies*, 3 (1972), 1-24. Roethke's search for his poetic identity is a "futile circling" between the poles of self-conscious guilt and the "light" or the soul. His narrow range of images and vision make his achievement slighter than is usually thought.

McLeod, James R. "Bibliographic Notes on the Creative Process and Sources of Roethke's 'The Lost Son' Sequence." *Northwest Review: Theodore Roethke Special Issue*, 11 (1971), 97-111. Traces the growth of understanding and admiration for Roethke's Lost Son Narratives and provides a 102-item bibliography of biographical and critical comments.

McMichael, James. "The Poetry of Theodore Roethke." *Southern Review*, n.s. 5 (1969), 4-25. Reprinted in *Profile of Theodore Roethke*, ed. William Heyen (Columbus, Ohio: Charles E. Merrill, 1971). Discusses the role of the mind and other "mediators" in Roethke's journey out of the self toward God, giving most attention to the "North American Sequence."

——. "Roethke's North America." *Northwest Review: Theodore Roethke Special Issue*, 11 (1971), 149-59. Finds that, through the metaphoric description of the journey and the landscape, the sequence enacts the poet's and the reader's own escape from the self and discovery of what the soul actually is.

Martz, Louis L. "A Greenhouse Eden." In *Theodore Roethke: Essays on the Poetry*, edited by Arnold Stein, pp. 14-35. Seattle: University of Washington Press, 1965. Reprinted in Martz's *The Poem of the Mind: Essays on Poetry—English and American* (New York: Oxford University

Press, 1966), pp. 162-82. Demonstrates how all Roethke's best poems, regardless of their genre or style, reveal a center of divine light in the depths of the often troubled psyche.

MAXWELL, J. C. "Notes on Theodore Roethke." *Notes and Queries,* n.s. 16 (1969), 265-66. Discusses lines in "Big Wind," "The Waking," and "The Dying Man" and argues with some previous interpretations of these and other Roethke poems.

MAZZARO, JEROME. "Theodore Roethke and the Failure of Language." *Modern Poetry Studies,* 1 (1970), 73-96. Reprinted in *Profile of Theodore Roethke,* edited by William Heyen (Columbus, Ohio: Charles E. Merrill, 1971), pp. 47-64. Complains that Roethke's experiments in various styles are evidence of his inability to find his "true voice."

MEREDITH, WILLIAM. "A Steady Stream of Correspondences—Theodore Roethke's Long Journey Out of the Self." In *Theodore Roethke: Essays on the Poetry,* edited by Arnold Stein, pp. 36-53. Seattle: University of Washington Press, 1965. Examines *Open House* and *The Lost Son and Other Poems* for evidence of Roethke's determination to find a nonrational, organic order hidden in the world around him, rather than succumb to an artificial identity or to emotional chaos.

MILLS, RALPH J., JR. "In the Way of Becoming: Roethke's Last Poems." In *Theodore Roethke: Essays on the Poetry,* edited by Arnold Stein, pp. 115-35. Seattle: University of Washington Press, 1965. Reprinted in Mills's *Creations Very Self: On the Personal Element in Recent American Poetry* (Fort Worth: Texas Christian University Press, 1969), pp. 48-66. Interprets Roethke's later poems, especially the "North American Sequence" and "Sequence, Sometimes Metaphysical," as presentations of an "arduous but successful quest for mystical illumination."

————. "Theodore Roethke: the Lyric of the Self." In *Poets in Progress,* edited by Edwin Hungerford, pp. 3-23. Evanston: Northwestern University Press, 1962. Reprinted as "Theodore Roethke" in *Contemporary American Poetry* (New York: Random House, 1966), pp. 48-71. Examines poems representative of the stages through which Roethke's work developed: from the early expressions of psychological need, through his poetic versions of a child's deepest questionings and an adult's need for human bonds, to the final presentations of visionary experience.

PEARCE, ROY HARVEY. "Theodore Roethke: The Power of Sympathy." In *Theodore Roethke: Essays on the Poetry,* edited by Arnold Stein, pp. 167-99. Seattle: University of Washington Press, 1965. Reprinted in *Historicism Once More* (Princeton: Princeton University Press, 1966). Traces through the entire canon Roethke's search for "self-knowledge and self-realization," which the poet achieves by ever-increasing understanding of the complexity of the external world and of how he can construct a bridge between that world and his inner world through "the power of sympathy."

PHILLIPS, ROBERT. "The Inward Journeys of Theodore Roethke." In *The Confessional Poets*. Carbondale: Southern Illinois University Press, 1973. Pp. 107-27. Develops the contention that Roethke's poems repeatedly conclude with descriptions of mystical experience and that for Roethke these experiences were sham.

PINSKY, ROBERT. *The Situation of Poetry*. Princeton: Princeton University Press, 1976. Pp. 118-29. Contrasts the rhetorical techniques of John Clare's "Badger" with those of Roethke's "Orchids," concluding that Clare earns the empathy he claims with the object whereas Roethke does not.

PORTER, KENNETH. "Roethke at Harvard, 1930-31 and the Decade After." *Northwest Review: Theodore Roethke Speical Issue*, 11 (1971), 139-48. Reminiscences of an early acquaintance of Roethke's, with some interesting political nuances.

RAMSEY, JAROLD. "Roethke in the Greenhouse." *Western Humanities Review*, 26 (1972), 35-47. Develops the idea that in order for the greenhouse, recovered through memories of childhood, to help the poet integrate and mature his own spirit, the "dark cellar of beginnings and endings must be faced and surmounted."

RANSOM, JOHN CROWE. "On Theodore Roethke's 'In a Dark Time.'" In *The Contemporary Poet as Artist and Critic, Eight Symposia*, edited by Anthony Ostroff, pp. 26-35. Boston: Little, Brown, 1964. Examines "In a Dark Time" in relation to Roethke's earlier poems and interprets it as a terse dramatization of the poet's suffering and ultimate acceptance of God's existence and of the rightness of death.

ROSENTHAL, M. L. *The New Poets: American and British Poetry Since World War II*. New York: Oxford University Press, 1967. Pp. 112-18. An evaluation of Roethke's work that sees a decline after the Greenhouse Poems caused by Roethke's overly ambitious efforts to capture mystical experiences (which Rosenthal finds unconvincing) and by Roethke's limiting of his subject matter to the fluctuations of his own sensibility.

SCOTT, NATHAN A., JR. "The Example of Theodore Roethke." In *The Wild Prayer of Longing: Poetry and the Sacred*. New Haven: Yale University Press, 1971. Pp. 76-118. Develops in full detail the idea that Roethke's descriptions of plants and animals should be understood in the context of existential theology, which reveals their constant evocation of Being itself and their avoidance of systematic moralizing and traditional mysticism.

SLAUGHTER, WILLIAM R. "Roethke's 'Song.'" *Minnesota Review*, 8 (1968), 342-44. Finds that "Song," beginning with the line "I met a ragged

man," enacts Roethke's reuniting the creative child in himself with the
"ragged man" of the external world by "prostrating himself in the
position of sexual intercourse and humility in religion."

SNODGRASS, W. D. " 'That Anguish of Concreteness'—Theodore Roethke's
Career." In *Theodore Roethke: Essays on the Poetry*, edited by Arnold
Stein, pp. 78-93. Seattle: University of Washington Press, 1965. Views
Roethke's career as an example of the modern failure to benefit from
the great physical and emotional energies that Western man has
released. Roethke briefly achieved control over the energies of the
unconscious mind in the Lost Son Narratives, but afterward sought
only a static nirvana, free from all concreteness and form.

SOUTHWORTH, JAMES G. "Theodore Roethke's *The Far Field*." *College
English*, 27 (1966), 413-18. Finds *The Far Field* to be Roethke's final
epical version of the triumph of life.

————. "The Poetry of Theodore Roethke." *College English*, 21 (1960),
326-30, 335-38. Traces the parallels between Roethke's psychological
growth and the development of his poetry as both move from
constriction to freedom.

SPENDER, STEPHEN. "The Objective Ego." In *Theodore Roethke: Essays on
the Poetry*, edited by Arnold Stein, pp. 3-13. Seattle: University of
Washington Press, 1965. Distinguishes between Roethke's authentic
voice, which is that of the child absorbed in nature, and his inauthentic
voice, which is that of an egotist overwhelmed by his burdens.

STAPLES, HUGH B. "Rose in the Sea-Wind: A Reading of Theodore Roethke's
'North American Sequence.' " *American Literature*, 26 (1964), 189-
203. Examines the new dimensions Roethke brought into his work with
the "North American Sequence," in which he projects his own search
for form on the American past and the American landscape. Roethke
develops the "Sequence" through a series of antinomies, such as body
and spirit, form and formlessness, and the past and the present.

STEIN, ARNOLD. "Roethke's Memory: Actions, Visions, and Revisions."
Northwest Review: Theodore Roethke Special Issue, 11 (1971), 19-31.
Traces Roethke's growth from exasperation to stillness, which he
achieved by recovering in memory the greenhouse of his childhood, a
world that he can never literally enter again. Detailed discussion of a
passage in "Meditations of an Old Woman" and passages from the
notebooks.

THURLEY, GEOFFREY. *The American Moment: American Poetry in Mid-
Century*. New York: St. Martin's Press, 1978. Pp. 91-105. Provides
personal reactions to the "neurotic" egotism in passages from various
poems in *The Lost Son*, but neglects to consider the meanings added
to these passages by the surrounding sequences.

TRUESDALE, C. W. "Theodore Roethke and the Landscape of American
Poetry." *Minnesota Review*, 8 (1968), 345-58. Places Roethke in the
tradition of American romanticism (especially with Whitman, Tho-

reau, and Twain) and holds that his growth as a poet was linked with his rediscovery of his own America.

VERNON, JOHN. "Theodore Roethke's *Praise to the End!* Poems." *Iowa Review*, 2 (1971), 60-79. Reprinted in *The Garden and the May: Schizophrenia in Twentieth-Century Literature and Culture* (Urbana: University of Illinois Press, 1973), pp. 159-90. Reads the Lost Son Narratives as expressions of the pain that accompanies awareness of the self's separation from the world and as Roethke's attempts to reachieve wholeness.

WAGGONER, HYATT HOWE. *American Poets: From the Puritans to the Present.* Boston: Houghton Mifflin, 1968. Pp. 564-77. Details the close similarities, and several differences, between passages in Roethke's poetry and the ideas of American Transcendentalists, especially Emerson.

WAIN, JOHN. "The Monocle of My Sea-Faced Uncle." In *Theodore Roethke: Essays on the Poetry*, edited by Arnold Stein, pp. 54-77. Seattle: University of Washington Press, 1965. Discusses Roethke's single-minded concentration on finding some source of personal salvation within himself, which he does find with joy and thanksgiving.

WESLING, DONALD. "The Inevitable Ear: Freedom and Necessity in Lyric Form, Wordsworth and After." *Journal of English Literary History*, 36 (1969), 544-61. Discusses the organic form of "Meditation at Oyster River," demonstrating that descriptive details and apparent structural breaks represent the movement of the poet's mind.

WOLFF, GEORGE. "Roethke's 'Root Cellar.'" *The Explicator*, 29 (1971), item 47. Interprets "Root Cellar" as the description of a threatening enclosure that becomes a protective one, a central pair of images in Roethke's work.

———. "Syntactical and Imagistic Distortions in Roethke's Greenhouse Poems." *Language and Style*, 6 (1973), 281-88. Defines the effects of ungrammatical sentences and unvisualizable images in the Greenhouse Poems.

Index

Roethke's works are listed alphabetically.

150

811.54
R719

112 556

SOUTHERN FICTION PRIOR TO 1860: AN ATTEMPT AT A FIRST-HAND BIBLIOGRAPHY

By

JAMES GIBSON JOHNSON

PHAETON PRESS

New York

1968

Originally Published 1909
Reprinted 1968

Library of Congress Catalogue Card Number 67-30804

Published by PHAETON PRESS

TO MY WIFE
EMMA HART JOHNSON

PREFACE.

"Whoever thinks a faultless piece to see,
Thinks what ne'er was, nor is, nor e'er shall be."

How well I have accomplished my task, remains for others
to say. But one word of caution to my critics: Before passing an unfavorable opinion upon this piece of work, let them
lay this monograph aside and then make one at first-hand
similar to it. By that time I am inclined to think their darts
will be harmless.

In every instance I have done all in my power to get back
to the sources—the novels themselves in the first editions.
I assume no responsibility for the correctness of the titles and
dates of books I have not seen. But little confidence can be
placed in the dates and titles as given by various encyclopedias
and books on American literature. This is especially true of
books written on Southern literature by Southern authors in
recent years. Most of these I have found absolutely worthless
when accuracy is at stake. Two notable exceptions are the
Life of Simms, by W. P. Trent, and the Virginia Edition of
Poe, by Dr. James A. Harrison. These two gentlemen have
made every effort to reach first-hand results. Nothing has
been added to the results reached by Dr. Harrison, and no
errors have been discovered in his dates or titles.

As to the matter included herein, the lines have not been
drawn at the novel alone; but novels, tales, tragedy, comedy,
short stories in prose and verse, and metrical romances have
been included. No account is taken of books written in foreign
languages, but a few translations have been listed.

I have cited every notice and review that I could find in
available Southern magazines and also in a few Northern

ones. There yet remains an unexploited field, the excellent collection of *ante-bellum* Southern newspapers in the Library of Congress. Many volumes have been found by chance. Several advertisements appearing in the novels themselves have been reproduced for obvious reasons. I have indicated the present location of every book that I have personally examined.

During my resident work at the University of Virginia I have had the pleasure of receiving instruction from the following gentlemen: Dr. M. W. Humphreys, Dr. Noah K. Davis, Dr. Charles W. Kent, Dr. James A. Harrison, Dr. R. H. Wilson, Dr. E. B. Setzler, Professor Thomas Fitz-Hugh, and Dr. W. H. Faulkner. To each of them I express my gratitude for their helpfulness to me.

In the actual preparation of this monograph, I am indebted to Dr. Kent for suggesting the subject, for general guidance, and for his ever ready aid in procuring the necessary books by purchase when possible. To Mr. John S. Patton, Librarian of the University of Virginia, and Miss Anna S. Tuttle, Assistant Librarian, I am indebted for aid in obtaining material by loans from other libraries, and also for many helpful suggestions. I have always profited by Mr. Patton's sane judgment, while Miss Tuttle's enthusiastic interest in my work has been a constant source of inspiration to me. I am under obligations to the Library of Congress both for the loan of books and for granting me special favors while working there. It is a genuine pleasure to work under such conditions as are offered by this library. Brown University has furnished many rare volumes not to be found elsewhere. The Virginia State Library has lent a few volumes. Dr. John W. Wayland has given aid by calling my attention to some helpful books, while his advice on many points has enriched my results. Dr. James A. Harrison, with whom I have had many conferences, has given me many valuable hints. My obligation to others is acknowledged at various places.

In conclusion I wish to express my high appreciation of what Dr. Kent has done for me. His power and enthusiasm as a teacher have meant much to me,—more than words can convey.

JAMES GIBSON JOHNSON.

University of Virginia,
October 22, 1908.

TABLE OF CONTENTS.

REFERENCE WORKS.

The following list contains but a small number of the reference works consulted in the preparation of this monograph. Where an abbreviation is used, this precedes the name of the author or work.

Adams, Oscar Fay: A Dictionary of American Authors. Fourth edition, revised and enlarged. Boston & New York, Houghton, Mifflin & Co., 1901. U. Va. A mine of condensed facts.

Allibone.—Allibone, S. Austin: Dictionary of American Authors. 3 vols. Phila., J. B. Lippincott & Co., 1871. U. Va.; Congress. Supplement, by John Foster Kirk. 2 vols. Phila., J. B. Lippincott & Co., 1891. U. Va.; Congress. This work is full of valuable information and almost equally full of useless errors.

Appleton.—Appleton's Cyclopædia of American Biography. 6 vols. New York, D. Appleton & Co., 1894. U. Va.; Congress. In general accurate.

The Atlantic Monthly, vols. I-VI. U. Va.

Bradshaw, Dr. S. E.: On Southern Poetry Prior to 1860. 12mo. Richmond, Va., B. F. Johnson Publishing Co., 1900. U. Va.

Davidson.—Davidson, James Wood: The Living Writers of the South. 12mo. New York, Carleton, 1869. Congress. This volume is invaluable for the student of Southern literature.

DeBow's.—DeBow's Commercial Review, 1846-1860. U. Va.; Congress.

Duyckinck.—Duyckinck, E. A. and Geo. L.: Cyclopædia of American Literature, edited to date by M. Laird Simmons. 2 vols. Phila., Wm. Rutter & Co., 1875. U. Va.

Forrest, Mary: Women of the South Distinguished in Literature, illustrated with portraits on steel. New York, Derby & Jackson, 1861. Two copies, U. Va.

Fortier, Alcée: Louisiana Studies, Literature, Customs, and Dialects, History and Education. New Orleans. Published by F. F. Hansell & Bro., 1894. U. Va.

Harper's Magazine, vols. I-XXII. U. Va.

Harrison, Dr. James Albert: The Complete Works of Edgar Allan Poe. 17 vols., 16mo. New York, Thomas Y. Crowell & Company, Publishers, 1902. U. Va.

Hart, John S.: A Manual of American Literature. Phila., Eldredge & Brother, 1873. U. Va.

Hart.—Hart, John S.: Female Prose Writers of America, with portraits, biographical notices, and Specimens of their writings. New edition, revised and enlarged. Phila., E. H. Butler & Co., 1855. Congress. Contains accurate and sympathetic estimates of: Caroline Gilman, Maria J. McIntosh, Mary S. B. Shindler, Caroline Lee Hentz, Louisa S. McCord, E. D. N. Southworth, Julia C. R. Dorr, and Mary Elizabeth Lee.

Lamb's Biographical Dictionary of the U. S., edited by John Howard Brown. 7 vols. Boston, 1901. Congress. Accurate and discriminating.

Loshe, Dr. Lillie Deming: The Early American Novel. 8vo. New York, The Columbia University Press, 1907. U. Va.

Manly, Louise: Southern Literature from 1579-1895. Richmond, Va., B. F. Johnson Publishing Co., 1900. U. Va. Contains a valuable list of names.

Minor, Benjamin Blake: The Southern Literary Messenger, 1834-1864. New York & Washington, The Neale Publishing Company, 1905. U. Va. Mr. Minor was editor and proprietor of the Messenger from 1843 to 1847.

Moore, Hight C.: The Poetic Literature of North Carolina. Reprinted from the North Carolina Magazine, October, 1907. Dr. E. A. Alderman's Library.

The National Cyclopædia of American Biography. 13 vols. New York, James T. White & Co., 1892-1906. U. Va.; Congress.

Owen: Ala.—Owen, Thomas McAdory: A Bibliography of Alabama, pp. 777-1248 of the Annual Report of the American Historical Association, 1897. U. Va.

Owen: Miss.—Owen, Thomas McAdory: A Bibliography of Mississippi, pp. 633-828 of the Annual Report of the American Historical Association, vol. 1, 1899. U. Va.

Painter, Dr. F. V. N.: Poets of Virginia. B. F. Johnson Publishing Co., Richmond, Va., 1907. U. Va.

Rogers, Dr. E. R.: Four Southern Magazines (DeBow's Review, The Southern Review, The Southern Quarterly Review, The Southern Literary Messenger). Richmond, The Williams Printing Company, 1902. U. Va.

Roorbach: Bibliotheca Americana (a Catalogue of American Publications, including reprints and original works). This with its supplements, 7 vols., 8vo., covers the period from 1820 to 1865. Congress.

Russell's Magazine, April, 1857—March, 1860 (vols. I-VI). Charleston. U. Va.

Rutherford.—Rutherford, Mildred Lewis: The South in History and Literature. A Handbook of Southern Authors from the Settlement of Jamestown, 1607, to Living

Writers. Atlanta, Ga., The Franklin-Turner Co., 1907.
U. Va.; Congress; J. G. Johnson. Has a valuable list
of names.

The Southern Literary Journal and Monthly Magazine.
Charleston, 1835-1838. Congress. Contains much valuable information concerning Southern writers.

So. Lit. Mess.—The Southern Literary Messenger, 1834-1864.
U. Va.; Congress. No serious student of Southern literature can dispense with this magazine.

So. Quar. Rev.—The Southern Quarterly Review, 1842-1856.
Congress; U. Va. (incomplete set). Contains much information about Southern books in its critical notices.

Stockbridge, John C.: A Catalogue of the Harris Collection
of American Poetry with Biographical and Bibliograph-
ical Notes. Providence, Providence Press Company,
Printers, 1886. U. Va.

So. Wri.—Tardy, Mrs. Mary T. (Ida Raymond, pseud.):
Southland Writers. Biographical and Critical Sketches
of the Living Female Writers of the South, With extracts
from their writings, by Ida Raymond. 2 vols., 8vo.,
paged continuously, pp. 973. Phila., Claxton, Remsen &
Haffelfinger, 1870. Congress.

Li. Fe. Wri.—Tardy, Mrs. Mary T. (Ida Raymond): The
Living Female Writers of the South. Edited by the
author of "Southland Writers." 8vo., pp. 568. Phila.,
Claxton, Remsen & Haffelfinger, 1872. Congress; J. G.
Johnson. These volumes are of especial interest and
value.

Thomas.—Thomas, Ella Marshall: Virginia Women in Literature, a Partial List. Richmond, B. F. Johnson Publishing Company, 1902. U. Va. A valuable and
suggestive monograph.

Thompkins, Hamilton B.: Bibliography of the Works of George H. Calvert. 12mo., pp. 15. Newport, R. I., 1900. Congress.

Trent.—Trent, W. P.: William Gilmore Simms. Boston and New York, Houghton, Mifflin and Company, 1892. Two copies, U. Va.

Wegelin: E. A. F.—Wegelin, Oscar: Early American Fiction, 1774-1830. Being a compilation of the titles of American Novels written by writers born in or residing in America, and published previous to 1831. Stamford, Conn. Published by the Compiler, 1902. U. Va.

Wegelin: E. A. P.—Wegelin, Oscar: Early American Plays, 1714-1830. A Compilation of the titles of plays and dramatic poems written by authors born in or residing in North America previous to 1830. Second edition revised. New York, The Literary Collector Press, 1905. U. Va.

Wegelin, Oscar: A List of the Separate Writings of William Gilmore Simms of South Carolina. 8vo., pp. 31. New York, 1906. Congress.

All the above works by Wegelin are invaluable. He has sought and obtained a high degree of accuracy in his productions.

A LIST OF AUTHORS, WITH THEIR WORKS
IN CHRONOLOGICAL ORDER.

———

The following abbreviations are used for libraries:

Congress, for the Library of Congress;

Harris, for the Harris Collection of American Poetry at Brown University;

U. Va., for the Library of the University of Virginia.

The names of other libraries are self-explanatory. Wherever the word Congress, Harris, U. Va. or the name of any other library is appended to a book or magazine it must be construed as meaning that the writer has personally examined the book or magazine in question.

All reviews and notices in the Southern Literary Messenger, the Southern Literary Journal, the Southern Rose, the Southern Literary Gazette, the Southern Quarterly Review, Russell's Magazine, the Atlantic Monthly, Sartain's Magazine, and DeBow's Review were discovered by the writer. The same responsibility applies to all novels, tales, dramas, and short stories cited as being published in any of the above magazines.

———

Anonymous.
> 1840. Abbot: or, "The Hermit of the Falls." So. Lit. Mess., September, 1840, pp. 687-699. W. C. P. South Carolina.

Adams, Francis Cobham, of Charleston, S. C.
> 1856. Justice in the By-Ways. A Tale of Life. 12mo. New York. See Adams, 3; Allibone Supplement, 10.

Anonymous.

    1844. The Age of Brass: or, The Fum Dynasty: Containing the Political Morals of Certain Political Characters. A Satire in Six Cantos. Canto I, The Introduction; II, The Conspiracy; III, The Magician; IV, The Guard; V, Fum's Dream; VI, The Great Man's Friend. By Nobody Nothing, of Nowhere. A Member of the Young Men's Whig Conv'n, 1840. 12mo., pp. 48. Baltimore. Published by George W. Wilson. Woods & Crane, Printers. Harris. A political satire. In pencil on title-page, James Alexander Young.

Anonymous.

    1837. The Age of Humbugs: The Grand Tour, and Other Original Poems. By the author of the "Snowy Daughter." 12mo., pp. 52. Wheeling. Times Press. E. W. Newton & Co., Printers. Harris. The Age of Humbugs, pp. 5-27, a satire on American life and manners.

Alexander, J. Bell, Ala.

    1852. Malice: A Tale of Real Life in the South; 8vo., pp. 91; Mobile, Strickland and Benjamin. See Owen: Ala.; also DeBow's, July, 1852, p. 108.

Alexander, James Waddell, 1804-1859. Va.

    1838. The American Mechanic, by Charles Quill. 16mo., pp. 285. Philadelphia, Henry Perkins. Congress.

    1843. The Working-Man, by Charles Quill. 16mo., pp. 287. Philadelphia, Perkins & Purves. Congress.

    "Author of more than 30 juvenile works, written mostly for the Sunday School Union," among which are Frank Harper, Carl, the Young Emigrant, Only Son. Hart, Amer. Lit., 258.

Anonymous.

    1849. Alfred and Inez; or, The Siege of St. Augustine: A Drama, in five acts. 12mo., pp. 172. Mobile,

Thompson and Harris. Founded on the invasion of Florida by the Carolinians in 1702. See Owen: Ala.

Allston, Washington, 1779-1843. S. C., Eng., Mass.
    1841. Monaldi: A Tale, 8vo., pp. 253. Boston, Charles C. Little and James Brown. Congress. U. Va. Another copy, 12mo., pp. 278. Boston, Ticknor & Fields, 1856. Congress. Reviewed in So. Lit. Mess., April, 1842, pp. 286-289; an exhaustive review in So. Quar. Rev., October, 1843, pp. 394-414.

Anderson, Florence, of Glen Ada, near Harrodsburg, Ky. Va., Ky.
    1858. Zenaida, by Florence Anderson. 12mo., pp. 374. Philadelphia, J. B. Lippincott & Co. Congress.

Anderson, R. H., of Richmond, Va. See Minor, So. Lit. Mess., p. 217.
    1860. Bricks. So. Lit. Mess., December, 1860, pp. 451-462.

Arrington, Alfred W. ("Charles Summerfield"), 1810-1867. N. C., Mo., Ark.
    1847. The Desperadoes of the Southwest; Containing an account of The Cane-Hill Murders, Together with the Lives of Several of the Most Notorious Regulators and Moderators of that Region. 8vo., pp. 48. New York, William H. Graham. 2 copies, Congress.
    1849. The Lives and Adventures of the Desperadoes of the Southwest; Containing an account of the Duelists and Dueling. Part one same as edition of 1847; part second is entitled: An Appeal from The Dead to the Living. 8vo., pp. 98. New York, William H. Graham. Congress.
    1856. The Rangers and Regulators of the Tanaha: or,

Life Among the Lawless. A Tale of the Republic of Texas. 12mo., pp. 397. New York, Robert M. DeWitt. Congress. U. Va. Reprinted in 1884 as: A Faithful Lover, A Novel. 12mo., pp. 396. New York, G. W. Carleton & Co. Congress.

Bagby, George W., 1828-1883; Va.

1858. The Letters of Mozis Addums to Billy Ivvins. So. Lit. Mess., 1858, vol. 26: pp. 121-125; 187-192; 251-256; 383-388; vol. 27: pp. 55-60; 200-204; 367-373; 422-428. Reprinted in "Selections from the Miscellaneous Writings of Dr. George W. Bagby," 2 vols., 8vo., pp. 400-412. Richmond, Whittet & Shepperson, 1884-1885. U. Va. The Letters of Mozis Addums, vol. II, pp. 40-162.

1860. Blue-Eyes and Battlewick, A Winter's Tale, by the Author of Mozis Addums' Letters. Printed in the So. Lit. Mess., vol. 30, pp. 55-71; 99-119; 182-201; 273-294; 353-375.

Baldwin, Joseph G., 1811-1864. Ala., Cal.

1853. The Flush Times of Alabama and Mississippi. A Series of Sketches. New York, D. Appleton & Co. See So. Lit. Mess., December, 1853, pp. 778-779. Seventh edition, 12mo., pp. 330. New York, D. Appleton & Co., 1854. U. Va. 20,000 copies were sold in six months from publication. See So. Lit. Mess., 1854, p. 125. Edition of 1887, 11th thousand, 12mo., pp. 330. San Francisco, Bancroft-Whitney Co. Congress.

1852. Sketches of the Flush Times of Alabama, So. Lit. Mess., 1852, pp. 433-438; 558-565; 746-756.

Sketches of the Flush Times of Alabama and Mississippi, So. Lit. Mess., 1852, pp. 674-681; also So. Lit. Mess., 1853, pp. 10-15; 65-74; 86-90; 214-222; 332-338; 409-417; 465-474; 553-560; 599-605.

1854. Old Uncle John Rosser and the Billy Goat, So. Lit. Mess., 1854, pp. 120-123.

1854. General Gym and Colonel Burrows, in the same, pp. 228-234.

Barrow, Mrs. Frances Elizabeth Mease ("Aunt Fanny"), 1822-   . S. C., N. Y.

1857. The Lost Found and Clara C. By Aunt Fannie. Philadelphia, Amer. Bap. Pub. So.

1857. The Pious Mother and Her Dutiful Daughter; the Lives of Emily Ross and Ellen Merwin. By the author of The Lost Found, &c. Charleston, So. Bap. Pub. So. See So. Lit. Mess., February, 1857, p. 160.

1860. Little Pet Books (a collection of tales). 3 vols., New York.

Barrymore, William.

1818(?). The Fatal Snow Storm; a Romantic Drama in Two Acts. Cumberland Minor Theatre, vol. XIII, pp. 34. London. Congress.

Gilderoy; or The Bonnie Boy; a Romantic Drama, in Two Acts, Cumberland Minor Theatre, vol. VIII, pp. 54. London. Congress.

Wallace; The Hero of Scotland. An Historical Drama in three acts. Modern Standard Drama, 12mo., pp. 30. Boston. Congress.

Anonymous.

1790 (cir.). The Battle of Eutaw Springs. A Drama in Five Acts. 8vo., pp. 52. Charleston. A play with a similar title was written by W. ·Ioor. Wegelin: E. A. P.

Bennett, Mrs. Martha Haines Butt (née Butt, Miss Martha Haines, of Norfolk, Va.).

1853. Antifanaticism: A Tale of the South. 12mo., pp.

268. Phila., Lippincott, Grambo & Co. Congress. This tale is a reply to "Uncle Tom's Cabin."

Pastimes with Little Folks. Written before the war. See Davidson, p. 42.

1859. Leisure Moments (a collection of short tales, essays, and sketches). New York, E. D. Long & Co. See Tardy: So. Wri., p. 806, *et seq.*

Bien, Herman M. Miss.?

1860. Samson and Delilah; or, Dagon stoops to Sabaoth: a Biblio-Romantic Tragedy, in Five Acts. 12mo. San Francisco. See Allibone Supplement, 145.

Blake, Mrs. Lillie Devereux Umsted. 1835-   . N. C., N. Y.

1859. Southwold. A novel, by Mrs. Lillie Devereux Umsted. 12mo., pp. 257, New York. Rudd & Carleton.

Blount, Annie R. Ga.

1859. The Sisters. A story published in the "Newbern (N. C.) Gazette." It was awarded the $100 medal for "the best story" to be published in a Southern paper. See Tardy: So. Wri., I, p. 432; also Li. Fe. Wri., p. 183. W. G. Simms, Rev. B. Craven, and Jno. R. Thompson were the judges.

Botsford, Edmund, of Georgetown, S. C.

1808. Sambo and Toney, a Dialogue in Three Parts. 16mo., pp. 46. Georgetown, (S. C.). Printed by Francis M. Baxter. Harris. This is a prose dialogue.

Bowen, Mrs. Sue Petigru King, 1824-1875. S. C.

1854. Busy Moments of An Idle Woman. Contents: Edith; An Every-Day Life; The Widow; Old Maidism Versus Marriage; An Episode in the Life of A Woman of Fashion. 12mo., pp. 285. New York, D. Appleton & Co. Congress. Good review in So. Quar. Rev., January, 1854, pp. 212-213; see also p. 268.

1855. Lily, A Novel. 12mo., pp. 330. New York, Harper & Brothers. Congress. Reviewed in Harper's Magazine, 12:115.

1859. Sylvia's World, and Crimes which the Law Does Not Reach. Both in one volume. 12mo., pp. 384. New York, Derby & Jackson. Congress. Reviewed in Russell's Mag., October, 1859, p. 95.

Crimes which the law does not reach:

No. I.—Gossip, Russell's Magazine, October, 1857, pp. 47-51;

No. II.—A Marriage of Persuasion, Russell's Magazine, November, 1857, pp. 111-115;

No. III.—A Male Flirt, December, 1857, pp. 201-211;

No. IV.—The Best Friend, January, 1858, pp. 355-365.

Brackenridge, Hugh Henry, 1748-1816.   Penn., Md.

1776. The Battle of Bunker Hill, A Dramatic Piece in Five Acts, in heroic measure by a gentleman of Maryland. 18mo., pp. 49. Phila., printed by R. Bell. Congress.

1806. The Battle of Bunker Hill, Etc. Reprinted, slightly curtailed, in the Author's Gazette Publications, pp. 281-303. Congress.

Bradley, Mrs. Mary E. N., 1835-   . Va.

1855. Bessie; A Story For Girls.

1856. Bread Upon the Waters. 13mo., pp. 252. New York, Gen. Prot. Episc. S. S. Union. Congress.

1857. Douglass Farm; A Juvenile Story of Life in Virginia. 12mo., pp. 202. New York, D. Appleton & Co. Congress; U. Va.

1860. Arthur and Other Stories. 18mo., pp. 134. New York, Gen. Prot. Episc. S. S. Union & Church Book Soc. Congress.

Brisbane, Abbott Hall, 1805-1861. S. C.
>   1848. Ralphton; or, The Young Carolinian of 1776. A
>   Romance on the Philosophy of Politics. 12mo., pp.
>   242. Charleston, Burgess & James. Congress.

Brown, William Hill, 1766-1793. Died in N. C.
>   —— A Tragedy founded on the death of Major John
>   André.
>   —— A Comedy.
>   1807. Ira and Isabella; or, The Natural Children, A
>   Novel founded in fiction, A Posthumous work.
>   By the late William H. Brown of Boston. 12mo.,
>   pp. 118. Congress. See Allibone, vol. I, p. 260;
>   also, Moore's Poetic Literature of North Carolina.

Bryan, Daniel, of Rockingham Co., Va.
>   1813. The Mountain Muse: Comprising The Adven-
>   tures of Daniel Boone; and the Power of Virtuous
>   and Refined Beauty, by Daniel Bryan of Rocking-
>   ham County, Virginia. 16mo., pp. 252. Harri-
>   sonburg. Printed for the Author by Davidson
>   and Bourne. U. Va., Congress. The Adventures
>   of Boone, a metrical tale, pp. 13-232. The popu-
>   larity of the book is attested by the list of more
>   than 1350 subscribers, whose names are appended
>   to the end of the work.

Burk, John (Daly),   -1808. Ireland, Va.
>   1797. Bunker-Hill; or The Death of General Warren.
>   An Historic Tragedy in five acts, as played in the
>   theatres in America for fourteen nights, with un-
>   bounded applause. 12mo., pp. 55. New York.
>   Printed by T. Greenleaf. Congress.
>   1817. Another copy, 18mo., pp. 44. New York. Pub-
>   lished by D. Longworth, at the Dramatic Reposi-
>   tory, Shakespeare-Gallery, 1817. Congress, U. Va.
>   1891. Another copy, with an introductory essay by B.
>   Matthews, pp. 82. New York, The Dunlap So-

ciety, 1891. This edition is No. 15 of the Dunlap
Society publications. Edition of 190 copies, with
facsimile title pages of early editions: New York,
1797 and 1817. Congress.

1798. Female Patriotism; or, The Death of Joan D'Arc:
An Historical Play in V. Acts, By John Burk,
author of Bunker-Hill, Prince of Susa and other
Dramatic Pieces. 12mo., pp. 40. New York, R.
M. Hurtin. Congress; Harris.

1807. Bethlem Gabor, Lord of Transylvania, or The Man
Hating Palatine; an Historical Drama, in three
acts. 18mo., pp. 49. Petersburg (Va.), Sommer-
velle & Conrad. Congress; Harris.

Cabell, Julia Mayo, Va.

1852. An Odd Volume of Facts and Fictions. In Prose
and Verse. By Julia Mayo Cabell. Richmond,
Nash & Woodhouse. J. W. Culley, Printer. Contains several tales. See So. Lit. Mess., June, 1852,
p. 383.

Calvert, George Henry, 1803-1880. Md.

1834. Don Carlos. A Dramatic Poem. Translated from
Schiller. 12mo., pp. 203. Baltimore. Harris.

1840. Count Julian; a Tragedy. 12mo., pp. 69. Baltimore. Harris.

1840. Cabiro, A Poem. Cantos I & II. 12mo., pp. 47.
Baltimore. Harris.

1856. Comedies: The Will and the Way, in five acts;
Like unto Like, in three acts. 12mo., pp. 125.
Boston, Philips, Sampson & Co. Congress; Harris.

1860. Joan of Arc; a Poem in Four Books. 16mo., pp.
108. Privately printed; later (1883) published at
Boston; sq. 12mo., pp. 108. Boston, Lee & Shep-
ard; New York, C. T. Dillingham. Congress.

Campana, Giacomo S.

1857. Mora; or, The Mysterious Child. By Giacomo S.

Campana. So. Lit. Mess., October, 1857, pp. 290-303. Signed Harrisonburg, Va. Sept. 21st.

Carpenter, William Henry, 1813-1899. England, Md. Resided for almost seventy years in America.

1850. Ruth Eversley, the Betrothed Maiden: A Tale of the Virginia Massacre. 12mo., Phila.

1851. The Regicide's Daughter. 18mo., Phila.
See Allibone Sup. I, 294; Adams, 456.

Caruthers, Dr. William A., 1800-1846. Va., Ga. He died in 1846, not in 1850. See So. Lit. Mess., 1846, pp. 63 and 764.

1834. The Kentuckian in New York. Or, The Adventures of Three Southerns. By A Virginian. 2 vols., 12mo., pp. 223-219. New York, Harper & Brothers. U. Va.

1835. The Cavaliers of Virginia; or, The Recluse of Jamestown. An Historical Romance of the Old Dominion. By the Author of "The Kentuckian in New York." 2 vols., 12mo., pp. 228-246. New York, Harper & Brothers. U. Va.; Congress. Reviewed in So. Lit. Mess., March, 1835, pp. 385-386.

1845. The Knights of the Horse-Shoe; A Traditionary Tale of the Cocked Hat Gentry in the Old Dominion, by the author of the "Cavaliers of Virginia," &c., &c. 8vo., 2 vols. in one, pp. 248. Wetumpka, Alabama. Printed and published by Charles Yancey. Dr. B. W. Green (Univ. of Va.) possesses a copy of the first edition of this book. See So. Lit. Mess., January, 1846, p. 63; also, December, p. 764; So. Quar. Rev., April, 1846, p. .531.

1882. Another copy, .4to., pp. 80, Harper's Franklin Square Library. New York, Harper & Bros., 1882. U. Va., and Dr. B. W. Green's Library.

Chivers, Thomas Holley, 1807-1858. Ga.
  1834. Conrad and Eudora; or, The Death of Alonzo.
    A Tragedy. 16mo., pp. 144. Phila. Harris.
  1837. Nacoochee or The Beautiful Star with other
    poems. 12mo., pp. 143. New York, Spalding &
    Shepard., Congress; Harris. Nacoochee, pp.
    1-31, is a portion of a metrical romance; Mala-
    volti; or The Downfall of the Alamo, pp. 116-143,
    is a narrative poem.
  1853. Atlanta; or the True Blessed Island of Poesy. A
    Paul Epic. In Three Lustra. By. T. H. Chivers,
    M. D. (Copyright secured). 12mo., pp. 18.
    Macon, Georgia. Printed at the Georgia Citizen
    Office. See So. Lit. Mess., June, 1853, pp. 379-
    382.
  1858. The Sons of Usna: A Tragic Apotheosis in Five
    Acts. Phila.

Anonymous.
  1843. The Clairwoods. A True Tale. So. Lit. Mess.,
    July, 1843, pp. 401-407. Signed S. S. Charlottes-
    ville, April, 1843.

Clemens, Jeremiah, 1814-1865. Ala.
  1856. Bernard Lile; An Historical Romance Embracing
    the Periods of the Texas Revolution, and the
    Mexican War. 12mo., pp. 287. Phila., J. B. Lip-
    pincott & Co. Congress.
  1858. Mustang Gray; A Romance. 12mo., pp. 296.
    Phila., J. B. Lippincott & Co. Congress. Deals
    with the Mexican War. Reviewed in Russell's
    Mag., October, 1857, p. 285.

    "The leading object of 'Bernard Lile' was to
    show that no strength of will, no genius, no gifts
    of fortune and no accomplishments, are sufficient
    of themselves to save us from the greatest errors
    in our journey through the world. In "Mustang

Gray" this idea is carried still farther, and I have
endeavored to show that no associations, no natural
gentleness of disposition and no pious training in
early life, will suffice to prevent us from yielding
to the temptations of passion." Author's preface
to Mustang Gray.

1859. The Rivals; a Tale of the Times of Aaron Burr
and Alexander Hamilton. Phila., J. B. Lippincott
& Co. Congress. Reviewed in Russell's Mag..
March, 1860, p. 565.

1900. Reprinted in 1900 as: An American Colonel. A
Story of Thrilling Times During The Revolution
and the Great Rivalry of Aaron Burr and Alexander Hamilton. 12mo., pp. 315. Akron, Ohio,
Wolfe Pub. Co. Congress.

Cobb, Joseph Beckham, 1819-1858. Ga.

1850. The Creole: or, Siege of New Orleans. An Historical Romance, Founded on the Events of 1814-
15. 8vo., pp. 130. Phila., A. Hart. Congress.
Noticed in So. Quar. Rev., July, 1850, p. 538.

1851. Mississippi Scenes; or Sketches of Southern and
Western Life and Adventure, Humorous, Satirical and Descriptive, including the Legend of
Black Creek. 12mo., pp. 250. Phila., A. Hart.
Congress. Noticed in So. Lit. Mess., September,
1851, p. 584. Based on real scenes and characters;
also includes The Innkeeper's Wife; A Story of
the Revolution.

Colcroft, Henry Rowe.

1843. Alhalla, or the Lord of Talladega. A Tale of the
Greek (Creek) War. With some selected Miscel-
lanies, chiefly of early date. By Henry Rowe Colcroft. 12mo., pp. 116. New York and London,
Wiley and Putnam. See Owen, Ala. 874.

—2

Collens, T. Wharton, 1812-1879. La.

    1836. Martyr Patriots (written 1833). A Tragedy in five Acts.

        "It celebrates the death of Villeré and Lafrénère, who in 1759 resisted the transfer of Louisiana from France to Spain, and were shot for their rebellion." Davidson. See also Fortier: Louisiana Studies, p. 101.

Cooke, John Esten, 1830-1886. Va.

    1852. Pine Fork Plantation; a Chronicle of Old Days in the Old Dominion. By Pen Ingleton, Esq. So. Lit. Mess., 1852, pp. 357-370; 417-429.

    1852. Chronicles of the Valley of Virginia. By Pen Ingleton, Esq. I. The Storming of Winchester Jail. So. Lit. Mess., 1852, pp. 459-467. II. Bachelor Smith. Do., pp. 529-534. On internal evidence I assign the above to Cooke.

    1854. Leather Stocking and Silk; or, Hunter John Myers and His Times. A Story of the Valley of Virginia. 12mo., pp. 408. New York, Harper & Brothers. Congress. Noticed in So. Lit. Mess., September, 1854, p. 576.

    1854. The Youth of Jefferson, or a Chronicle of College Scrapes at Williamsburg in Virginia A D 1764. 12mo., pp. 249. New York, Redfield. Congress; U. Va. Noticed in So. Lit. Mess., September, 1854, p. 576.

    1854. The Virginia Comedians; or, Old Days in the Old Dominion. Edited from the MSS. of C. Effingham Esq. Two vols. in one, 12mo. New York, D. Appleton & Co. Reviewed in So. Lit. Mess., October, 1854, p. 638.

    1883. Edition of 1883, 2 vols. in one, 12mo., pp. 332-282. New York, D. Appleton & Co. U. Va.

        Reissued, vol. I as: Beatrice Hallam, A Novel. 12mo., pp. 332; vol. II as: Captain Ralph, a Sequel to Beatrice Hallam. 12mo., pp. 282. New York, G. W. Dillingham & Co. U. Va.

1855. Ellie; or The Human Comedy. By John Esten Cooke, Author of "The Virginia Comedians," "Leather Stocking and Silk," "The Youth of Jefferson," Peony, &c. With illustrations after designs by Strother. 12mo., pp. 576. Richmond, A. Morris. Congress; U. Va. Reviewed in So. Lit. Mess., August, 1855, p. 519.

1856. The Last of the Foresters; or, Humors on the Border; a Story of the Old Virginia Frontier. 12mo., pp. 419. New York, Derby & Jackson; Cincinnati, H. W. Derby & Co. Congress. Reviewed in So. Lit. Mess., August, 1856, p. 158.

1857. Estcourt; or, The Memoirs of a Virginia Gentleman. Russell's Magazine, vol. I, 1857, pp. 16-26; 108-122; 202-217; 305-319; 397-409; 490-500; and vol. II, 1857, pp. 20-33.

1858. May-Days at Rackrack Hall. By John Esten Cooke. So. Lit. Mess., May, 1858, pp. 340-350.

1859. Henry St. John Gentleman or "Flower of Hundreds" in the county of Prince George, Virginia. A Tale of 1774-'75. A Sequel to The Virginia Comedians. 12mo., pp. 503. New York, Harper & Brothers. Congress (card). Reprinted (1884) as: Bonnybel Vane, Embracing the History of Henry St. John Gentleman. 12mo., pp. 503. New York, Harper & Brothers. Congress. Dr. B. W. Green. Reviewed in So. Lit. Mess., October, 1859, pp. 316-318.

1859. Greenway Court; or, The Bloody Ground (copyright secured). Published in the So. Lit. Mess., 1859, vol. 28, pp. 265-277; 337-354; 419-436; vol. 29, pp. 33-51; 113-130; 187-205; 249-268; 353-375; 440-465. Signed John Esten Cooke, Richmond, May 23d, 1859.

1868. Published as: Fairfax; or, The Master of Greenway Court. A Chronicle of the Valley of the
Shenandoah. 12mo., pp. 405. New York, Carleton & Co. Congress; U. Va.

Cooke, Philip Pendleton, 1816-1850. Va.
1847. Froissart Ballads, and other Poems. 16mo., pp.
216. Phila. The Ballads, pp. 13-157 (a translation). Congress.
1848. The Two Country Houses, So. Lit. Mess., vol. 14,
pp. 307-318; 349-356; 436-450. Erisicthon, pp.
721-726.
1848. The Gregories of Hackwood. So. Lit. Mess., vol.
14, pp. 537-543; 612-622.
1849-50. The Chevalier Merlin. An Original Novel. So.
Lit. Mess., vol. 15, pp. 326-335; 417-426; 473-
481; 569-578; 641-650; 727-734; vol. 16, pp. 42-52.
Abruptly terminated by the death of the author on
January 20, 1850. "His last published effort was
'The Chevalier Merlin,' the singularly beautiful
story of the fortunes of Charles XII. as given by
Voltaire, with an interwoven plot of rare interest."
So. Lit. Mess., vol. 16, pp. 125-126. See So.
Lit. Mess., June, 1858, pp. 418-432, for "Recollec-
tions of P. P. Cooke."

Cooke, Philip St. George, 1809-1895. Va.
1851-1853. Scenes Beyond the Western Border. By a
Captain of U. S. Dragoons. So. Lit. Mess., 1851,
1852, 1853.

1856. Scenes and Adventures in the Army; or Romance
of Military Life. By P. St. G. Cooke, Colonel
Second Dragoons, U. S. A. 12mo., pp. 432.
Philadelphia, Lindsay and Blakiston.

Anonymous.
1849. Cordora. A Poetical Romance. By F. S. M.

12mo., pp. 86. St. Louis, Mo. Republican Steam Power Press. Harris. The poem Cordora pp. 1-73; the remainder of the volume fugitive pieces.

Cowden, Mrs. V. G., of Mobile, Ala.
    1860. Ellen; or The Fantastic's Daughter. Mobile, S. H. Goetzel & Co. See So. Lit. Mess., December, 1860, p. 476, and January, 1861, p. 80.

Crafts, William, 1787-1826. S. C. N. Y.
    1819. The Sea Serpent; or, Gloucester Hoax. A Dramatic Jeu D'Esprit, in Three Acts. Copy-Right Secured According to Law. 12mo., pp. 34. Charleston. Printed and Published by A. E. Miller. No. 101, Queen-Street. Congress; Harris.
    1820. Sullivan's Island, the Raciad, and Other Poems. Reprinted. 8vo., pp. 100. Charleston. Printed by T. B. Stephens, 8, Tradd-St. Harris. Sullivan's Island, pp. 3-12; The Raciad, pp. 13-22; also contained in A Selection in Prose and Poetry from the Miscellaneous Writings of the late William Crafts to which is prefixed a memoir of his Life. 12mo., pp. 384. Charleston. Printed by C. C. Sebring and J. A. Burgess. 1828. U. Va.

Cranch, Christopher Pearse, 1813-1892. Va., Mass.
    1840. A Poem Delivered in the First Congregational Church in the Town of Quincy, May 25, 1840. The Two Hundredth Anniversary of the Incorporation of the Town, by Christopher Pearse Cranch. 8vo., pp. 26. Boston, James Munroe and Company. Congress.
    1856. The Last of the Huggermuggers. 12mo. Boston.
    1857. Kobboltozo: A Sequel to the Last of the Huggermuggers, with illustrations, by Christopher Pearse Cranch. 12mo., pp. 95. Boston, Phillips, Sampson and Company. Congress.

Custis, George Washington Parke, 1781-1857. Md., Va.

> 1828. Indian Prophecy. A National Drama in Two Acts, founded on a most interesting and romantic occurrence in the life of General Washington. 16mo., pp. 35. Georgetown. See Wegelin: E. A. P.

> 1830. Pocahontas; or, The Settlers of Virginia, A National Drama, in three Acts. Performed at the Walnut Street Theatre, Philadelphia, twelve nights, with great success. By George Washington Custis Esq., of Arlington House, Author of the Rail Road, Pawnee Chief, &c. &c. Philadelphia edition, narrow 12mo., pp. 47. Phila., C. Alexander. Congress; Harris.

Cutler, Mrs. Lizzie Petit, 1831-1902. Va., N. Y.

> 1855. Light and Darkness; or The Shadow of Fate. A Story of Fashionable Life. New York, D. Appleton & Co. Noticed in Harper's Mag., 11 : 694; also So. Lit. Mess., October, 1855, p. 639.

> 1856. Household Mysteries; A Romance of Southern Society. By Lizzie Petit, of Virginia, Author of "Light and Darkness." New York, D. Appleton & Co. Reviewed in So. Lit. Mess., vol. 23, September, 1856, pp. 239-240. See vol. II, March-April, 1902, pp. 39-40, of Things and Thoughts (Winchester, Va.) for an estimate of Mrs. Cutler by S. A. Brock Putnam. U. Va.

Cutter, George Washington.

> 1848. Buena Vista : and Other Poems. By G. W. Cutter. 12mo., pp. 168. Cincinnati, Morgan & Oerend, Printers. Harris. Preface Signed, Covington, Kentucky, Dec. 1847. Buena Vista, pp. 13-23 is a spirited war ballad; The Creation of Woman, pp. 63-72 is an exquisite piece of description.

Dabney, Richard, 1787-1825.   Louisa County, Virginia.

    1843. Rhododaphne; or the Thessalian Spell.   A Poem,
        So. Lit. Mess., 1843, pp. 329-340; 408-417.

        "A Literary Lady placed in my hands a few
        days since a copy of Rhododaphne or the Thessa-
        lian Spell; a poem which issued from the Phila-
        delphia press about 25 years since; and which I
        well remember at the time to have read with un-
        usual delight.   It is probable that this copy is the
        only one which has escaped the destruction of time,
        and I therefore send it to the Messenger to be pre-
        served and circulated in its pages."   From the in-
        troductory note in the Messenger.   Reprinted from
        the Messenger.   8mo., pp. 21, no date and no
        place.   U. Va.

Anonymous.

    1837. The Dade Asylum; or Mental Monument to Major
        Dade, and those who have fallen in the Florida
        War.   For the Educating of the Yeomanry of the
        South.   An Excerpt from the "Seminoliad."   A
        Poem by A Soldier of the Line.   The proceeds
        pledged for the founding of the Dade Asylum.
        18mo., pp. 40.   Charleston, S. C.   Printed by
        Thomas J. Eccles, 122 King-Street.   Harris.

Daveiss, Mrs. Mary Thompson, 1814-   . Ky.

    —— Roger Sherman, A Tale of '76.

    —— Woman's Love. See Appleton II: 81.

Anonymous.

    1804. Delavel, A Novel.   16mo. Newbern, N. C.   See
        Wegelin: E. A. F.

Anonymous.

    1844. De Mortier; A Tale of the French Revolution.   So.
        Lit. Mess., January, 1844, pp. 52-60.   Dated Rich-
        mond, Oct. 21, 1843.

Dimitry, Alexander, 1805-1883. La.
    1830-35. Many Short Stories for annuals under the pen-
        name "Tobias Guarnerius."

Doddridge, Dr. Joseph, 1769-1826. Va.
    1823. Logan, The Last of the Race of Skikellemus, Chief
        of the Cayuga Nation. A Dramatic Piece. To
        which is added the Dialogue of the Backwoodsman
        and the Dandy, First recited at the Buffaloe Semi-
        nary, July the 1st, 1821, by Dr. Joseph Doddridge.
        12mo., pp. 47. Buffaloe Creek, Brooke County, Va.
        Printed for the Author, by Solomon Sala at the
        Buffaloe Printing Office. This copy can be found
        in the Harris Collection.
    1868. Reprinted from the Virginia Edition of 1823, with
        an Appendix relating to the Murder of Logan's
        Family, for William Dodge, by Robert Clarke &
        Co., Cincinnati. 4to., pp. 76. Congress; U. Va.;
        Harris.

Anonymous. Some one of Albemarle County, Virginia.
    1841. Don Paez and Other Poems. By a Virginian.
        12mo., pp. 150. New York, W. H. Graham, Tri-
        bune Building. Don Paez is a poem of more than
        2000 lines arranged in the Spenserian stanza, and
        in *Duans* instead of cantos. So. Lit. Mess., July,
        1847, pp. 441-446. Harris. Don Paez pp.1-83.

Dorr, Julia Caroline Ripley, 1825-   . S. C., Vt., N. Y.
    1848. Isabel Leslie (a tale which was awarded a $100
        prize by Sartain's Magazine).
    1854. Farmingdale, A Tale. 2 vols., 12mo.: also 2 vols.
        in one, 12mo. New York.
            This tale came out under the name of Caroline
        Thomas. See Allibone, III, 2386.
    1856. Lanmere. A Tale. 12mo., pp. 447. New York,
        Mason Brothers. Congress (card). See Supple-
        ment to Allibone, I, p. 503.

"Mrs. Dorr has been a most industrious writer. Her tales, novelettes, and poems, published in various first-class literary journals and magazines from 1848 to the present time (1871) would form a score of medium sized volumes." Living Female Writers of the South, p. 477.

Dorsey, Mrs. Anna Hanson, 1815-1896. D. C., Md.

1846. Tears of The Diadem: or, The Crown and the Cloister. A Tale of the White and Red Rose. By Mrs. Anna H. Dorsey, Authoress of "The Student of Blenheim Forest" &c. 16mo., pp. 223. New York, E. Dunigan. Congress.

1847. The Student of Blenheim Forest; or The Trials of a Convert.

1867. Second revised edition. 12mo., pp. 346. Baltimore, J. Murphy & Co. Congress.

1852. Woodreve Manor; or, Six Months in Town. A Tale of American Life, to suit the Merits and the Follies of the Times. 12mo., pp. 334. Phila., A. Hart. Congress.

1856. Conscience; or, The Trials of May Brooke. An American Catholic Tale. 2 vols., 18mo. New York.

1885. New Edition. See Allibone, Supplement, I, p. 503.

1857. Oriental Pearl; or, The Catholic Emigrant. 32mo. (translated into German and republished in Vienna).

According to Roorbach's Bibliotheca Americana 1820-1852 (Congress), The Sisters of Charity, 18mo., and The Oriental Pearl, or the Catholic Emigrant, were published before 1849. See Appleton II, p. 206, and Li. Fe. Wri., p. 14, for further information.

Drake, Benjamin, 1794-1841. Ky., Ohio.

1838. Tales and Sketches, from the Queen City. 16mo., pp. 180. Cincinnati, E. Morgan & Co. Congress.

Dubose, Catharine Anne Richards ("Lelia Cameron"), 1826-
. Ga.
>1858. The Pastor's Household (a prose story for the
young). New York, Sheldon & Co. See Tardy:
So. Wri. I, p. 411; Li. Fe. Wri., pp. 175-176; Appleton II, 238.

Duke, Seymour R., of New Orleans.
>1838. Osceola; or, Facts and Fiction; A Tale of the
Seminole War, by a Southerner. 12mo., pp. 150.
New York, Harper & Brothers. Congress. Time
1813-1838.

Dupuy, Eliza Anne, 1814-1881. Va., La.
>1843. The Conspirator, a Tale of Blennerhassett's Island.
See So. Lit. Mess., 1845, p. 392.
>1849. Celeste. The Pirate's Daughter. A Tale of the
Southwest by the Author of "The Conspirator,"
&c. &c. 8vo., pp. 152. Cincinnati & St. Louis,
Stratton & Barnard. Congress. First edition in
1845 (?). See So. Lit. Mess., 1845, p. 392, where
it is announced as being in the press.
>1850. The Conspirator. 12mo., pp. 299. New York,
D. Appleton & Co.; Phila., Geo. S. Appleton. Congress. Noticed in So. Quar. Rev., January, 1851,
p. 280.
>1852. Adventures of a Gentleman in Search of Miss
Smith. 8vo., Cincin. Title in Roorbach's Bibliotheca Americana.
>1852. Florence; or, The Fatal Vow. See DeBow's, July,
1852, p. 108.
>1854. Emma Walton: or Trials and Triumph by the
author of "The Conspirator," "The Separation,
The Divorce, and Coquette's Punishment,"
"Celeste," "Florence" &c. &c. 8vo., pp. 179. Cincinnati, J. A. & U. P. James. Congress.
>1854. Asleigh: A Tale of the Olden Time, by the author

of "Emma Walton," "Florence," "Celeste, the
Pirate's Daughter," &c. &c. 8vo., pp. 112. Cincinnati, H. B. Pearson. Congress.

1855. The Country Neighborhood. 8vo., pp. 110. New
York, Harper & Brothers. Congress.

1856. The Huguenot Exiles; or, The Times of Louis
XIV. A Historical Novel. 12mo., pp. 453. New
York, Harper & Brothers. Congress.

Between 1855 and 1858. The Planter's Daughter, A Tale
of Louisiana. 12mo. New York. Title in Roorbach's Bib. Amer.

1860. Autobiography of a Skeleton. A serial in the
"Ledger," New York. See Davidson, p. 176.

Eastman, Mrs. Mary Henderson, 1818-   . Va.

1852. Aunt Phillis's Cabin; or, Southern Life As It Is.
12mo., pp. 280. Phila., Lippincott, Grambo & Co.
Congress; U. Va.

1856. Sketches of Fashionable Life. 12mo., pp. 394.
Phila., Lippincott, Grambo & Co. Congress.

Ellinjay, Louise. Va.

1859. Rising Young Men and Other Tales. Title taken
from card catalogue of U. Va. Virginiana. This
valuable collection of Virginia Literature was destroyed by fire when the library was burned in
1895.

Elliott, William, of Beaufort, S. C., 1788-1863.

1846. Carolina Sports by Land and Water; including incidents of Devil Fishing, Wild Cat, Deer, and Bear
Hunting &c. &c. 12mo., pp. 172. Charleston,
Burges & James. Congress. Real incidents, but
read like fiction.

1859. Another copy, 12 mo., New York, Derby & Jackson. Congress. Reviewed in So. Quar. Rev.,
July, 1847, pp. 67-90. See So. Lit. Mess., June,

1846, p. 384: Russell's Mag., January, 1860, p. 381.

1850. Fiesco, A Tragedy by an American. 12mo., pp. 64. New York. Printed for the Author. See Duyckinck, I: 797.

Anonymous.

1818. Essays, Religious, Moral, &c., by a Lady. 12mo., pp. 242. Charleston. Among other things this volume contains: A Tyrant's Victims, A Tragedy in Five Acts; The Young Carolinians; or, Americans in Algiers; A Play in Five Acts; The Orphans; A Play in Five Acts. See Wegelin: E. A. P.

Falkner, W. C., 1826-1889. Tenn., Miss.

1851. The Spanish Heroine; A Tale of War and Love. Scenes Laid in Mexico. 12mo., pp. 136. Cincin., I, Hart & Co. Congress. Time, 1840, *et seq.*

1853. Henry and Ellen. See Pub. of Miss. State Hist. Asso., 1900, vol. III, pp. 113-125, for biography by Bondurant. U. Va.

Farmer, C. M. Va.

1847. The Fairy of the Stream and Other Poems. 8vo., pp. 167. Richmond, Harrold & Murray. Contains Alceste (an Eastern tale). See review in So. Lit. Mess., February, 1848, pp. 123-128; also Painter's Poets of Virginia, p. 119.

Anonymous.

1807. The Female Enthusiast. A Tragedy in Five Acts by a Lady. 12mo., pp. 51. Charleston, J. Hoff. Wegelin: E. A. P.

Field, Joseph M., 1810-1856. Eng., Mo., Ala.

1847. The Drama in Pokerville; The Bench and Bar of Jurytown, and Other Stories. 12mo., pp. 200. Phila., Carey & Hart. Congress. Also bound in

a volume with Chronicles of Pineville, by William
Tappan Thompson, 12mo., pp. 200. Phila., A.
Hart, late Carey & Hart, 1850. Congress.

Flagg, Edmund, 1815-1890. Me., Mo., Ky., Miss., Va.
1842. Carrero, or the Prime Minister, A Novel; Francois
of Valois, A Novel.
1848. The Howard Queen, a Novel.
1849. Edmond Dantes, a sequel to Monte Christo.
1850. Blanche of Artois.
Also several dramas. See Duyckinck, Adams,
Allibone and Appleton.

Anonymous.
1842. Florence Courtland. By a Young Lady of Virginia. See So. Lit. Mess., July, pp. 468-480;
October, pp. 629-643. Signed *Maia*.

Anonymous.
1839. Florence, The Maid; or, A Woman's Vengeance.
A (pseud.) Historical Tragedy. 12mo., pp. 92.
Charleston. Harris.

Ford, Mrs. Sallie Rochester, 1828-1902. Ky.
1857. Grace Truman; or, Love and Principle. 12mo.,
pp. 499. New York, Sheldon, Blakeman & Co.;
Chicago, S. C. Griggs & Co.; St. Louis, Wm.
Crowell; Louisville, Kirk & Clark. Congress.
1860. Mary Bunyan, The Dreamer's Blind Daughter. A
Tale of Religious Persecution. 12mo., pp. 488.
New York, Sheldon & Co.; Boston, Gould & Lin-
coln. Congress. Noticed in So. Lit. Mess., vol. 31,
July, 1860, p. 79.

French, James S., of Virginia.
1836. Elkswatawa; or, The Prophet of the West. A
Tale of the Frontier. 2 vols., 12mo., pp. 244-254.
New York, Harper & Brothers. Congress. U.
Va. The preface to this tale is dated January 27,

1836, Jerusalem, Southampton Co., Va. The historic time is 1794-1811. Reviewed in So. Lit. Jour., vol. 3, p. 152; and So. Lit. Mess., vol. 2, August, 1836, pp. 589-592.

French, Mrs. L. Virginia Smith, 1830-1881. Md., Tenn.
1859. Iztalilxo, the Lady of Tula, a Tragedy, in five acts of which the scene is in Mexico; the time before the Spanish Discovery; the Characters, the mysterious Tezcucons. See Davidson, 205; Forrest, 442.

Furman, Richard.
1859. The Pleasures of Piety and Other Poems. By Richard Furman. 12mo., pp. 220. Charleston, S. C. S. G. Courtenay & Co. Publishers. The Pleasures of Piety, pp. 9-120. Rawlings Institute Library.

Gayarré, Charles Etienne Arthur, 1805-1895. La.
1854. School for Politics; A Dramatic Novel. 12 mo. New York, D. Appleton & Co. Congress (card). See Harper's Mag., 9: 710. "The design is to satirize the politics, morals and manners of its day. Scene Baton Rouge; Characters: the governor, senators, representatives and politicians in general of the state." Davidson, p. 217; see also Fortier's Louisiana Studies, p. 102.

Anonymous.
1846. Gertru, or The Maid of Charleston. A Poem in four Cantos. By a Citizen of Perry County, Alabama. Printed by C. Yancey, Wetumpka, Alabama. See So. Lit. Mess., January, 1847, pp. 52-57, for a review of this metrical romance.

Gilman, Caroline Howard, 1794-1888. Mass., S. C.
1834. Recollections of a New England Bride and Housekeeper. 16mo., pp. 155. New York. Congress. Chiefly concerned with domestic economy.

1838. Recollections of a Southern Matron. 12mo., pp. 268. New York, Harper & Brothers. Congress; U. Va. Appeared as a serial in the Southern Rose-Bud and the Southern Rose, 1835-1837. Congress.

1839. Tales and Ballads. 16mo., pp. 190. Boston, William Crosby & Co. Congress; U. Va.

1840. Love's Progress. 12mo., pp. 171. New York, Harper & Brothers. Congress. Appeared as Love's Progress, or Ruth Raymond, in the Southern Rose, May 26, 1838, to April 13, 1839.

1852. Recollections of a New England Bride and of a Southern Matron. New edition, revised. Recollections of a Southern Matron, pp. 5-311; Recollections of a New England Bride and Housekeeper, pp. 312-403; one vol., 12mo. New York, G. P. Putnam & Co. Congress.

1856. Poetry and Prose for the Young. The First and Last Oath; with Other Stories. By Caroline Howard. Charleston, So. Bap. Pub. Society. Noticed in So. Lit. Mess., vol. 24, May, 1857, p. 398.

Godfrey, Thomas, Jr., 1736-1763. B. Phila.; d. N. C. Finished Prince of Parthia during a three-years' residence in N. C.

1765. Juvenile Poems on Various Subjects. With the Prince of Parthia, A Tragedy. By the Late Mr. Thomas Godfrey, Junr. of Philadelphia. 8vo., pp. 223. Phila., Henry Miller. Congress; Harris. The Prince of Parthia, pp. 90-223 of this volume. This play was written before 1759.

Goulding, Rev. Francis Robert, 1810-1881. Ga.

1844. Little Josephine (a Sunday school story). New York.

1852. Robert and Harold; or, The Young Marooners on the Florida Coast. 12mo., pp. 422. Phila., William S. Martien. Congress.

1880. The Young Marooners on the Florida Coast; or, Robert and Harold, New and enlarged edition. 12mo., pp. 446. Phila., Alfred Martien. Congress. Reviewed in So. Quar. Rev., vol. 24, July, 1853, p. 284.

Grayson, William J., 1788-1863. S. C.
1858-1859. Marion, A Narrative Poem. Published in Russell's Magazine, 1858, pp. 212-218; 1859, 313-321; 406-414; 505-509.
1860. Marion, a Narrative Poem.
1907. Reprinted in "Selected Poems by W. J. Grayson," selected and compiled by Mrs. William H. Armstrong (his daughter). 12mo., pp. 148. New York & Washington. The Neale Publishing Co. 1907. U. Va. Marion, pp. 85-139.

Gregory, James ("Capt. Seaworthy").
1851. Bertie; or, Life in the Old Field. A Humorous Novel, with a letter to the author from Washington Irving. 12mo., pp. 242. Phila., A. Hart. Congress. Scene N. C.; resembles "Mississippi Scenes" by Cobb. See So. Lit. Mess., September, 1851, p. 584.

Griffith, John T. Miss.
—— The Fawn's Leap, A Novel. See Owen: Miss., p. 718.

Hall, Everard.
1809. Nolens Volens; or, The Biter Bit. 12mo., pp. 92. Newbern, N. C. See Wegelin: E. A. P.

Harby, Isaac, 1788-1828. S. C.
1807. Alexander Severus.
1807. The Gordian Knot; or, Causes and Effects.
1819. Alberti. A Play. 12mo., pp. 55. Charleston. Harris.

1829. A Selection from the Miscellaneous Writings of Isaac Harby. 8vo., pp. 287. Charleston, J. S. Burges. Congress. Alberti, a play in five acts (scene Florence, Italy, time a day and night, 1480 A. D.), pp. 8-54 of this volume.

Harney, John Milton, of Bardstown, Ky., 1789-1825. Del., Tenn., La., Ky.

1816. Crystalina; A Fairy Tale, by an American, in six cantos. 12mo., pp. 112. New York, G. F. Hopkins. Congress; Harris. "This poem is founded chiefly, on the superstitions of the Highlanders of Scotland, and was finished as early as 1812." Preface by the author.

Harris, George W., 1814-1869. Penn., Tenn.

1843. Humorous Stories Contributed to the New York "Spirit of the Times."

1858-1861. Sut Lovingood Papers, contributed to Nashville journals.

Some of the above appeared as:

1867. Sut Lovingood. Yarns Spun by a "Nat'ral Born Durn'd Fool." Warped and Wove For Public Wear. 12mo., pp. 299. New York, Dick and Fitzgerald. Congress; U. Va.

Hayward, Ann, of Kemper Co., Miss.

1842. Emma Stanley, A Novel. By Ann Hayward of Kemper County, Miss. See Owen: Miss., p. 725.

Heath, James Ewell, c. 1812-1880. Va.

1828. Edge-hill; or, The Family of the Fitzroyals. A Novel, by a Virginian. 2 vols. in one; 12mo., pp. 222-224. Richmond, T. W. White. Congress; Va. State Library. Reviewed in Southern Literary Gazette (Charleston), New Ser., 1829, pp. 33-34.

—3

Hentz, Mrs. Caroline Lee Whiting, 1800-1856.   Mass., N. C., Ala., Fla.

—— Lamorah; or, The Western Wilds.   Published in a newspaper in Cincinnati.

—— Constance of Werdenberg.   See Lamb's Biog. Dic. of U. S., 1901, vol. IV, p. 26; also Hart's Female Prose Writers, p. 162.

1833. Lovell's Folly, A Novel by the author of "De Lara," "Lamorah" &c.   12mo., pp. 333.   Cincinnati, Hubbard & Edmonds.   Congress.

1835. The Village Pastor's Wife.   So. Lit. Mess., March, 1835, pp. 359-365.

1843. De Lara; or, The Moorish Bride, A Tragedy, in Five Acts.   12mo., pp. 79.   Tuscaloosa, Ala., Woodruff & Olcott.   Harris.   Awarded a prize of $500, offered by Mr. Pelby of the Boston Theatre.   See So. Quar. Rev., October, 1843, pp. 521-522.   Written in 1831.   Scene, A Spanish Castle on the frontier of Granada.

1845. A Legend of the Silver Wave.   Published in Southern and Western Monthly Magazine and Review (Simm's Monthly Magazine), Charleston, S. C., October, 1845, vol. II, pp. 255-264.

1846. Aunt Patty's Scrap Bag.   Phila., Carey & Hart.

1872. Edition of 1872.   12mo., pp. 322.   Phila., T. B. Peterson & Brothers.   Congress.   First written in 1844 for the Philadelphia Saturday Courier.   Also contained in The Lost Daughter and Other Stories of the Heart.   See So. Lit. Mess., November, 1846, p. 704.

1848. The Mob Cap.

1850. Linda; or, The Young Pilot of the Belle Creole. A Tale of Southern Life.   By the author of the prize story "The Mob Cap," "The Pedlar," Aunt Patty's Scrap Bag &c.   12mo., pp. 276.   Phila., A. Hart, late Carey & Hart.   Congress.

1881. Another copy. 12mo., pp. 276. Phila., T. B.
Peterson & Brothers. Congress.

1889. Another copy. 12mo., pp. 276. Phila., T. B.
Peterson & Brothers. Congress; U. Va. Edition
of 1889 contains biographical sketch of the author.

1851. Rena; or, The Snow Bird.

1889. Edition of 1889. 12mo., pp. 275. Phila., T. B.
Peterson & Brothers.

1852. Marcus Warland; or, The Long Moss Spring. A
Tale of the South, by the author of "The Mob
Cap," "Linda," "Rena," &c. &c. 12mo., pp. 287.
Phila., A. Hart, late Carey & Hart. 2 copies,
Congress. Reviewed in So. Quar. Rev., July, 1852,
p. 257. See DeBow's, July, 1852, p. 108.

1852. Eoline; or, Magnolia Vale; or, The Heiress of
Glenmore. 12mo., pp. 261(?).

1889. Edition of 1889. 12mo., pp. 261. Phila., T. B.
Peterson & Brothers. Congress.

1853. Wild Jack; or, The Stolen Child: and Other Sto-
ries. Including the Celebrated Magnolia Leaves.
12mo., pp. 277. Phila., A. Hart, late Carey &
Hart. Congress. Contents: Wild Jack or The
Stolen Child; Bell and Rose; Percy or the Banished
Son; The Little Brown Boy; Selim, An Oriental
Tale; Howard, The Apprentice Boy; The Black
Mask; A Tale of the Land of Flowers; Magnolia
Leaves; A Trip to the Bay; Paradise of the Dead;
The Sex of the Soul.

1853. The Victim of Excitement &c. 12mo., pp. 257.
Phila., A. Hart, late Carey & Hart. Congress.
Contents: The Victim of Excitement; The Blind
Girl's Story; The Parlour Serpent; The Shaker
Girl; The Rainy Evening; Three Scenes in the Life
of a Belle; The Fatal Cosmetic; The Abyssinian
Neophyte; The Village Anthem; The Bosom Ser-

pent; My Grandmother's Bracelet; The Mysterious Reticule; Love After Marriage.

1853. Helen and Arthur; Miss Thusa's Spinning Wheel. A Novel. 12mo., pp. 238. Phila., A. Hart, late Carey & Hart.

1853. Ugly Effie; or, The Neglected One And The Beauty.

1854. The Planter's Northern Bride. 2 vols., 12mo., pp. 300-281. Phila., A. Hart. Congress (card). See So. Quar. Rev., July, 1854, p. 255; DeBow's Rev., 1854, p. 443 (January-June).

1854. Love After Marriage and Other Stories.

1855. The Flowers of Elocution; a Class Book. 12mo., pp. 322. Phila., Charles DeSilver. Public Library, Washington, D. C. Contains scenes from the following dramas: De Lara, pp. 248-272; Lamorah, or the Western Wild, pp. 272-293; Constance of Werdenberg, or the Heroes of Switzerland, pp. 294-322.

1855. Robert Graham. A Novel. A Sequel to Linda. 12mo., pp. 256. Phila., Parry & McMillan, Successors to A. Hart, late Carey & Hart. Congress.

1855. Another copy: Robert Graham. A Sequel to "Linda." 12mo., pp. 256. Phila., T. B. Peterson. U. Va. See So. Lit. Mess., May, 1855, p. 328.

1856. The Lost Daughter and Other Stories of the Heart.

1870. Edition of 1870. 12mo., pp. 308. New York, The Federal Book Company Publishers. Congress. Contents: The Lost Daughter; The Maiden of Judea; The Pea-Green Taffeta; The Purple Satin Dress; The Red Velvet Bodice; The Snow Flakes; The Soldier's Bride; De Lara's Bride; The Premature Declaration of Love; Aunt Patty's Scrap Bag.

1856. Courtship and Marriage; or, The Joys and Sorrows of American Life. 12mo., pp. 522. Phila., T. B. Peterson. Congress. Contents: The Pet

Beauty; The Fortunes of a Young Physician; The
Two Sisters and the Two Uncles; The Mob Cap,
or, My Grandmother's Trunk; The Pedler, The
Sequel to the Mob Cap; The Beauty Transformed;
The Drunkard's Daughter; Father Hilario, the
Catholic; The Tempted; Aunt Mercy; The Village
Pastor's Wife; Thanksgiving Day; The Stranger
at the Banquet.

1856. Ernest Lindwood; A Novel. Twentieth Thousand.
12mo., pp. 467. Boston, John P. Jewett & Co.;
Cleveland, Jewett, Proctor & Worthington; New
York, Sheldon, Blakeman & Co. Congress.

1869. Another copy: Ernest Lindwood; or, The Inner
Life of the Author. 12mo., pp. 466. Phila., T. B.
Peterson & Brothers. 1869. Congress.

1856. The Banished Son; and Other Stories of the Heart.
12mo., pp. 277. Phila., T. B. Peterson. Contents:
The Banished Son; Wild Jack or the Stolen Child;
Bell and Rose; The Little Brown Boy; Selim, an
Oriental Tale; Howard, the Apprentice Boy; The
Black Mask; A Tale of the Land of Flowers; Mag-
nolia Leaves; The Paradise of the Dead; The Sex
of the Soul; A Trip to the Bay. Compare Wild
Jack; or the Stolen Child, 1853. Noticed in Har-
per's Mag., 14: 121.

The following advertisement appears on the back
cover of Robert Graham (1855; Congress):

Novels and Tales, By Caroline Lee Hentz. New
Edition in Ten Volumes. 12mo., paper covers, $5;
cloth gilt, $7.50.

I. Linda; or, The Pilot of the Belle Creole. A Tale
of the South. Fifth Edition. 1 vol. 276 pp.

II. Rena; or, The Snow Bird. A Tale of Real Life.
Fifth Edition. 1 vol. 273 pp.

III. Marcus Warland; or, The Long Moss Spring. A
Tale of the South. Sixth Edition. 1 vol. 287 pp.

IV. Eoline; or, Magnolia Vale. A Novel. Fifth Edition. 1 vol. 257 pp.

V. Wild Jack; or, The Stolen Child. A Sketch from Life. Together with Bell and Rose, &c. Third Edition. 1 vol. 277 pp.

VI. Helen and Arthur; or, Miss Thusa's Spinning-wheel. A Novel. Third Edition. 1 vol. 280 pp.

VII. The Victim of Excitement, The Parlour Serpent, and Other Novelettes. Second Edition. 1 vol. 272 pp.

VIII. The Planter's Northern Bride. A Novel. 2 vols. 600 pp.

IX. Robert Graham: A Sequel to Linda. 1 vol. 256 pp.

Parry & McMillan, Publishers, Phila.

Still further information may be found in the advertisements in Robert Graham (1855, U. Va.). See also biography of Mrs. Hentz in the introduction (pp. III-XVIII) to Linda (edition of 1881, U. Va.) for a discussion of her works by one who knew her.

Hentz, Nicholas Marcellus, 1797-1856. France, Mass., N. C., Ala., Fla.

1825. Tadeuskund; or, The Last King of the Lenape. An Historical Tale. 12mo., pp. 276. Boston, Cummings, Hilliard & Co. Printed by Hillard & Metcalf. Congress.

Herndon, Mrs. Mary E., 1820-   . Ky.

1853. Louise Elton; or, Things Seen and Heard. A Novel. 12mo., pp. 407. Phila., Lippincott, Grambo & Co. Congress. Dedicated to Jefferson Davis. Noticed in So. Quar. Rev., 24, October, 1853, p. 542.

1855. Oswyn Dudley. Cincinnati.

Holbrook, Silas Pinkney, 1796-1835. S. C.
   1834. Sketches of a Traveller. See Appleton, III: 231;
      Duyckinck, I: 869-870.

Holmes, Isaac Edward, 1796-1867. S. C.
   1822. Recreations of George Telltale (consisting of sto-
      ries, essays, and descriptive sketches). Charleston,
      S. C. See Appleton, III: 242.

Holmes, Mary Jane Hawes. Mass., Ky.
   1854. Tempest and Sunshine. 12mo., pp. 381. New
      York, D. Appleton & Co. Congress. See So.
      Quar. Rev., July, 1854, pp. 267-268; Harper's,
      9: 278.
   1855. The English Orphans; or, A Home in The New
      World. 12mo., pp. 331. New York, D. Appleton
      & Co. Congress. See So. Quar. Rev., July, 1855,
      pp. 253-254.
   1855. The Homestead on the Hillside, and Other Tales.
      12mo., pp. 379. New York, Miller, Orton & Mulli-
      gan. Congress. Contents: The Homestead on
      the Hillside; Rice Corner; The Gilberts; or Rice
      Corner Number Two; The Thanksgiving Party
      and its Consequences; The Old Red House Among
      the Mountains; Glen's Creek; The Gable-Roofed
      House at Snowden.
   1856. Lena Rivers. 12mo., pp. 416. Auburn, N. Y.
      Congress.
   1857. Meadow Brook. 12mo., pp. 380. New York,
      Miller, Orton & Co. Congress.
   1859. Dora Deane; or, The East India Uncle; and Mag-
      gie Miller; or, Old Hagar's Secret. 12mo., pp.
      474. New York, C. M. Saxton. Congress (card).
   1860. Cousin Maude and Rosamond. 12mo., pp. 374.
      New York, Saxton, Baker & Co.

Homes, Mrs. Mary Sophie Shaw ("Millie Mayfield"), c. 1830- . Md., La.

>   1857. Carrie Harrington; or, Scenes in New Orleans. New York. Tardy, So. Wri., vol. I, p. 269; Li. Fe. Wri., pp. 110-116.

Hooper, Johnson J., 1815-1863. N. C., Ala.

>   1846. Some Adventures of Captain Simon Suggs, Late of the Tallapoosa Volunteers; together with "Taking the Census" and Other Alabama Sketches, by a Country Editor. 12mo., pp. 201. Phila., Carey & Hart. Congress.

>   1851. Widow Rugby's Husband and Other Tales of Alabama. 12mo., pp. 169. Phila., A. Hart. Congress (card).

Hulse, Georgie A. (afterwards, 1853, Mrs. McLeod), 1835-1890. Fla., Md.

>   1851. Sunbeams and Shadows, and Buds and Blossoms; or, Leaves from Aunt Minnie's Portfolio. 12mo., pp. 262. New York, D. Appleton & Co. Congress. Contents: Sunbeams and Shadows; or, Leaves from Aunt Minnie's Portfolio; pp. 9-134; Buds and Blossoms, sequel to Sunbeams and Shadows; pp. 135-262. See So. Lit. Mess., September, 1851, p. 583.

>   1857 (Ante). Ivy Leaves from An Old Homestead. Prose and verse.

>   1857. Mine and Thine; or, The Step Mother's Reward. New York, Derby & Jackson. Tardy: So. Wri., 943.

Hungerford, James, of Maryland.

>   1859. The Old Plantation and What I Gathered There in An Autumn Month. 12mo., pp. 369. New York, Harper & Bros. Congress. Time 1832. The author had gone to a plantation on the Chesapeake to

escape from cholera in Baltimore. His book gives
an account of Maryland plantation life. See So.
Lit. Mess., March, 1859, p. 240.

Hunt, Rev. Thomas P. A native of Charlotte County, Vir-
ginia. 1794-   .
—— It Will Not Injure Me.
—— Death By Measure.
—— History of Jesse Johnson and His Times.
—— Wedding-Days of Former Times.
—— Liquor Selling a System of Fraud; etc.
  The above are temperance tales. Hart 318; Alli-
bone, I : 922.

Hunter, Mrs. Martha Featon, 1800-1866. Essex County, Va.
  1848. Sketches of Southern Life. So. Lit. Mess., pp.
    470-475; 630-635; 744-751.
  1849. Pp. 70-76; 158-164.
  1849-1851. The Seldons of Sherwood. So. Lit. Mess.,
    1849, pp. 389-398; 484-492; 612-622; 664-673;
    710-720;
  1850. Pp. 14-26; 100-112; 153-161; 222-228; 281-288;
    341-349; 441-448; 483-495; 649-659; 720-727;
  1851. Pp. 54-63; 184-188; 233-241; 305-317; 355-372.
    Scene eastern Va.; time 1790 *et seq.*
  1852. The Clifford Family; or, A Tale of the Old Do-
    minion, by one of her daughters. 12mo., pp. 430.
    New York, Harper & Brothers. U. Va. Noticed
    in So. Lit. Mess., 1852, p. 576.
      The dates of the following cannot at present be
    fixed; but evidently some of them appeared before
    1860.
—— Eveline Neville.
—— Thomas Jackson.
—— Walter Seyton.
—— Lilias and Her Cousins.
    See Thomas, p. 26.

Anonymous.

>1860. Ida Randolph, of Virginia. A Poem in Three Cantos. 12mo., pp. 60. Philadelphia, Willis P. Hazard, 724 Chestnut Street. Harris. In pencil on title-page, Caleb Harlan.

Imlay, Gilbert, c. 1755-   . N. J., Ky.

>1793. The Emigrants, or the History of an Expatriated Family, being a Delineation of English Character and Manners written in America. London. Title taken from Loshe's Early American Novel. Compare J. W. Townsend's Kentuckians in History and Literature. pp. 13-25. Brown University, the British Museum, The Filson Club (Louisville, Ky.), and the N. Y. Public Library have copies of this work.

Ingraham, Joseph Holt, 1809-1860. Me., Miss.

>1835. The Southwest. By a Yankee. 2 vols., 12mo., pp. 276-294. New York, Harper & Brothers. Congress. See So. Lit. Mess., vol. 2, pp. 122-123.

>1836. Lafitte: the Pirate of the Gulf. By the author of the South-West. New York, Harper & Brothers. Reviewed in So. Lit. Mess., vol. 2, 1836, pp. 593-596; also Southern Literary Journal, 1836, p. 485.

>1837. Spheeksphobia; or, The Adventures of Abel Stingflyer A. M. A Tragic Tale. By the author of "Lafitte" and the South-West. So. Lit. Mess., October, 1837, pp. 585-593.

>1838. Burton; or, The Sieges. A Romance by the Author of "The Southwest," and "Lafitte." 2 vols., 12mo., pp. 261-277. New York, Harper & Brothers. Congress. Reviewed in So. Lit. Mess., 1838, pp. 561-563; also in Southern Literary Journal, July, 1838, p. 76.

1839. Captain Kyd; or, The Wizard of the Sea.   First Edition.   2 vols.; boards, uncut.

1839. A Legend of the Mountain of the Burning Stone; A Story of the First Montezuma.   By the author of Lafitte, "Capt. Kyd," &c.   In two parts.   So. Lit. Mess., December, 1839, pp. 781-787.   See Montezuma below.

1841. The Quadroone; or, St. Michael's Day, by the author of "Lafitte," "Captain Kyd," "Burton," &c. 2 vols., 12mo., pp. 244-218.   New York, Harper & Brothers.   Congress.

1842. Edward Austin; or, The Hunting Flask.   A Tale of the Forest and Town, by J. H. Ingraham, author of Lafitte, Quadroone, Dancing Feather, &c. 12mo., pp. 66.   Boston, F. Gleason.   Congress.

1843. Jemmy Daily; or, The Little News Vender.   8vo., Boston.

1844. The Midshipman; or, The Corvette and Brigantine. A Tale of Sea and Land, by J. H. Ingraham, Esq., author of Lafitte the Pirate, Dancing Feather, &c. 8vo., paper, pp. 64.   Boston, F. Gleason.   Congress.

1844. Arnold; or, The British Spy: A Tale of Treason and Treachery.   8vo., paper, pp. 25.   In the same volume: The Bold Insurgent, A Tale of the Year 1768 (1676), pp. 25-39.   Boston.   Published at the "Yankee Office."   Congress.

1844. The Miseries of New York; or, The Burglar and Counsellor.   By Professor J. H. Ingraham, author of Lafitte, The Child of the Sea, Mark Manly, Frank Rivers, Howard, Black Ralph, &c.   8vo., paper, pp. 48.   Boston.   Published at the "Yankee Office."   Congress.

1845. Montezuma, The Serf; or, The Revolt of the Mexitili.   A Tale of the Last Days of the Aztec Dynasty, by the author of "Lafitte," "Kyd," Burton,

The Quadroone, &c. 8vo., 2 vols. in one, pp. 122-116. Boston, H. L. Williams. Congress.

1845. Norman; or, The Privateersman's Bride. A Sequel to "Freemantle," by J. H. Ingraham, Esq., author of Montezuma, the Serf, Forrestal, Beautiful Cigar Vender, Rafæl, Frank Rivers, Herman de Ruyster, &c. 8vo., paper, pp. 48. Boston. Published at the "Yankee Office." Congress.

1845. Rafæl; or, The Twice Condemned. A Tale of Key West, by Prof. Ingraham. 8vo., paper, pp. 45. Boston, H. L. Williams, at the "Yankee Office." Congress.

1846. Bonfield; or, The Outlaw of the Bermudas. A Nautical Novel. By J. H. Ingraham, Esq., Author of Montezuma, The Dancing Feather, Paul Deverell, Grace Weldon, &c. 8vo., pp. 98. Boston, H. L. Williams; Louisville, J. A. Penton. Congress.

1846. Grace Weldon; or, Frederica, the Bonnet-Girl: A Tale of Boston and Its Bay. 8vo., paper, pp. 108. Boston, H. L. Williams. Congress. This tale is a sequel to "Jemmy Daily."

1846. Leisler; or, The Rebel and King's Man. A Tale of the Rebellion of 1689. 8vo., paper, pp. 90. Boston, H. L. Williams. Congress.

1846. The Mysterious State-Room; a Tale of the Mississippi. 8vo., paper, pp. 50. Boston, Gleason Publishing Hall. Congress.

1846. The Odd Fellow; or, The Secret of Association, and Foraging Peter. By J. H. Ingraham, Esq., author of The Midshipman, Edward Austin, Scarlet Feather, &c. 8vo., paper, pp. 82. Boston, U. S. Pub. Co. Headquarters, F. Gleason. The Odd Fellow, pp. 1-39; Foraging Peter, pp. 41-82. Congress.

1846. The Spectre Steamer and Other Tales by J. H. Ingraham. 8vo., pp. 100. Boston, U. S. Pub. Co. Congress. Contents: The Spectre Steamer; or, Hugh Northup's Oath, A Tale of the Mississippi. The Frigate's Tender, a Tale of the Last War. The Cascade; or, The Exile's Rock, a Tale of the Valley of the Kennebec. Ildefonse; the Noble Polish Maiden, a Tale of Warsaw. The French Jew; or, "Killing Time" in the Jersies, taken down from the mouth of Tom King. The Lottery Ticket. Annette, the Heiress; or, The Foraging Party, A Tale of the Last War. Donna Inezetta; or, The Duke's Daughter, A Tale of Spain. The Bivouac; or, A Night at the Mouth of the Ohio, A Sketch of Western Voyaging. The Hand of Clay; or, The Sculptor's Task, A Tale of Mysteries. Otho Visconti; or, The Bridal Present. My Uncle the Colonel, with the Story of My Uncle's Friend, the Pick Pocket.

1847. Beatrice, The Goldsmith's Daughter. A Story of the Reign of the Last Charles. 8vo., pp. 93. Boston, Williams Bros. Congress.

1847. The Dancing Feather; or, The Amateur Freebooters; A Romance of New York. 8vo., pp. 92. Boston, H. L. Williams. Congress.

1847. In the same volume: Morris Græme; or, The Cruise of the Sea-Skipper, A Sequel to the Dancing Feather (copyrighted 1843). 8vo., pp. 50-92. Boston, Williams Bros.

1847. Neal Nelson; or, The Siege of Boston. 8vo., pp. 48. Boston, Williams Bros. Congress.

1847. Edward Manning; or, The Bride and the Maiden. 8vo., pp. 120. Boston, Williams Bros. Congress.

1847. Paul Perril, The Merchant's Son; or, The Adventures of a New-England Boy Launched Upon Life. 8vo., parts I and II, pp. 104-96. Boston, Williams Bros. Congress.

1847. Ringold Griffitt; or, The Raftsman of the Susque-hannah. A Tale of Pennsylvania. 8vo., pp. 100. Boston, F. Gleason. Congress.

1847. The Truce; or, On and Off Soundings. A Tale of the Coast of Maine. 8vo., pp. 103. Boston, Williams Bros. Congress.

1848. Mark Manly; or, The Skipper's Lad. 8vo., paper, pp. 75. New York, Williams Bros. Congress.

1848. Jennette Alison; or, The Young Strawberry Girl. A Tale of the Sea and the Shore. 8vo., pp. 100. Boston. Published by F. Gleason. In the same volume are found: Gallant Tom; or, The Perils of a Sailor ashore and afloat, A Nautical Romance of Wonderful Interest, pp. 100. Boston, Jones's Publishing House; and Neal Nelson, pp. 48. U. Va.

1850. Forrestal; or, The Light of the Reef. A Romance of the Blue Waters. 8vo., pp. 58. In the same volume: May Wilbur; or, The Deacon and the Widow's Daughter, pp. 59-93. New York, Morning Star Office. Congress.

1851. Nobody's Son; or, The Life and Adventures of Percival Mayberry. Written by himself. Complete in one volume. 12mo., pp. 225. Phila., A. Hart. Congress.

1854. Reissued in 1854 as: The Life and Adventures of Percival Mayberry. An Autobiography. 12mo., pp. 225. Phila., T. B. Peterson. Congress.

1857. The Prince of the House of David; or, Three Years in the Holy City. Revised and Corrected by the author. 12mo., pp. 454. New York, Pudney & Russell, Publishers (Copyright 1855). U. Va.

1883. Another copy. 12mo., pp. 472. Boston, Roberts Bros. 1883. Congress.

1859. The Pillar of Fire; or, Israel in Bondage. 12mo.,

pp. 596. New York, Pudney & Russell Publishers. U. Va. Preface dated, Holly Springs, Miss., January 1, 1859.

1887. Edition of 1887. 12mo., pp. 596. Boston, Roberts Bros. Congress.

1860. The Throne of David; From the Consecration of the Shepherd of Bethlehem to the Rebellion of Prince Absalom. 12mo., pp. 603. Phila., G. G. Evans. Congress. See So. Lit. Mess., June, 1860, p. 476.

1860. The Sunny South; or, The Southerner at Home, embracing Five Years' Experience of a Northern Governess in the Land of the Sugar and the Cotton. By Kate Conyngham. Edited by Prof. J. H. Ingraham of Miss. 12mo., pp. 526. Phila., G. G. Evans. Congress.

The following advertisements are reproduced for two reasons: first, in order that the bibliography of Ingraham's works may be as complete as possible; and second, in order that the date of the first appearance of some of his works may be more definitely fixed.

In The Miseries of New York, 1844, on back cover:

Morris Græme; or, The Cruise of the Sea-Slipper. A Sequel to the Dancing Feather;

Mark Manly; or, The Skipper's Lad. A Tale of Boston in the Olden time. Deals with events immediately preceding the Revolution;

Fanny; or The Hunchback and the Roue;

Frank Rivers; or, The Dangers of the Town. A Story of Temptation, Trial and Crime. This story is founded on events in the Lives of Richard P. Robinson and Ellen Jewett;

White Wing; or, *El Pirata of Rigolets*. A

Story of New Orleans. By Professor Ingraham. "This is undoubtedly the most ably written and deeply interesting of all this popular author's works;"

Eleanor Sherwood; or, The Beautiful Temptress. By Professor Ingraham. A story of great interest and full of incident;

Howard; or, The Mysterious Disappearance. A Tale of the Tripolitan War. By Professor Ingraham;

Rodolphe in Boston. By Professor Ingraham. "The Yankee for Saturday June 30th (1844?), Contains the First chapter of a splendid new Romance, written by Professor Ingraham, entitled Steel Belt; or, The Three Masted Galeta."

On back cover of Montezuma; The Serf; 1845; part I: Original works pub. by Henry L. Williams. By Professor J. H. Ingraham, Esq.; Norman; or, The Privateersman's Bride; The Dancing Feather; Morris Græme; The Beautiful Cigar Girl; Herman De Ruyter; Frank Rivers; Mary Wilbur; Black Ralph; Harry Harefoot (or, The Three Temptations); Charles Blackford (or, The Adventures of a Student); Estelle; or, The Conspirator; Mark Manly; a Tale of Boston; Rafæl, a Tale of Key West; Safta (Santa?) Claus; Will Terrill; Diary of a Hackney Coachman. (This and the preceding volumes are 12½ cents each.); Alice May; or, The Lost of Mount Auburn. (6¼ c.); Forrestal; or, The Light of the Reef. (25c.); Marie, The Fugitive. (12½ c.).

Montezuma, Part II, inside front cover:

Great Original Works By J. H. Ingraham Esq.

Paul Deverell: or, Two Judgments For One Crime.

The Silver Bottle; or, The Adventures of "Little

Marlboro." This work is printed in handsome stye, in two numbers; price 12½ cents each.

The East Indian: or, The Privateersman's Mate: A nautical romance.

Montezuma, Part III, on back cover:

La Bonita Cigarrera; or, The Beautiful Cigar-Vender. A Tale of New York. Founded on the Mysterious Disappearance of a lovely and ill-fated "Cigar Girl."

Herman De Ruyter; or, The Mystery Unveiled. A Sequel to the "Beautiful Cigar Girl."

In Bonfield, 1846, on back cover, a novel entitled: "The Ringdove" by Ingraham, is announced to appear in Williams' Pictorial Weekly Omnibus.

In Grace Weldon, 1846, on back cover: The Lady of the Gulf. A Romance of the City and the Seas by J. H. Ingraham, 25 cents.

On back cover of The Mysterious State Room, 1846: The Young Artist and the Bold Insurgent, by J. H. Ingraham, 12½ cents.

In Leisler, 1846, on back cover: Rivingston; or The Young Ranger Hussar.

On back cover of Paul Perril, 1847, the following are advertised as written by Ingraham: Lady of the Gulf, 25c; Winwood, 25c; Olph; or The Wreckers, 25c; Berkley, or The Lost and the Redeemed, 25c; Ringdove; or The Privateer and the Cutter, 25c; Silver Ship of Mexico, 25c; The Surf Skiff; or The Heroine of the Kennebec; The Texan Ranger, 25c; The Silver Ship; Marie, the Fugitive; Bertrand; A Sequel to Marie; William Terril.

Ioor, William.

1805. Independence; or Which Do You Like Best, the

—4

Peer, or The Farmer? A Comedy in Five Acts. (Founded on the Novel of "The Independent") and performed at the Theatre, Charleston, with unbounded applause. By William Ioor of St George, Dorchester, South-Carolina. Copy-right secured according to law. 8vo., pp. 70. Charleston. Printed for the Author, By G. M. Baunetheau, No. 3, Broad Street. (Price one Dollar). M,DCCCV. Harris.

1807. The Battle of Eutaw Springs and Evacuation of Charleston; or, the Glorious 14th of December, 1782. A National Drama in Five Acts. 8vo., pp. 59. Charleston. Printed for the Author. Played in Charleston Theatre in 1817. Wegelin: E. A. P.

Jackson, Henry R., 1810-   . Ga.

1850. Tallulah and Other Poems. 12mo., pp. 235. Savannah, Ga. John M. Cooper. Tallulah, pp. 19-42. Harris.

Janney, Samuel M., 1801-1880. Va.

1839. The Last of the Lenapé and Other Poems. 12mo., pp. 180. Phila., Henry Perkins; Boston, Perkins & Martin. Preface dated: Occoquan Va. 12th mo., 4th, 1838. Harris.

Jervey, Mrs. Caroline Howard Gilman Glover, 1823-1877. S. C.

1858. Vernon Grove; or, Hearts As They Are (Copyright secured). So. Lit. Mess., vol. 26, 1858: pp. 33-51; 99-118; 193-215; 273-287; 360-382; 433-450; vol. 27, 1858: pp. 33-48; 95-111.

1858. Vernon Grove; or, Hearts As They Are. A Novel. New York, Rudd & Carleton. See So. Lit. Mess., November, 1858, pp. 397-398; also, February, 1859, pp. 148-149. Noticed in The Atlantic

Monthly, January, 1859, p. 133. U. Va. A very favorable review. Published under the signature Caroline Howard.

Johnson, John.

1792. The Rape of Bethesda; or The Georgia Orphan House Destroyed. A Poem. By John Johnson. 12mo., pp. 16. Charleston. Printed by Markland & McIver. No. 47, Bay, MDCCXCII. Harris.

Jones, John Beauchamp, 1810-1866. Md., Pa., Va.

1842. Wild Western Scenes: A Narrative of Adventures in the Wilderness, Forty Years Ago. No. 1. pp. 44. New York, S. Colman; Baltimore, N. Hickman. Noticed in So. Lit. Mess., January, 1842, p. 104.

1842. Wild Western Scenes: A Narative of Adventures in the Western Wilderness. 12mo., pp. 263. Phila. Congress (card).

1845. Wild Western Scenes: A Narrative of Adventures in the Western Wilderness, Forty Years Ago: Wherein the Conduct of Daniel Boone, the Great American Pioneer is Particularly Described. Also: Minute accounts are given of Bear hunts—deer and buffalo hunts—Desperate Conflicts with savages—wolf hunts—fishing and fowling adventures—encounters with serpents, &c., &c., By A Squatter. 8vo., pp. 248. Phila., E. Ferrett & Co. Congress.

1856. New Stereotype edition, Altered, revised, and Corrected, illustrated with sixteen engravings from Original designs. 12mo., pp. 263. Phila., J. B. Lippincott & Co. Congress.

1859. Another copy. 12mo., pp. 263. Phila., J. B. Lippincott & Co. Congress. 100,000 copies were sold up to 1859. See so. Quar. Rev., January, 1852, p. 259, from which it would seem that an edition came from the press of Lippincott, Grambo & Co. in 1851.

1847. Book of Visions.

1849. Rural Sports. A Tale, in Four Parts. A Poem. Phila., Charles Marshall. See So. Lit. Mess., June, 1849, p. 372, for an excellent review.

1852. The Spanglers and Tingles; or, The Rival Belles. A Tale, unveiling some of the mysteries of society and politics as they exist at the present time in the United States. 12mo., pp. 270. Phila., A. Hart, late Carey & Hart. Congress.

1878. Reissued in 1878 as: The Rival Belles.

1852. Adventures of Col. Gracchus Vanderbomb, of Sloughcreek, in Pursuit of the Presidency; also, The Exploits of Mr. Numerius Plutarch Kipps, his private secretary. 12mo., pp. 202. Phila., A. Hart, late Carey & Hart. Congress.

1853. The Monarchist: An Historical Novel embracing real Characters and romantic adventures. 12mo., pp. 336. Phila., A. Hart. Congress. See So. Quar. Rev., July, 1853, pp. 269-270.

1854. Life and Adventures of a Country Merchant. A Narrative of his Exploits at home, during his travels, and in the cities. Designed to amuse and instruct. 12mo., pp. 396. Phila. Congress.

1854. Freaks of Fortune: or, The History of Ned Lorn. 12mo., pp. 401. Phila., T. B. Peterson. Congress.

1855. The Winkles; or, The Merry Monomaniacs. An American Picture with portraits of the natives. 12mo., pp. 424. New York, D. Appleton & Co. Congress. Noticed in DeBow's, July-December, 1855, p. 119.

1856. Wild Western Scenes, Second Series. The War-Path: A Narrative of adventures in the wilderness; with minute details of the captivity of sundry persons; amusing and perilous incidents during their abode in the wild woods; fearful battles with Indians; ceremony of adoption into an Indian family; encounters with wild beasts and rattlesnakes, &c. 12mo., pp. 335. Phila., J. B. Lippincott & Co. Congress.

1859. Wild Southern Scenes, A Tale of Disunion; and Border War. 12mo., pp. 502. Phila., T. B. Peterson & Brothers. Congress; U. Va. See advertisement at the beginning of the above edition (1859, Congress; U. Va.), where four pages of criticisms from the contemporary press are printed.

1861. Reissued in 1861 as: Secession, Coercion, and Civil War, the Story of 1861. 12mo., pp. 502. Phila., T. B. Peterson & Brothers. Congress; U. Va.

Anonymous.
1846. Kawanda, The Mute. A Tale. So. Lit. Mess., 1846, pp. 33-43; 95-104; 112-120. Signed J. F. K. Maryland.

1847. Some Scenes from the Life of a Fastidious Man. So. Lit. Mess., 1847, pp. 147-151; 231-236. Signed J. F. K.

Kennedy, John Pendleton, 1795-1870. Md.
1832. Swallow Barn; or, A Sojourn in the Old Dominion, in two volumes. 12mo., pp. 312-320. Phila., Carey & Lea. Congress.

1851. Revised edition, with twenty plates, 12mo., pp. 506. New York, G. P. Putnam. Congress. Reviewed in So. Quar. Rev., vol. 21, January, 1852, pp. 71-86 (by G. B. S. of Charleston, S. C.); also in So. Lit. Mess., vol. 17, December, 1851, p. 764.

1856. Another copy, same, 1856. Congress.

1872. Another copy, 12mo., pp. 506. New York, G. P. Putnam and Sons. U. Va.

1893. Another copy, 12mo., pp. 506. New York, G. P. Putnam's Sons. U. Va.

1835. Horse Shoe Robinson; a Tale of the Tory Ascendency, by the author of "Swallow Barn." 2 vols., 12mo., pp. 325-298. Phila., Carey, Lea, and Blanchard. Congress.

1852. Revised edition. 12mo., pp. 598. New York, G. P. Putnam. Congress. Reviewed in the Southern Literary Journal, 1836, p. 206, Congress; also in So. Quar. Rev., vol. 22, July, 1852, pp. 203-220. See also So. Lit. Mess., vol. 1, May, 1835, pp. 522-524; and vol. 18, July, 1852, p. 448.

1872. Another copy. 12mo., pp. 598. New York, G. P. Putman's Sons. U. Va.

1893. Another copy. 12mo., pp. 598. New York, G. P. Putnam's Sons. U. Va.

1838. Rob of the Bowl: A Legend of St. Inigoe's, by the author of "Swallow Barn," "Horse Shoe Robinson," &c. 2 vols., 12mo., pp. 270-275. Phila., Lea & Blanchard. Congress.

1854. Revised edition. 12mo., pp. 432. Phila., J. B. Lippincott Co. Congress. Noticed in So. Lit. Mess., vol. 20, May, 1854, p. 319.

1872. Another copy. 12mo., pp. 432. New York, G. P. Putnam and Sons. U. Va.

1840. Quodlibet: Containing some annals thereof, with an authentic account of the origin and growth of the borough and the sayings and doings of sundry of the townspeople; interspersed with sketches of the most remarkable and distinguished characters of that place and its vicinity. Edited by Solomon Secondthoughts, Schoolmaster, from original MSS. indicted by him, and now made public at the request and under the patronage of the great new

light Democratic Central Committee of Quodlibet.
12mo., pp. 250.   Phila., Lea. & Blanchard.   Congress.

1860. Second edition.   12mo., pp. 267.   Phila., J. B.
Lippincott & Co.   Congress.

1866. Third edition.   12mo., pp. 268.   New York.   Published by Hurd and Houghton.   U. Va.

Ketchum, Annie Chambers, 1824-   .   Ky., Tenn.
1855. Nelly Bracken, A Novel.   Phila.
1859-1861. Rillo Motto (a romance contributed to the
Lotus, Memphis).   See Appleton III: 528.

Ladd, Mrs. Catharine Stratton ("Minnie Mayflower,"
"Alida," "Arcturus," "Moina"), 1809-   .   Va.,
S. C.
1845. Emma Clifford; or, The Temptation and the
Triumph.   By Moina.   So. Lit. Mess., November,
1845, pp. 673-683.
1840-1860. Tales (contributed to periodicals).   See Li.
Fe. Wri., pp. 489-490.

Lamar, John Basil, 1819-1862.   Ga.
1851. Polly Pea-Blossom's Wedding and Other Tales,
by Hon. J. B. Lamar and R. M. Charlton.   See
DeBow's, May, 1851, p. 604.

Lamar, Mirabeau B.
—— Sally Riley.   In Two Cantos.   Canto 1, 1825;
Canto II, 1843.   Pp. 76-104 of Verse Memorials
by Mirabeau B. Lamar.   8vo., pp. 224.   New
York.   Published by W. P. Fetridge & Co., 1857.
Congress.

Anonymous.
1821. The Land of Powhatan.   By a Virginian.   18mo.,
pp. 120.   Baltimore, Fielding Lucas, Jr.   U. Va.;
Harris.

Lee, Mary Elizabeth, 1813-1849. S. C.

> 1840. Social Evenings; or, Historical Tales For Youth. 18mo., pp. 260. Boston, Marsh, Capen, Lyon and Webb. Congress. Good review in So. Quar. Rev., vol. 2, October, 1842, pp. 531-532.
>
> The following translations and adaptations from French and German by Miss Lee appeared in the So. Lit. Mess.
>
> 1845. Walpurgis Night; or The First Night of May (translated from the German of Zschokke). May, 1845, pp. 267-278.
>
> 1845. Green and Black Tea (from the German of Sternberg). July, 1845, pp. 443-445.
>
> 1845. Marie D'Enambuc. A Tale of the Antilles (Altered from the French). September, 1845, pp. 539-549.
>
> 1845. Five Eras of a Woman's Life (From the German of Zschokke). October, 1845, pp. 633-642.
>
> 1845. The Prediction. (From the French). December, 1845, pp. 713-714.
>
> 1846. The Death Knell. (From the German of Tramlitz). January, 1846, pp. 11-18.
>
> 1846. The Indian's Revenge. A Legend of Toccoa. January, 1846, pp. 25-26. This is an original piece, not a translation.
>
> 1846. The Hyacinth. A Flower from the "Bouquet for the Friends of Nature." (From the German of Flanke.) Pp. 295-308.
>
> 1846. Aaron's Rod; or The Young Jewess. (From the German). Pp. 488-495; 554-560.
>
> 1846. The Balsan, A Tale. (From the German of Hanke). Pp. 616-626; 672-681; 725-733.
>
> 1847. Julia Gonzaga. A Tale of Italy, (From the German of Tromlitz). Pp. 281-291.
>
> 1848. The Statute of Santa Maria (Translated from Pièrre Chevalier.) Pp. 29-33.

1848. A Tale of Heligoland (From the German of
Wachsman). Pp. 281-292.

1848. The Gray Lady. (From the German.)   Pp. 409-
420.

Lees, Thomas J. Va.
1831. The Musings of Carol: Containing an essay on
liberty: the desperado, a tale of the ocean, and
other original poems. 18mo., pp. 178. Wheeling
(Va.). Congress; Harris.

Lehmanowski, L. F.
1840. The Fall of Warsaw. A Tragedy. 18mo., pp. 59.
Annapolis, Md. Harris.

Leigh, J. E., of Memphis, Tenn.
1849. Lilienhorn, A Dramatic Poem. So. Lit. Mess.,
November, 1849, pp. 681-684. A short dramatic
piece dealing with Gustavus III, of Sweden, 1792.

Levy, Samuel Yates, of Savannah, Ga., 1827-   .
1856. The Italian Bride. A Play—in Five Acts. Written for Miss Eliza Logan, and published for private
distribution. The scene is laid in Venice. 12mo.,
pp. 132. Savannah, J. M. Cooper and Co. (for
private distribution). Congress; Harris. Reviewed
in So. Lit. Mess., vol. 23, August, 1856, pp. 145-
149.

Lewis, John. Va., Ky.
1844. Young Kate; or The Rescue. By a Kentuckian.
New York, Harper & Brothers. Depicts frontier
life in Western Virginia, the Kanawha Valley, etc.
A good review in So. Lit. Mess., July, 1844, pp.
447-448.

Anonymous.
1856. The Literary Wife. By F. G. R. D. of Charlottesville, Va. So. Lit. Mess., December, 1856, pp.
400-410.

Logan, Cornelius A., 1800-1853. Va.

> The following plays: The Wag of Maine; The Wool Dealer; Yankee Land; Removing the Deposits; An Hundred Years Hence; etc., etc. Also many prose tales for the periodicals. Hart 222.

Longstreet, Augustus Baldwin, 1790-1870. Ga., La., S. C., Miss.

> 1835. Georgia Scenes, Characters, Incidents, &c., in the first half century of the republic. By a Native Georgian. 12mo., pp. 235. Augusta. Printed at the S. R. Sentinel Office. U. Va. Contents: Georgia Theatrics; The Dance; The Horse Swap; The Character of a Native Georgian; The Fight; The Song; The Turn Out; The "Charming Creature" as a Wife; The Gander Pulling; The Ball; The Mother and Her Child; The Debating Society; The Militia Company Drill ("This is from the pen of a friend who has kindly permitted me to place it among the Georgia Scenes. It was taken from the life, and published about twenty years ago. The Author"); The Turf; An Interesting Interview; The Fox Hunt; The Wax Works; A Sage Conversation; The Shooting Match. The first edition of this book is very rare; the University of Virginia has just obtained a copy. A full and careful review may be found in So. Lit. Mess., February, 1836, pp. 287-292. The work is also reviewed in the Southern Literary Journal, 1836, p. 368. Congress.

> 1840. Georgia Scenes, Characters, Incidents, &c., in the First Half Century of the Republic. By a Native Georgian. Second edition. With original illustrations. 12mo., pp. 214. New York, Harper & Bros. Congress; U. Va.

> —— Another copy. Narrow 12mo., pp. 238. Congress.

—— Another copy. New edition, from new plates, with original illustrations. 12mo., pp. 297. New York, Harper & Bros. Congress.

1844. Darby Anvil. So. Lit. Mess., January, 1844, pp. 43-52. This was taken from an obscure Georgia paper, and sent to the Messenger by some one of Ashly River.

Lorraine, Miss A. M. of Abingdon, Virginia.

1828. Donald Adair. A Novel, By a Young Lady of Virginia, in two volumes. 12mo., pp. 162-170. Richmond, Peter Cottom. U. Va.

1841. Donald Adair: A Novel. By Miss A. M. Lorraine, Abingdon, Washington County, Virginia. In two volumes, Second edition. 12mo., pp. 162-170. Richmond: Published by Peter Cottom. U. Va.

McCabe, John Collins, 1810-1875. Va.

1835. Scraps, by John Collins McCabe. 12mo., pp. 192. Richmond, J. C. Walker. Va. State Library. "This little volume from the Richmond press, consists of various poems and half a dozen tales and legends in prose." So. Lit. Mess., March, 1835, p. 386.

McClung, John Alexander, 1804-1859. Ky.

—— Camden, A Novel. In the preface to "Sketches of Western Adventure" (1832, Congress), the author confesses that he wrote the above novel several years before.

McCord, Louisa S., 1810-1880. S. C.

1851. Caius Gracchus. A Tragedy, in five acts. 12mo., pp. 128. New York, H. Kernot. Congress; Harris. Noticed in DeBow's, August, 1851, p. 224.

McCoy, Mrs. Catharine Webb Towles Barber, 1823-
Mass., Ala., Ga.

    1857. The Three Golden Links. Crossville, Ga.

    1859. Tales for the Freemason's Fireside. New York.
See Davidson, p. 33; Tardy, So. Wri. II: 594;
Li. Fe. Wri., pp. 283-284.

McIntosh, Maria Jane, 1803-1878. (Aunt Kitty.) Ga., N. J.

    1841. Blind Alice (written 1838).

    1843. Jessie Graham.

    1843. Florence Amos.

    1843. Grace and Clara.

    1843. Ellen Leslie.

        The above were published as "Aunt Kitty's"
Tales in 1847. Lamb's Biog. Dic., vol. V, p. 255.

    1843. Conquest and Self-Conquest; or, Which Makes the
Hero? 18mo., pp. 216. New York. Congress
(card). See So. Lit. Mess., April, 1844, p. 252.

    1843. Woman An Enigma; or, Life and Its Revealings.
By the author of Conquest and Self-Conquest, &c.
18mo., pp. 238. New York, Harper & Bros. Congress.

    1845. The Cousins; a Tale of Early Life. By the Author
of "Conquest and Self-Conquest" &c. 18mo., pp.
205. New York. Congress (card).

    1845. Praise and Principle; or, For What Shall I Live?
Noticed in So. Lit. Mess., September, 1845, p. 576.

    1846. Two Lives; or, To Seem and To Be. By Maria J.
McIntosh, author of Conquest and Self-Conquest,
"Praise and Principle" "Woman," "An Enigma,"
&c., &c. 12mo., pp. 318. New York, D. Appleton
& Co.; Phila., Geo. S. Appleton. Congress.

    1865. Another copy. 12mo., pp. 262. New York, D.
Appleton & Co. Congress.

    1848. Charms and Counter Charms.

    1864. Eight edition. 12mo., pp. 400. New York. Congress (card). See So. Quar. Rev., April, 1850, p. 247, for the character of her novels.

1851. Evenings at Donaldson Manor; or, The Christmas Guest. 8vo., pp. 286. Beautifully illustrated. New York, D. Appleton & Co.; Phila., Geo. S. Appleton. Congress. See So. Quar. Rev., January, 1851, pp. 295-296: So. Lit. Mess., October, 1852, p. 639.

1853. The Lofty and the Lowly; or, Good in All and None All-Good. 2 vols., 12mo., pp. 299-323. New York, D. Appleton & Co. Congress. Begun in 1850; finished Dec. 1, 1852. See So. Quar. Rev., July, 1853, p. 268.

1855. Second edition in 1855 as: Alice Montrose, A Tale. 3 vols., 12mo., pp. 304-320-319. London, Richard Bentley. Congress.

1855. Emily Herbert; or, The Happy Home. 18mo., pp. 165. New York, D. Appleton & Co. Congress (card). Noticed in So. Lit. Mess., December, 1854, p. 772.

1855. Rose and Lillie Stanhope; or, The Power of Conscience. 18mo., pp. 152. New York. Congress (card).

1856. Violet or The Cross and the Crown. 12mo., pp. 448. Boston. Congress (card).

1859. Meta Gray; or, What Makes Home Happy. By the Author of Aunt Katy's Tales. 12mo., pp. 207. New York, D. Appleton & Co. Congress. See Li. Fe. Wri., pp. 223-229 for a discussion of her works.

1860. A Year with Maggie and Emma. A True Story. Edited by Maria J. McIntosh. 18mo., pp. 137. New York, D. Appleton & Co. See Atlantic Mo. Dec. 1860, p. 764.

McSherry, James, 1819-1869. Md.

1847. Père Jean, or The Jesuit Missionary; a Tale of the

North American Indians. 24mo., pp. 256. Baltimore, J. Murphy; Dublin, R. Grace & Sons. Congress.

1860. Another copy, under the title, Father Laval; or The Jesuit Missionary, a Tale of the North American Indians. 16mo., pp. 216. Baltimore and London. Congress.

1851. Willitoft; or, The Days of James the First. A Tale (republished in German, Frankfort-on-the-Main, 1858). See Appleton, IV: 161.

Anonymous.

1839. The Maid of Florence; or, A Woman's Vengeance. A Pseudo-Historical Tragedy, in Five Acts. 12mo., pp. 92. Charleston. Printed by S. S. Miller, 50 East-Bay. Harris. "Scene, Florence. Period, close of 13th Century."

Marks, Elias, M. D., 1790-1886. Columbia, S. C.

1850. Elfreide of Guldal. A Scandinavian Legend, &c. 12mo., pp. 186. N. Y. Harris. Hart, 370.

Meek, Alexander Beaufort, 1814-1865. Ala.

1839. Florence Lincoln: a Novelette. In the Southron, February-May, 1839.

1855. The Red Eagle. A Poem of the South. 12mo., pp. 108. New York, D. Appleton & Co. Congress; Harris. Noticed in So. Lit. Mess., December, 1855, p. 764. Reviewed in the same, February, 1856, pp. 107-109.

Anonymous.

1838. Mexico versus Texas, a Descriptive Novel, most of the characters of which consist of living persons. By a Texan. 8vo., pp. 548. Phila. Advertised in catalogue No. 23 of the Americus Book Co., Americus, Ga., February, 1908, at $4.00.

Miles, George Henry, 1824-1871. Md.

    1849. Loretto, or the Choice (a short story that was awarded a $50 prize, and published in the "Catholic Mirror").

    1859. Loretto, or the Choice. A Story written for the old and for the young. In four parts. Tenth stereotype edition, revised and enlarged by the author. 12mo., pp. 324. Baltimore, Kelly, Hedian & Piet. Congress.

    1870. Another copy. 12mo., pp. 371. Baltimore, Kelly, Hedian & Piet, 1870. Congress.

    1850. Mohammed, The Arabian Prophet. A Tragedy in five acts. The scene partly in Mecca, and partly in Medina. 12mo., pp. 166. Boston, Phillips, Sampson & Co. Congress. Excellent review in So. Quar. Rev., November, 1850, pp. 375-384; also So. Lit. Mess., May, 1851, pp. 325-326. "This drama was awarded a $1,000 prize, over nearly one hundred competitors, as being the best American drama."

    1851. The Governess; or, The Effects of Good Example, an Original Tale, being a Leaf From Every-Day Life. 16mo., pp. 256. Baltimore, Hedian & O'Brien. Congress.

    1853. De Soto, The Hero of the Mississippi; A Tragedy in Five Acts. By George H. Miles of Baltimore. See review in So. Quar. Rev., October, 1853, pp. 450-451.

    1857. Mary's Birthday; or The Cynic. A Play in three acts, by George H. Miles, author of Mohammed, De Soto, Senor Valiente, Blight and Bloom, &c. 12mo., pp. 3-36. Modern Standard Drama. New York, R. S. French. The Modern Standard Drama, v. 30. Congress; Harris.

    1858. (Copyright). Senor Valiente. A Comedy in five acts, by George H. Miles, author of De Soto, Mohammed, Mary's Birthday, &c. 12mo., pp. 52. Boston, W. V. Spencer. The Modern Standard Drama, v. 35. Congress; Harris. Preface dated January 1, 1859.

—— Cromwell, a Tragedy.

1860-1861. The Seven Sisters (Founded on the secession of the seven cotton States), had a long run at Laura Keene's Theatre in New York, 1860-1861.

Miller, Stephen Franks, 1810-1867. N. C.

1860. Wilkins Wilder, or the Successful Man. 12mo., Philadelphia. Appleton 4: 329; Allibone Supplement, 1115.

Milward, Mrs. Maria Georgia.

1839. The Bachelor Beset; or, The Rival Candidates. So. Lit. Mess., November, 1839, pp. 751-757.

1840. Mrs. Shooter's Party. So. Lit. Mess., 1840, pp. 61-68. Signed M. G. M. See p. 232 of this number of the So. Lit. Mess.

1840. The Yellow Blossom of Glynn. So. Lit. Mess., July, 1840, pp. 505-514. Signed, Savannah, Ga.

1841. Country Annals. So. Lit. Mess., January, 1841, pp. 37-48; February, pp. 119-122.

1843. The Winter Nights' Club. So. Lit. Mess., January, 1843, pp. 38-56. Signed, Florence, Georgia.

1846. Mrs. Sad's Private Boarding House. So. Lit. Mess., pp. 690-698. Signed, Oswichee, Ala.

Minor, Mrs. B. B. Va.

1843. The Fatal Effects of Insincerity. So. Lit. Mess., October, 1843, pp. 606-617. Signed L. V.

1844. The Prize Tale. Stephano Colonna, or Love and Lore. A Tale of the Fifteenth Century. So. Lit. Mess., May, 1844, pp. 277-282; June, pp. 349-356; July, pp. 426-434. Signed L. V... L. V... is La Visionnaire, Mrs. B. B. Minor, née Virginia

Maury Otey. See Minor: The So. Lit. Mess.,
p. 110; p. 125, *et seq.* U. Va.

Mitchell, John Kearsley, M. D., born at Shepardstown, Va.
1798-1858. Va., Pa.

1839. Indecision, a Tale of the Far West; and Other
Poems. 12mo., pp. 212. Phila., E. S. Carey &
A. Hart. Congress; Harris. Indecision, pp. 13-
144; a metrical tale. Reviewed in So. Lit. Mess.,
May, 1839, pp. 351-355.

Anonymous.

1860. The Mock Auction. Ossawatomie Sold, a Mock
Heroic Poem. With portraits and tableaux, illus-
trative of characters and actions of the world-re-
nowned Peter Funks. 12mo., pp. 261. J. W. Randolph, 121 Main Street, Richmond, Va. Harris.
See So. Lit. Mess., June, 1860, pp. 422-432.

Moore, John S.

1847. Abrah, the Conspirator. A Tragedy. 16mo., pp.
51. Washington, W. Adam. Congress; Harris.

Mosby, Mrs. Mary Webster, of Richmond, Va. ("Mrs. M. M.
Webster"), 1792-1844. Va.

1840. Pocahontas. A Legend, with historical and traditionary notes by Mrs. M. M. Webster. 12mo., pp.
220. Phila., H. Hooker. Congress; Va. State
Library. A metrical romance, or narrative poem,
in five books. Noticed in So. Lit. Mess., November, 1840, p. 780. Reviewed in the same, January,
1841, p. 78.

Anonymous.

1840. The Motherless Daughters. A Tale—in Three
Chapters. By a Virginian. So. Lit. Mess., July,
1840, pp. 531-545; September, 1840, pp. 612-622.
Ascribed to George E. Dabney of Washington
College. See p. 783 of the So Lit. Mess. above.

—5

Munford, Col. Robert. Va.

>   1798. A Collection of Plays and Poems, by the late Col.
>   Robert Munford, of Mecklenberg County in the
>   State of Virginia, now first published together.
>   12mo., pp. 171. Petersburg, W. Prentis. Con-
>   gress. The Candidates; or, The Humors of a
>   Virginia Election, A Comedy, in three acts, pp.
>   9-51; The Patriots. A Comedy in five acts, pp.
>   53-132.
>
>   There are two copies of the above volume listed
>   as being in the Harris Collection at Brown Uni-
>   versity.
>
>   1798. A Collection of Plays and Poems. 12mo., pp. 206.
>   Petersburg.
>
>   1798. The same: 12mo., pp. 189. Richmond, Va. This
>   volume must be wrongly assigned to Robert in-
>   stead of William Munford, whose work note below.

Munford, William, 1775-1825. Va.

>   1798. Poems and Compositions, in Prose on Several Oc-
>   casions, by William Munford of the county of
>   Mecklenburg, and State of Virginia. 12 mo., pp.
>   189. Richmond. Printed by S. Pleasants, Jun.
>   Congress; U. Va. Almoran and Hamet, A
>   Tragedy founded on an Eastern Tale of that name,
>   pp. 25-107 of the above volume.

Anonymous.

>   1821. Nature and Philosophy. A Drama adapted from
>   the French, by a Citizen of Richmond. 12mo., pp.
>   28. Richmond.
>
>   1830. Another copy. 16mo., pp. 33. New York. See
>   Wegelin, E. A. P.

Neville, Laurence, (pseud?) Va.

>   1855. Edith Allen; or Sketches of Life in Virginia. By
>   Laurence Neville. Richmond, J. W. Randolph,

Publisher. See So. Lit. Mess., January, 1856, p. 79.

1856. Lilias, A Novel. By the author of Edith Allen. So. Lit. Mess., vol. 23, July to December, 1856; pp. 115-131; 191-207; 257-269; 337-357; 419-434; vol. 24, January to June, 1857: pp. 35-46; 113-130; 191-203; 294-306; 381-390; 425-432; vol. 25, July to December, 1857: pp. 104-112; 171-177; 336-345.

Newman, Burkett J. Va., Ky.

1859. The Eagle of Washington: A Story of the Revolution. A Poem in three Cantos. 12mo., pp. 152. Louisville, Morton & Griswold. Harris.

Nott, Henry Junius, of Columbia, S. C., 1797-1837.

1834. Novellettes of a Traveller; or, Odds and Ends from the Knapsack of Thomas Singularity, Journeyman Printer. Edited by Henry Junius Nott. 2 vols., 12mo., pp. 228-203. New York, Harper & Bros. Congress. Contents, vol. 1: Biographical Sketch of Thomas Singularity, by Jeremiah Hopkins, Journeyman Printer; The Andalusian Rope-Dancer; The Solitary; vol. II: Cock Robin; The Shipwreck; The Counterfeiters; The French Officer. See Southern Literary Journal, October, 1835, p. 78. Congress.

Nourse, James Duncan, 1817-1854. Ky., Mo.

1846. The Forest Knight, A Novel.

1848. Levenworth. A Story of the Mississippi and the Prairies, by James Duncan Nourse author The Forest Knight &c. 8vo., pp. 143. Louisville, Geo. W. Noble, Publisher. Congress. Scene: Texas, Mexico, &c.; time, 1815-1846.

Anonymous.

1854. The Only Son. By a Virginian. So. Lit. Mess., February, 1854, pp. 89-105.

Anonymous.
    1845. Onslow; or, the Protégé of an Enthusiast. An
        Historical Traditionary Tale of the South. By a
        gentleman of Alabama. Phila., G. B. Zieber & Co.
        "Sumter and other patriots of the South are in-
        troduced" in this work from the pen of *Doct.
        Oliver,* of Montgomery, Alabama. So. Lit. Mess.,
        January, 1846, p. 63.

Page, J. W. Va.
    1853. Uncle Robin, in His Cabin in Virginia, and Tom
        without one in Boston. By J. W. Page. 12mo.,
        pp. 299. Richmond, J. W. Randolph. U. Va.
        See So. Quar. Rev., October, 1853, pp. 539-540.

Peacock, J. S., M. D. Miss.
    1855. The Creole Orphans, A Novel. 12 mo. New Or-
        leans. See Davidson, p. 408.
    1857. The Creole Orphans; or, Lights and Shadows of
        Southern Life. 12mo. New York. See David-
        son, p. 408.

Peck, William Henry, 1830-   . Ga., La.
    1857. Antoinette de Bordelaire, a Tale. See Davidson,
        p. 410.
    1859. The Brother's Vengeance. See Davidson, p. 410.
    1860. The Conspirators of New Orleans. See Ruther-
        ford, p. 865. "He has contributed many tales and
        romances to periodicals." See Appleton, IV, p.
        696.

Phelps, Mrs. Almira Hart Lincoln, Principal of Patapsco In-
        stitute, Md., 1793-1884. Conn., Md.
    1833. Caroline Westerley. 16mo. This volume is No.
        16 of Harper's Boy's and Girl's Library Allibone
        II, 1575.
    1848. Ida Norman; or, Trials and Their Uses. Vol. I,
        12mo., pp. 272. Baltimore, Cushing & Brother.
        Congress.

1854. Complete edition. Ida Norman; or Trials and their Uses. Two volumes in one. 12mo., pp. 432. New York, Sheldon, Lampart & Blakeman. Congress.

"The first volume of this work was commenced in the autumn of 1846, and read in parts, weekly, to the author's pupils, with the design of imparting moral instruction under a form more interesting to the young than that of didactic essays,——The second volume is now added in order to complete the story of 'Trials and their Uses.'" Author's preface, dated July 15, 1854. See excellent review in So. Quar. Rev., April, 1848, pp. 331-346.

Pise, Charles Constantine.

1831. The Indian Cottage: a Unitarian Story. By the author of Father Rowland &c. &c. 16mo., pp. 159. Baltimore. Published by F. Lucas, Jun. Congress.

1831. Father Rowland, A North American Tale, Second Edition, Enlarged. 16mo., pp. 195. Baltimore. Published by Fielding Lucas, Jr. Congress.

1833. The Pleasures of Religion and Other Poems, by Charles Constantine Pise, D. D. 12mo., pp. 251. Philadelphia. Published by E. L. Carey & A. Hart. Congress. Contains several narrative poems.

Poe, Edgar Allan, 1809-1849. Va., Md.

1833. MS. Found in a Bottle. Baltimore Saturday Visiter, October 12, 1833.

1835. Berenice. So. Lit. Mess., March, 1835.
Morella. So. Lit. Mess., April, 1835.
Some Passages in the Life of a Lion. (Lionizing.) So. Lit. Mess., May, 1835.
Hans Pfaall. So. Lit. Mess., June, 1835.

The Assignation. (The Visionary.) So. Lit. Mess., July, 1835.

Bon-Bon. So. Lit. Mess., August, 1835.

Shadow, A Parable. So. Lit. Mess., September, 1835.

Loss of Breath. So. Lit. Mess., September, 1835.

King Best. So. Lit. Mess., September, 1835.

1836. Metzengerstein. So. Lit. Mess., January, 1836.

The Duc De L'Omelette. So. Lit. Mess., February, 1836.

Four Beasts in One; The Homo-Cameleopard. So. Lit. Mess., March, 1836.

A Tale of Jerusalem. So. Lit. Mess., April, 1836.

1837. Narrative of A. Gordon Pym. So. Lit. Mess., January, February, 1837.

1838. Ligeia. The American Museum, September, 1838.

How to Write a Blackwood Article. The American Museum, December, 1838.

A Predicament. The Scythe of Time. The American Museum, December, 1838.

1839. The Devil in the Belfrey. Philadelphia Saturday Chronicle and Mirror of the Times, May 18, 1839.

The Man That Was Used Up. A Tale of the late Bugaboo and Kickapoo Campaign. Burton's Gentleman's Magazine, August, 1839.

The Fall of the House of Usher. Burton's Gentleman's Magazine, September, 1839.

William Wilson. Burton's Gentleman's Magazine, October, 1839.

Silence (Siope)—A Fable. Baltimore Book, 1839.

The Conversation of Eiros and Charmion. Burton's Gentleman's Magazine, December, 1839.

1840. The Journal of Julius Rodman, being an account of the first passage across the Rocky Mountains of North America ever achieved by civilized man.

Burton's Gentleman's Magazine, January-June, 1840.

Mystification (Von Jung).

Why the Little Frenchman Wears his Hand in a Sling.

The Business Man (Peter Pendulum). Burton's, February, 1840.

The Man of the Crowd. Burton's, December, 1840.

1841. The Murders in the Rue Morgue. Graham's, April, 1841.

A Descent into the Maelström. Graham's, May, 1841.

The Island of the Fay. Graham's, June, 1841.

The Colloquy of Monos and Una. Graham's, August, 1841.

Never Bet the Devil Your Head. Graham's, September, 1841.

Three Sundays in a Week. Philadelphia Saturday Evening Post, November 27, 1841.

1842. Eleonora, The Gift, 1842.

The Oval Portrait. Graham's, April, 1842.

The Mask of the Red Death. Graham's, May, 1842.

The Landscape Garden. Snowden's Lady's Companion, October, 1842.

The Mystery of Marie Rogêt (A Sequel to The Murders in the Rue Morgue). Snowden's, November, December, 1842.

1843. The Pit and the Pendulum. The Gift, 1843.

The Tell-Tale Heart. The Pioneer, January, 1843.

The Gold-Bug. Prize Story of the Philadelphia Dollar Newspaper, June 21-28, 1843.

The Black Cat. The Phila. U. S. Sat. Post, August 19, 1843.

1844. The Elk. (Morning on the Wissahiccon.) The Opal, 1844.

A Tale of the Ragged Mountains. Godey's Lady's Book, April, 1844.

The Spectacles.

Diddling Considered as one of the exact Sciences.

The Balloon Hoax. The New York Sun, April 13, 1844.

Mesmeric Revelation. Columbian Magazine, August, 1844.

The Premature Burial. Appeared in August, 1844, in an unknown Philadelphia periodical.

The Oblong Box. Godey's, September, 1844.

Thou Art The Man. Godey's, November, 1844.

The Literary Life of Thingum Bob, Esq., Late Editor of The Goosetherumfoodle. By Himself. So. Lit. Mess., December, 1844.

The Angel of the Odd. An Extravaganza. Columbia Magazine, October, 1844.

1845. The Purloined Letter. The Gift, 1845.

The System of Dr. Tarr and Prof. Fether. Graham's, November, 1845.

The Thousand-and-Second Tale of Scheherazade. Godey's, February, 1845.

Some Words with a Mummy. American Whig Review, April, 1845.

The Power of Words. Democratic Review, June, 1845.

The Imp of the Perverse. Graham's, July, 1845.

The Facts in the Case of M. Valdemar. American Whig Review, December, 1845.

1846. The Cask of Amontillado. Godey's, November, 1846.

1847. The Domain of Arnheim. Columbian Magazine, March, 1847.

1849. Mellonta Tauta. Godey's, February, 1849.

Hop Frog. The Flag of Our Union, 1849.

   For the dates and titles of the tales given above, the Virginia Edition of Poe's Works by Dr. James A. Harrison has been followed. To this edition the reader is referred for fuller information on Poe.

1850. The Works of the late Edgar Allan Poe: with Notices of his Life and Genius. By N. P. Willis, J. R. Lowell, and R. W. Griswold. In two volumes. 12mo., pp. 483-495. New York, J. S. Redfield. 2 copies, U. Va.

Anonymous.

1814. The Power of Christianity; or, Abdallah and Sabat. A Poem by a Lady. 16mo., pp. 46. Charleston.

Anonymous.

1839. The Prediction. A Tale of the Huguenots. By a Lady of Virginia. So. Lit. Mess., May, 1839, pp. 331-348.

Preston, Margaret Junkin, 1825-1899. Va.

1856. Silverwood. A Book of Memories. New York, Derby & Jackson. See So. Lit. Mess., January, 1857, p. 80.

Randolph, J. Thornton.

1852. The Cabin and the Parlor; or Slaves and Masters. By J. Thornton Randolph, illustrated. 12mo., pp. 324. Phila., T. B. Peterson. U. Va. See So. Lit. Mess., 1852, p. 703.

Requier, Augustus Julian, 1825-1887. S. C., Ala.

1842. The Spanish Exile, a Drama. Appeared when the author was but seventeen.

1846. The Old Sanctuary.

1860. Poems. By Augustus Julian Requier. 12mo., pp. 190. Philadelphia, J. B. Lippincott & Co. Harris; Congress. Crystalline—The Created, pp. 25-54; Marco Bozzaris. A Play in Three Acts, pp. 126-190. *"Scene of Action.* A small Grecian town near the heights of Agrapha;—afterwards the Camp of Carpenisse."

Rhodes, William H., 1822-   . N. C., Texas, Cal.

1846. The Indian Gallows, and Other Poems, in two parts by William H. Rhodes. 12mo., pp. 153. New York, Edward Walker. Congress. Part I, containing The Indian Gallows, a Poem, pp. 1-46; Part II, comprising a Tragedy and Miscellaneous Poems, relating chiefly to Scenes in Texas. Theodosia, The Pirate's Prisoner, A Tragedy, in three acts, pp. 51-100.

Rives, Mrs. William Cabell (Rives, Mrs. Judith Page Walker), 1802-1882. Va.

1842. Tales and Souvenirs of a Residence in Europe, by A Lady of Virginia. 12mo., pp. 301. Phila., Lea & Blanchard. Congress. Contents: A Tale of Our Ancestors, pp. 9-165; Fragments of a Journal, pp. 166-301. In this journal are interwoven: The Soldier's Bride, a Tale, and The Valley of Goldau, a Tale. Fact and fiction are mingled in both these. See So. Lit. Mess., 1842, pp. 236-237.

Robb, John S., of St. Louis, Mo.

1847. Streaks of Squatter Life, and Far West Scenes. A series of humorous sketches descriptive of incidents and characters in the wild west. To which are added other miscellaneous pieces by "Solitaire" (John S. Robb of St. Louis, Mo.), author of "Swallowing Oysters Alive." 12mo., pp. 187. Phila., T. B. Peterson. 2 copies, Congress.

1858. Reissued in 1858 as: Western Scenes; or, Life on the Prairie. A Series of humorous sketches, &c. 12mo., pp. 187. Phila. Congress.

1859. The Swamp Doctor's Adventures in the Southwest &c. &c. By "Madison Tensas M. D." and Solitaire (John S. Robb of St. Louis, Mo.). 12mo., pp. . Philadelphia, T. B. Peterson & Brothers. Congress.

Robertson, John, 1787-1873. Va.

1825. Virginia; or, The Fatal Patent. 12mo., pp. 68. Washington, Davis & Force. Harris. A metrical romance, in three cantos.

1842-1843. Riego; or, The Spanish Martyr, A Play in Five Acts. So. Lit. Mess., September, 1842, pp. 541-548; May, 1843, pp. 302-306; July, 1843, pp. 385-389. The fifth act is not printed, but is given in outline. "The theme attempted in this drama, is the Revolution in Spain,—that of 1820—and more particularly the fate of its ill-starred champion, Riego."

1850. Riego, or, The Spanish Martyr, A Tragedy: in Five Acts. Richmond, P. D. Bernard Printer and Publisher, (Just issued). Reviewed in So. Lit. Mess., September, 1851, pp. 533-543; So. Quar. Rev., April, 1852, pp. 539-541. See So. Lit. Mess., September, 1857, pp. 209-213, for a review of an "altered and abridged" edition issued by A. Morris, Richmond, Va.

1872. Riego; or, The Spanish Martyr. A Tragedy. 12mo., pp. 67. Richmond, Va. Harris.

Robinson, Fayette, d. 1859. Va., N. Y.

1853. Wizard of the Wave; A Romance. 8vo. N. Y., 1853. Allibone, 2: 1856; Adams 318.

Robinson, John. Va., Tenn.

1810. The Savage. By Piomingo, a headman and war-

rior of the Muscoguglee Nation. 12mo., pp. 311.
Phila., S. Manning. Congress (card). See American Historical Record, v. 3, p. 466, Congress, for an interesting account of Robinson's life, most of which was passed in Washington County, Va., and Carter County, Tenn. See Owen: Ala. 1126.

Anonymous.
  1836. Rose-Hill: a Tale of the Old Dominion. By a Virginian. 12mo., pp. 200. Phila., Key & Biddle. See So. Lit. Mess., February, 1836, p. 180. "It embraces some events connected with two (fictitious) families in the Western section of Virginia during the Revolution."

Royall, Mrs. Anne, 1769-1854. Va., Ala., D. C.
  1827. The Tennesseean, A Novel, Founded on Fact. 12mo., pp. 372. New Haven. Printed for the Author. Congress.

Ruffner, Henry, 1789-1861. Va.
  1839. Judith Bensaddi: A Tale. Second edition, revised and enlarged by the author. So. Lit. Mess., 1839, pp. 469-505.
  1839. Seclusaval; or The Sequel to the Tale of "Judith Bensaddi." So. Lit. Mess., 1839, pp. 638-662.
  1850. Judith Bensaddi: A Tale, Second edition revised and enlarged by the author. So. Lit. Mess., 1850, pp. 561-571; 585-596; 673-685; 732-743.
  1851. Seclusaval; or, The Sequel to the Tale of "Judith Bensaddi." So. Lit. Mess., 1851, pp. 25-36; 83-94; 161-169.
      "Ten years ago the author heard, at bed time, some extraordinary incidents that had befallen a young friend of his. The romantic character of these incidents excited his fancy so, that he could not sleep until a tale was fabricated out of the

materials, and the mind had unburdened itself by putting its conceptions on paper. After a hasty revision, this effusion of a restless imagination was sent to the press. It was published in a literary periodical of Philadelphia, and to the author's mortification, a good deal blurred by a foul typography. It was copied errors and all, into several country papers; and in spite of defects, whether in authorship or typography, the natural intent of the story caused it to be considerably admired. . . . This revision has more than doubled its size." From the preface to the second edition. So. Lit. Mess., July, 1839, p. 469.

Sawyer, Lemuel, 1777-1852.   N. C.
    1824. Blackbeard. A Comedy in Four Acts, founded on Fact. 16mo., pp. 66. Washington. Harris.
    18—. The Wreck of Honor, A Tragedy. 16mo., pp. 86. New York. Harris.

Schoolcraft, Mrs. Mary Howard.   S. C., N. Y.
    1860. The Black Gauntlet, A Tale of Plantation Life in South Carolina. 12mo., pp. 569. Phila., J. B. Lippincott & Co. Congress.

Schmucker, Samuel Mosheim (he wrote his name Smucker), 1823-1863.   Born at New Market, Va., died in Penn.
    1854. The Spanish Wife, A Play, with Memoir of Edwin Forest. 8vo., pp. 96. New York. Harris. See Appleton, V : 422.

Seawell, J.   Ala.
    1859. Valentia, A Play in five acts. 12mo., pp. 96. Mobile, Farrow & Dennett, Printers. See Owen: Ala. 1138.

Shindler, Mrs. Mary Stanley Bunce Palmer Dana, 1814-1883. S. C.

    1843. Charles Morton, or The Young Patriot; A Tale of the American Revolution. By Mary S. B. Dana. 16mo., pp. 236. New York, Dayton & Newman. Congress. See So. Quar. Rev., July, 1843, pp. 257-258.

    1844. The Young Sailor. New York, Harper & Brothers.

    1844. Forecastle Tom; or The Landsman Turned Sailor. By Mary S. B. Dana. See So. Lit. Mess., March, 1846, p. 190; also Li. Fe. Wri., pp. 475-477.

Shreve, Thomas H., 1808-1853. Va., Ky.

    1851. Drayton, A Story of American Life. 12mo., pp. 274. New York, Harper & Brothers. Congress; U. Va. See So. Lit. Mess., December, 1851, p. 764; Harper's, III, 710; and So. Quar. Rev., vol. 22, 1852, p. 263.

Simmons, James Wright. S. C.

    1821. The Maniac's Confession, &c. 12mo., pp. 96. Phila. Harris.

    1822. Blue Beard; or, The Marshal of France. 8vo., pp. 110. Phila. Harris.

    1822. The Exile's Return, &c. 12mo., p. 117. Phila. Harris.

    1852. The Greek Girl; a Tale in Two Cantos. 12mo., pp. 125. Boston & Cambridge, J. Munroe & Co. Congress; Harris. The story of a Greek maiden who was reduced to the condition of a Mohammedan slave. See So. Quar. Rev., July, 1852, p. 272; So. Lit. Mess., August, 1852, p. 511; Duyckinck, II, 456; Appleton, V, 533.

Simmons, William Hayne, 1785-   . S. C., Fla.—A brother of J. W. S.

    —— Onea, an Indian poem, published anonymously in

Charleston, S. C. See Duyckinck, II, 456; Appleton, V, 533.

Simms, William Gilmore, 1806-1870. S. C.

    1829. Vision of Cortes, Cain, and Other Poems. 16mo.,
        pp. 151. Charleston, James S. Burgess. Con-
        gress. The Cortes, a metrical tale, pp. 7-44 of this
        volume.

    1832. Atalantis, A Story of the Sea: in Three Parts.
        8vo., pp. 80. New York, J. & J. Harper.

    1848. Revised edition: Atalantis; A Story of the Sea.
        8vo., pp. 144. Phila. Congress. The Atalantis,
        a dramatic poem, pp. 1-72 of this volume, which
        also contains "The Eye and the Wing; Poems
        chiefly imaginative."

    1833. The Book of My Lady. A Melange. By a Bach-
        elor Knight. "Volti Subito." 12mo., pp. 334.
        Phila.

    1833. Martin Faber; the Story of a Criminal. 16mo.,
        pp. 189. New York, J. & J. Harper. Congress.

    1834. Guy Rivers: A Tale of Georgia, By the Author
        of Martin Faber. 2 vols., 12mo., pp. 278-321.
        New York, Harper & Brothers. Congress.

    1841. Another copy: Guy Rivers, The Outlaw. A Tale
        of Georgia, By W. Gilmore Simms, author of
        "Martin Faber," "The Yemassee," "Mellichampe,"
        &c. 8vo., pp. 213. London, 1841. The Roman-
        cist and novelist's library, new series, vol. 2, edited
        by William Hazlitt. Congress.

    1835. The Yemassee. A Romance of Carolina. 12mo.,
        pp. 222-242. New York, Harper & Brothers.
        Congress.

    1853. Another copy, new and revised edition, 1 vol.,
        12mo., pp. 454. New York, Redfield. Congress.
        See So. Lit. Mess., January, 1854, p. 64.

    1866. Another copy, 12mo., pp. 454. New York, W. J.
        Widdleton, Publisher, U. Va.

1835. The Partisan: A Tale of the Revolution. 2 vols., 12mo., pp. 244-276. New York, Harper & Brothers. Congress. Excellent review in So. Lit. Mess., January, 1836, pp. 117-121; also see notice in So. Lit. Mess., July, 1854, p. 446. See also So. Lit. Jour., I, 1835, pp. 284-285; 347-358.

1836. Mellichampe. A Legend of the Santee. 2 vols., 12mo., pp. 224-232. New York, Harper & Brothers. Congress.

1854. New and revised edition, 12mo., pp. 431. New York, Redfield. Congress.

1836. The Spirit Bridegroom by the Author of the Yemassee, Guy Rivers &c. Published in the So. Lit. Jour., vol. 3, pp. 193-209. Congress.

1837. Blondeville. By W. Gilmore Simms, From a Manuscript Drama. So. Lit. Mess., June, 1837, pp. 353-360.

1838. Richard Hurdis; or, The Avenger of Blood. A Tale of Alabama. 2 vols., 12mo., pp. 224-262. Phila.

1855. New and revised edition, 12mo., pp. 403. New York, Redfield. Congress.

1838 (July). Ipsistos. So. Lit. Jour., July, 1838, New Series, vol. 4, pp. 8-30. Congress.

1838. Pelayo: A Story of the Goth. 2 vols., 12mo., pp. 213-282. New York, Harper & Brothers. Congress. See So. Lit. Mess., 1838, pp. 535-538.

1838. Carl Werner, An Imaginative Story; with Other Tales of Imagination. 2 vols., 12mo., pp. 243-208. New York, George Ablard. Congress. Contents: Vol. I, Carl Werner; Ipsistos; The Star Brethren; Onea and Anyta; vol. II, Conrade Weickhoff; Logoochie; Jocassee; The Cherokee Embassage.

1839. The Damsel of Darien. 2 vols., 12mo., pp. 308-281. Phila., Lea and Blanchard. Congress.

1840. Border Beagles; a Tale of Mississippi. 2 vols., 12mo., pp. 300-337. Phila., Carey & Hart. Congress.

1855. New edition, 12mo., pp. 495. New York, Redfield. U. Va.

1841. The Kinsmen; or The Black Riders of the Congaree. A Tale. 2 vols., 12mo., pp. 241-275. Phila., Lea & Blanchard. Congress.

1854. Afterwards known as "The Scout; or the Black Riders of the Congaree." New and revised edition, 12mo., pp. 472. New York, Redfield. Congress. See So. Lit. Mess., May, 1859, p. 535, *et seq.*

1841. Confession; or, The Blind Heart. A Domestic Story. 2 vols., 12mo., pp. 251-257. Phila., Lea and Blanchard. Congress.

1856. New and revised edition, 12mo., pp. 398. New York, Redfield. U. Va.

1842. Beauchampe, or The Kentucky Tragedy. A Tale of Passion. 2 vols., 12mo., pp. 303-301. Phila., Lea & Blanchard. Congress.

1856. New and revised edition, 12mo., pp. 402. New York, W. J. Widdleton. U. Va.

1843. Donna Florida. A Tale. 16mo., pp. 97. Charleston, Burges & James. Congress. A metrical romance of the Don Juan type. Reviewed in So. Lit. Mess., January, 1844, pp. 18-22.

1844. The Prima Donna: A Passage from City Life. A short story (24 pages) forming the first number of Godey's Library of Elegant Literature. 8vo., Phila.

1845. Castle Dismal; or, The Bachelor's Christmas. A Domestic Legend. 12mo., pp. 192. New York.

1845. Helen Halsey, or The Swamp State of Conelachita. A Tale of the Borders. 12mo., pp. 216. New

York.   Republished as "The Island Bride," in Munro's Fireside Companion (New York, 1869).

1845. Count Julian; or, The Last Days of the Goth. A Historical Romance. 8vo., pp. 201. Baltimore and New York. A sequel to Pelayo.

1845. The Wigwam and the Cabin. First and second series, 12mo., pp. 233-238. New York. Congress. Contents: First series: Grayling, or "Murder Will Out." The Two Camps, A Legend of the Old North State; The Last Wager, or The Gamester of the Mississippi; The Arm-Chair of Tustenuggee, a Tradition of the Catawba; The Snake of the Cabin; Oakabitee, or the Choctaw Sampson; Jocassee, A Cherokee Legend; second series: The Giant's Coffin, or The Feud of Holt and Houston; Sergeant Barnacle, or The Raftsman of the Edisto; Those Old Lunes: or Which is the Madman?; The Lazy Crow, A Story of the Cornfield; Caloya, or The Loves of the Driver; Lucas de Ayllon.

1848. An edition entitled: Life in America; or, The Wigwam and the Cabin. 12mo., pp. 311. Aberdeen, George Clark & Son, and London, W. Brittain. 2 copies, Congress. Contents same as first series above, with "Mr. Green" and "How Would You Like It" added.

1856. New and revised edition, 12mo., pp. 472. New York, Redfield. Congress. Contents same as first and second series above. See So. Lit. Mess., March, 1857, p. 240.

1849. The Cassique of Accabee, a Tale of Ashley River, with other pieces. 16mo., pp. 112. Charleston, J. Russell; New York, G. P. Putnam. Congress. The Cassique of Accabee, pp. 5-38, a metrical tale. See So. Lit. Mess., November, 1849, p. 704.

1850. Flirtation at the Moultrie House, &c. 8vo., pp. 46. Charleston.

1850. The Lily and the Totem; or, The Huguenots in Florida. A Series of Sketches, picturesque and historical of the Colonies of Coligni, in North America, 1562-1570. First and second editions, 12mo., pp. 470. New York, Baker & Scribner. A copy of each, Congress. See Harper's Magazine, 1 : 718.

1851. Norman Maurice; or, The Man of the People. An American Drama, In Five Acts. 8vo., pp. 4-31. Richmond, J. R. Thompson. Congress; Harris.

1851. Printed in Southern Literary Messenger, 1851, pp. 193-199; 281-289; 339-344; 410-415; 467-472. See Harper's Magazine, 4 : 274.

1852. Printed as a supplement to the Southern Literary Gazette (Charleston), June 19 to July 31, 1852. Congress.

1853. Fourth edition, revised and corrected, 12mo., pp. 169. Phila. Congress. Contents of volume: Norman Maurice, pp. 4-125; Caius Marius, an Historical Legend; Bertram, an Italian Sketch; and the Death of Cleopatra.

1851. Katharine Walton; or, The Rebel of Dorchester. An Historical Romance of the Revolution in Carolina. 8vo., pp. 186 (double-column, fine print). Phila., A. Hart, late Carey & Hart. Congress.

1854. New and revised edition, 12mo., pp. 474. New York, Redfield. Congress. U. Va.

1852. Gleams after Glooms; or "Joy Cometh in the Morning." A Cottage Chronicle of Christmas in the South. By a Southron. So. Lit. Mess., 1852, pp. 267-278; 345-362.

1852. The Golden Christmas: A Chronicle of St. John's, Berkeley. Compiled from the Notes of a Briefless Barrister. 12mo., pp. 168. Charleston, Walker & Richards. Reviewed in So. Lit. Mess., May, 1852, p. 318.

1852. Printed as a supplement to Southern Literary Gazette (Charleston), January 24 to February 14, 1852, pp. 1-48 (pp. 1 & 2 missing). Congress.

1852. As Good as a Comedy; or, The Tennesseean's Story. By an Editor. 12mo., pp. 251. Phila., A. Hart, late Carey & Hart. Congress. A story of Georgia life and manners.

1852. Michael Bonham; or, The Fall of Bexar, A Tale of Texas, in five parts, by a Southron. 8vo., pp. 35. Richmond, J. R. Thompson. Congress; Harris. A dramatic tale recounting the incidents in the leaguer and taking of San Antonio de Bexar.

1852. Printed in So. Lit. Mess., 1852, pp. 89-96; 145-149; 234-240; 296-304; 342-349.

1852. The Sword and the Distaff; or, "Fair, Fat and Forty." A Story of the South at the Close of the Revolution. Printed as a supplement to the Southern Literary Gazette, Charleston, S. C., February 28 to November 6, 1852. Two copies of this supplement. Congress.

1853. The Sword and the Distaff; or, "Fair, Fat, and Forty." A Story of the South at the Close of the Revolution. 12mo., pp. 591. Phila., Lippincott, Grambo, & Co. Congress. Trent gives the date as 1852, Charleston, but says he did not examine the first edition; Wegelin gives it as 1852, Phila., but does not give the number of pages. The book was copyrighted in 1852, but this does not mean that it was necessarily published in book form that year.

1854. New and revised edition: "Woodcraft or Hawks about the Dovecote. A Story of the South at the

Close of the Revolution." 12mo., pp. 518. New York, Redfield. Congress.

1853. Poems, Descriptive, Dramatic, Legendary and Contemplative. 12mo., pp. 348-360. New York, Redfield. Congress. Volume I contains Norman Maurice, Atalantis, &c. See So. Lit. Mess., March, 1854, pp. 190-192.

1853. Marie De Berniere: A Tale of the Crescent City &c &c &c. 12mo., pp. 422. Phila., Lippincott, Grambo & Co. Congress. Contents: Marie De Berniere; The Maroon, A Legend of the Caribbees; and Maize in Silk, A Christmas Story of the South. The same volume was issued in 1855, as: "The Maroon; a Legend of the Caribbees, and other Tales." Phila., Lippincott, Grambo & Co. Congress.

1866. Marie De Berniere was issued in 1866, 12mo., pp. 114, as: "The Ghost of My Husband, A Tale of the Crescent City." New York, Chapman & Company. Congress. The Maroon deals with the Spanish in the Caribbean Sea in 1532.

1853(?). Vasconselos; A Romance of the New World.
1854(?).

1857. Edition of 1857 (copyright 1856), 12mo., pp. 531. New York, Redfield. 2 copies, Congress.

1854. The Legend of the Happy Valley and the Beautiful Fawn. By a Southron. So. Lit. Mess., 1854, pp. 396-403; 492-503.

1854. Southward Ho! A Spell of Sunshine. 12mo., pp. 472. New York, Redfield. Congress; U. Va. Noticed in So. Lit. Mess., January, 1855, p. 63.

1855. The Forayers or The Raid of the Dog-Days. 12mo., pp. 560. New York, Redfield. Congress.

1882. Another copy, 12mo., pp. 560. New York, A. C. Armstrong & Son. U. Va.

1856. Charlemont; or, The Pride of the Village. Tale of

Kentucky. 12mo., pp. 447. New York. Congress (card). See Russell's Mag., June, 1857, pp. 251-255. Preface dated Woodlands, S. C., December, 1855.

1885. New and revised edition, 12mo., pp. 447. Chicago and New York, Bedford, Clarke & Co. U. Va.

1856. Eutaw, A Sequel to the Forayers, or The Raid of the Dog-Days. A Tale of the Revolution. 12mo., pp. 582. New York, Redfield. Congress.

1859. The Cassique of Kiawah: A Colonial Romance. 12mo., pp. 600. New York, Redfield. Congress (card). Deals with South Carolina in 1684. See So. Lit. Mess., June, 1859, p. 476; also Russell's Mag., February, 1859, pp. 443-455 (for a selection); December, 1859, pp. 276-277 (for a review). The City Library of Charleston and the library of S. C. University, at Columbia, each have copies of this book, but the writer has been unable to see either of them.

The University of Virginia library possesses a set of Simms's romances in 17 volumes, 12mo., cloth. The Martin & Hoyt Co., Publishers, Atlanta, Georgia. Each volume bears this legend: "Presented to the Poe Alcove by Prof. Ed. S. Joynes through Prof. J. A. Harrison, 1901." The titles to the volumes are as follows: The Yemassee: A Romance of Carolina, New and Revised Edition. (Pp. 454.) The Wigwam and the Cabin, New and Revised Edition. (Pp. 472.) Charlemont; or, The Pride of the Village; A Tale of Kentucky. (Pp. 447.) Southward Ho! A Spell of Sunshine. (Pp. 472.) Guy Rivers: A Tale of Georgia. (Pp. 503.) Border Beagles: A Tale of Mississippi. (Pp. 495.) Beauchampe: or, The Kentucky Tragedy. A Sequel to Charlemont.

(Pp. 402.)   Richard Hurdis: A Tale of Alabama.
(Pp. 401.)   Confessions of the Blind Heart.   A
Domestic Story.   (Pp. 398.)   Woodcraft; or,
Hawks about the Dovecote.   A Story of the South
at the Close of the Revolution.   (Pp. 518.)   Eutaw: A Sequel to the Forayers; or, The Raid of
the Dog-Days.   A Tale of the Revolution.   (Pp.
582.)   The Scout; or, The Black Riders of the
Congaree.   (Pp. 472.)   The Forayers; or, The
Raid of the Dog-Days.   (Pp. 560.)   Katharine
Walton; or, The Rebel of Dorchester.   (Pp. 474.)
Mellichampe.   A Legend of the Santee.   (Pp.
431.)   The Partisan: A Romance of the Revolution.   (Pp. 531.)   Vasconselos: A Romance of
the New World.   (Pp. 531.)

According to Wegelin the New York Historical
Society has a fine collection of Simms's romances.
Brown University has a good collection of his
poems.   The Southern Literary Messenger contains many of his poems, and some of his dramas.

For good contemporary criticisms of Simms as
a poet and novelist, see So. Lit. Mess., 1838, pp.
528-535; 1856, pp. 280-285; 1859, pp. 355-370.

Sims, Alexander Dromgoole, 1803-1848.   Va., S. C.
1842. Bevil Faulcon.   A Tradition of the Old Cheraw.
Columbia, S. C., I. C. Morgan.   Reviewed in So.
Quar. Rev., July, 1843, pp. 249-251.

Skitt (pseud.).
1859. Fisher's River (North Carolina) Scenes and Characters: by Skitt, who was raised there: illustrated
by John M'Lenan.   16mo., pp. 269.   New York,
Harper & Bro.   See So. Lit. Mess., January, 1860,
p. 78; Atlantic Mo., January, 1860, p. 127.
1860. Duck Town, by "Skitt," who has been "thar."   So.
Lit. Mess., November, 1860, pp. 337-342.

Smith, William Russell, 1813-1896.   Ala.
>   1860. As It Is.   12mo., pp. 260.   Albany (N. Y.), Mun-
>   sell & Rowland.   Congress.   Facing the last page
>   is this announcement: "In press, and will be speed-
>   ily published, in a volume corresponding with this,
>   Love's Apprenticeship, being a sequel to As It Is."

Smythe, James M.
>   1857. Ethel Somers: or, The Fate of the Union.   By a
>   Southerner.   12mo., pp. 382.   Augusta, Ga., H.
>   D. Norrell.   Congress.   "This book is a defence
>   of the institution of Slavery."

Anonymous.
>   1855. A Southern Home (a juvenile story), Richmond,
>   A. Morris.   See So. Lit. Mess., February, 1855, p.
>   127; also advertisement in Ellie by J. E. Cooke
>   (U. Va.), p. 9.

Anonymous.
>   1860. Southern Sketches.   Richmond, J. W. Randolph.
>   "A first rate collection of humorous sketches of
>   Southern life, taken from various newspapers and
>   put in book form."   So. Lit. Mess., October, 1860,
>   p. 320.

Southworth, Emma D. E. N., 1819-1899.   D. C.
>   1849. Retribution; or, The Vale of Shadow.   8vo., pp.
>   108.   New York, Harper & Bros.   Congress (card).
>   Published also in the *National Era,* Washington,
>   D. C., the same year.
>   1850. The Deserted Wife; a Novel.   New York, Apple-
>   ton & Co.   See Harpers, 11:836; So. Lit. Mess.,
>   1855, p. 640.
>   1851. The Mother-in-Law; or, The Isle of Rays.   A Tale
>   by Emma D. E. N. Southworth, author of "Retri-
>   bution or the Vale of Shadows," "Shannondale,"
>   "The Deserted Wife" &c. &c.   New York, D.

Appleton & Co.; Phila., G. S. Appleton. Reviewed in So. Lit. Mess., June, 1851, p. 390; November, 1860, p. 400.

1851. Shannondale. 8vo., paper. New York, D. Appleton & Co. Reviewed in So. Lit. Mess., February, 1851, p. 128; also, So. Quar. Rev., April, 1851, p. 566.

1852. The Discarded Daughter; or The Children of the Isle. 2 vols., Phila., A. Hart. See DeBow's, October, 1852, p. 429, for title; also, So. Quar. Rev., October, 1852, p. 531; and Harper's, 5:713.

1852. Virginia and Magdalene; or, The Foster Sisters. 8vo., paper. Phila., A. Hart. See So. Quar. Rev., October, 1852, p. 541.

1852. The Foster Sisters.

1853. The Curse of Clifton. Phila., A. Hart. So. Quar. Rev., July, 1853, p. 266. See Hart, p. 215.

1853. Mark Sutherland. See Hart, p. 215.

1853. Old Neighborhoods and New Settlements, or, Christmas Evening Legends. By Emma D. E. N. Southworth, author of "The Curse of Clifton," "The Deserted Wife," "The Discarded Daughter," "Foster Sisters" &c &c. 12mo., pp. 370. Philadelphia, A. Hart, late Carey & Hart. Congress. Contents: The Better Way or the Wife's Victory; The Married Shrew; a Sequel to "The Better Way"; The Thunderbolt to the Hearth; Neighbors' Prescriptions; The Temptation; Across the Street; a New Year's Story; The Irish Refugee; New Year in the Little Rough-Cast House; Winny; The Fine Figure.

1854. The Wife's Victory; and Other Novellettes. 12mo., pp. 366. Phila., T. B. Peterson, and Bros. Congress. Same as above volume with the addition of another story: Sybil Brotherton; Or the Temptation.

1854. Lost Heiress. Phila., T. B. Peterson. Congress (card). See So. Lit. Mess., November, 1854, p. 712; also Harper's Mag., 10: 282.

1854. Hickory Hall. See Hart, p. 215.

1855. Missing Bride; or, Miriam the Avenger. Phila., T. B. Peterson. Congress (card). See So. Lit. Mess., July, 1855, p. 456.

1856. India: the Pearl of Pearl River. 12mo., pp. 402. Phila., T. B. Peterson. Congress.

1856. Retribution; a Tale of Passion. 12mo., Phila. Congress (card).

1858. The Three Beauties. 12mo. Phila. Congress (card).

1859. The Lady of the Isle. A Romance of Real Life. 12mo., pp. 598. Phila., T. B. Peterson and Brothers. 2 copies, Congress.

1860. The Haunted Homestead; and Other Novellettes. With an autobiography of the author. 12mo., pp. 29-292. Phila., T. B. Peterson & Bros. Congress (card).

1860. The Mother-in-Law. A Tale of Domestic Life. 12mo., pp. 497. T. B. Peterson & Bros. Congress (card).

The following advertisement appears in the back of "Wild Southern Scenes, a Tale of Disunion! and Border War!" By J. B. Jones, 1859. U. Va.

Published and for Sale by
T. B. Peterson & Brothers, Philadelphia.
Mrs. Southworth's Works.

The Two Sisters. This is Mrs. Southworth's last new work. Two vols., paper cover. Price $1.00; or bound in one volume, cloth, for $1.25.

The Three Beauties. Complete in two volumes,

paper cover. Price One Dollar; or bound in one volume, cloth, $1.25.

Vivia. The Secret of Power. Two volumes, paper cover. Price One Dollar; or one volume, cloth, for $1.25.

India. The Pearl of Pearl River. Two vols., paper cover. Price One Dollar; or bound in cloth, $1.25.

The Wife's Victory. Two volumes, paper cover. Price One Dollar; or bound in one volume, cloth, $1.25.

The Lost Heiress. Two volumes, paper cover. Price One Dollar; or bound in one volume, cloth, for $1.25.

The Missing Bride. Two volumes, paper cover. Price One Dollar; or bound in one volume, cloth, $1.25.

Retribution: A Tale of Passion. Two vols., paper cover. Price One Dollar; or in one vol., cloth, $1.25.

The Curse of Clifton. Two vols., paper cover. Price One Dollar; or bound in one volume, cloth, $1.25.

The Discarded Daughter. Two volumes, paper cover. Price One Dollar; or one volume, cloth, for $1.25.

The Deserted Wife. Two vols., paper cover. Price One Dollar; or bound in one vol., cloth, for $1.25.

The Belle of Washington. Two volumes, paper cover. Price One Dollar; or in cloth, for $1.25.

The Initials. A Love Story of Modern Life. Two vols., paper cover. Price $1.00; or in one volume, cloth, $1.25.

> The Dead Secret. Two volumes, paper cover.
> Price One Dollar; or bound in one volume, cloth,
> for $1.25.
>
> Kate Aylesford. Two volumes, paper cover. Price
> One Dollar; or bound in one volume, cloth, for
> $1.25.
>
> The whole of the above are also published in
> very fine style, bound in full Crimson, gilt edges,
> sides, backs, etc., making elegant presentation
> books. Price $2.00 a copy.

Stabler, E. (of Harewood, Md.).

> 1860. Forty-Four Years of the Life of a Hunter; Being
> Reminiscences of Meshach Browning, A Mary-
> land Hunter, roughly written down by himself.
> Revised and illustrated by E. Stabler of Harewood,
> Md. 12mo., pp. 400. Phila., J. B. Lippincott &
> Co. Congress. See Atlantic, Mo., December,
> 1859, pp. 770-773.

Strange, Robert, 1796-1854. Va., N. C.

> 1839. Eoneguski; or The Cherokee Chief. Was pub-
> lished in Washington, D. C., in 1839. It is a
> novel in two volumes, the scene of which is laid
> along the banks of the Homony Creek, a stream
> issuing "from a small range of mountains on the
> western side of the French Broad River, commonly
> called the Homony Hills." The story ends with
> the War of 1812. See Moore's Poetic Literature
> of N. C., p. 17, note.

Strong, George V. N. C.

> 1847. Francis Herbert; A Romance of the Revolution
> and Other Poems. 16mo., pp. 100. New York,
> Leavitt, Trow & Co. Library of the Univ. of
> N. C.

Strother, David Hunter, 1816-1888. Born in Martinsburg, Va. (now W. Va.); died at Charles Town, W. Va.

1853. The Blackwater Chronicle. A Narrative of An Expedition into the Land of Canaan, in Randolph County, Virginia, A country flowing with wild animals such as panthers, bears, wolves, elk, deer, otter, badger, &c, &c, with innumerable trout—By five adventurous gentlemen, without any aid of government, and solely by their own resources, in the summer of 1851. By "The Clerke of Oxenforde," with illustrations from life by Strother. 12mo., pp. 223. New York, Redfield. U. Va.

Anonymous.

1855. The Summer-Land: A Southern Story. By a Child of the Sun. New York, D. Appleton & Co. See So. Quar. Rev., April, 1855, p. 541.

Anonymous.

1835. A Tale of the West, founded on fact. So. Lit. Mess., 1835, pp. 437-445. Signed Lovingston, Va., March 25, 1835.

Anonymous—T. H. E. of Amelia County, Virginia.

1839. My Cousin Helen. Only a Sketch, by T. H. E. So. Lit. Mess., September, 1839, pp. 606-614.

1840. Mr. Lindsay's Manuscript, by T. H. E. So. Lit. Mess., March, 1840, pp. 169-181.

1840. The German's Daughter, by T. H. E. So. Lit. Mess., November, 1840, pp. 737-760. This tale called forth so many favorable criticisms in the newspapers of the day that the editor of the So. Lit. Mess. partially revealed the identity of the author: see So. Lit. Mess., 1840, p. 1, facing p. 848, where he says the above tale "is the production of a very interesting and talented young lady of Amelia County Va."

1841. The Autobiography of a Monomaniac, by T. H. E. So. Lit. Mess., October, 1841, pp. 665-685.

1842. Mrs. Latour. By a young lady of Virginia. In two parts, by T. H. E. So. Lit. Mess., August, 1842, pp. 485-508.

Taylor, George Boardman, 1832-1907. Va., Md., Italy.

1860. Kenny, by Geo. B. Taylor of Virginia. 18mo., pp. 176. New York, Sheldon & Co. Congress.

1860. Cousin Guy, by Geo. B. Taylor of Virginia. 18mo., pp. 173. New York, Sheldon & Co. Congress.

1860. Claiborne, by Geo. B. Taylor of Virginia. 18mo., pp. 180. New York, Sheldon & Co. Congress. Known as the "Oakland Stories." Their purpose is to give moral and religious instruction to the young. In Claiborne, volume IV, "Gustave," is announced as being in press.

Terhune, Mrs. Mary Virginia Hawes (Marion Harland), 1831-   . Va., N. Y.

——(?) Marrying for Prudential Motives.

1854. Alone. By Marion Harland. Author of "Robert Remer's Letters," "Kate Harper," &c &c. Richmond, A. Morris. See So. Lit. Mess., May, 1854, p. 320; June, pp. 380-381. The third edition is reviewed in the September issue, pp. 571-573; also in December, pp. 726-732, by some one at the University of Virginia. In March, 1856, p. 240, appears this notice: "Alone. By Marion Harland of Richmond, Virginia. Nineteenth Thousand. New York, J. C. Derby."

1855. The Hidden Path. By Marion Harland. Author of "Alone." New York, J. C. Derby. Reviewed in So. Lit. Mess., October, 1855, pp. 637-638; in March, 1856, p. 240, this notice appears: "The Hidden Path. By Marion Harland, Author of Alone. Seventeenth Thousand." See Harper's Mag., 11 : 694.

1857. Moss Side. 12mo. New York, Derby & Jackson.

1898. Edition of 1898, 12mo., pp. 434. New York, Dillingham & Co. Congress. Reviewed in So. Lit. Mess., October, 1857, pp. 319-320.

1860. Miriam.

1860. Nemesis. By Marion Harland. New York, Derby & Jackson. "Twelve thousand copies of this book were sold in less than a month after its publication." So. Lit. Mess., November, 1860, p. 398.

Thomas, Frederick William, 1811-1866. S. C., Md., Ala.

1835. Clinton Bradshaw; or, The Adventures of a Lawyer. Phila., Carey, Lea & Blanchard. Reviewed in So. Lit. Mess., December, 1835, p. 68.

1836. East and West. A Novel by the author of "Clinton Bradshaw." 2 vols. in one, 12mo., pp. 240-232. Phila., Carey, Lea & Blanchard. Congress.

1840. Howard Pinckney. A Novel. 2 vols., 12mo., pp. 227-216. Phila., Lea & Blanchard. Congress.

1841. Published in 1841 in The Romancist and Novelists Library, new series, vol. II, 8vo., pp. 159. London, John Clements. Congress.

1844. The Beechen Tree. A Tale Told in Rhyme. 12mo., pp. 95. New York, Harper & Brothers. Congress; Harris.

1849. Sketches of Character, and Tales Founded on Fact. 12mo., pp. 117. Louisville. Published at the office of the Chronicle of Western Literature and Art. Congress.

1852. An Autobiography of William Russell, by the author of Clinton Bradshaw. 8vo., pp. 119 (double column). Baltimore, Gobright, Thorne & Co. Congress. In the dedication the author says: "This narration has too much truth in it to be called fiction."

For a good estimate of some of Thomas's works, see So. Lit. Mess., 1838, pp. 297-301.

Thomas, Lewis Foulke, 1815-1868. Md., Ky., Mo.
>   1838. Osceola, A Tragedy (acted in St. Louis, Cincinnati, and New Orleans).
>   1857. Cortez, The Conqueror, A Tragedy, in five acts, founded on the Conquest of Mexico. 12mo., pp. 73. Washington, D. C., B. W. Ferguson. Congress; Harris.

Thomas, Martha McCannon, 1823-   . Md.
>   1854. Life's Lesson. A Tale. 12mo., pp. 398. New York, Harper & Brothers. Congress.

Thompson, William Tappan, 1812-1882. Ohio, Ga.
>   1840. Major Jones's Courtship: detailed with Other Scenes, Incidents, and Adventures, in a series of Letters by Himself.
>   1844. Second edition, greatly enlarged, with illustrations by Darley. 12mo., pp. 200. Phila., 1844 (copyright 1843), Carey & Hart. Congress.
>   1872. Another copy, square 12mo., pp. 190. T. B. Peterson & Brother. Congress.
>   1844. Chronicles of Pineville; embracing Sketches of Georgia Scenes, incidents, and Characters.
>   1852. Edition of 1852, 12mo., pp. 186, with 12 original engravings. Phila., Gretz & Buck. Congress. In the same volume is bound: The Drama of Pokerville, The Bench and Bar of Jury-Town, and Other Stories, by "Every point." (J. M. Field.) 12mo., pp. 200. Phila., A. Hart, late Carey & Hart, 1850.
>   1848. Major Jones's Sketches of Travel.
>   1850. Major Jones' Courtship; or, Adventures of a Christmas Eve. A Domestic Comedy in Two Acts. By Major Joseph Jones. 12mo., pp. 61. Savannah. Edward J. Purse. Harris. Scene— A Georgia Plantation.

Thorpe, Thomas Bangs. 1815-1878, Mass., La., N. Y.
  1845. The Big Bear of Arkansas, and Other Sketches,
      illustrative of Characters and Incidents in the
      South and South-West, edited by William T. Por-
      ter, with illustrations by Darley. 12mo., pp. 181.
      Philadelphia, Carey & Hart. Congress.
  1854. The Master's House; a Tale of Southern Life, by
      Logan. 12mo., pp. 301. New York, T. L. Mc-
      Elrath & Co. Congress. In pencil: "Thorpe,
      Thomas Bangs."
  1859. Major Thorpe's Scenes in Arkansas, Containing
      the whole of the Quarter Race in Kentucky; Bob
      Herring, the Arkansas Bee Hunter &c &c, By J.
      M. Field, Esq., of the St. Louis Reveille. 12mo.,
      pp.   Philadelphia, T. B. Peterson & Brothers.
      Congress.

Tiffany, Osmond, 1823-   . Md.
  1858. Brandon; or, A Hundred Years Ago. A Tale of
      the American Colonies. 12mo., pp. 285. New
      York, Stanford & Delisser. Congress.

Townsend, Mrs. Mary Ashley (Van Voorhiss) ("Xariffa").
      La.
  1859. The Brother Clerks, A Tale of New Orleans.

Tucker, George, 1775-1861. Va.
  1824. The Valley of Shenandoah; or, Memories of the
      Graysons. Reprinted in England and translated
      into German.
  1828. Second edition, 2 vols., 12mo., pp. 316-320. New
      York, Orville A. Roorbach. Congress.
  1827. A Voyage to the Moon; with Some Account of the
      Manners and Customs, Science and Philosophy of
      the People of Morosofia and Other Lunarians, by
      Joseph Atterley. 12mo., pp. 264. New York, E.
      Bliss. Congress. A satirical romance.

—7

Tucker, Nathaniel Beverley, 1784-1851. Va.

    1836. George Balcombe, A Novel. 2 vols., 12mo., pp. 282-319. New York, Harper & Brothers. Two copies, Congress. Reviewed in So. Lit. Mess., January, 1836, pp. 49-58.

    1836. The Partisan Leader; a Tale of the Future. By Edward William Sidney. In two volumes, 12mo., pp. 201-201. Washington City. Printed for the Publishers, by James Caxton. 1856. U. Va. This copy bears the date of 1856 but is a copy of the original edition, published in 1836, but bearing the imprint 1856. See So. Lit. Mess., January, 1837, pp. 73-89, for a long and scholarly review.

    1861. Reprinted as: A Key to the Disunion Conspiracy. The Partisan Leader. By Beverley Tucker of Virginia. Secretly Printed in Washington (in the year 1836) by Duff Green, for circulation in the Southern States, But afterwards suppressed. 2 vols. in one, 12mo., pp. 392. New York. Reprinted by Rudd & Carleton. Congress; U. Va. 2 copies.

    1862. The Partisan Leader: A Novel, and an Apocalypse of the Origin and Struggles of the Southern Confederacy. By Judge Beverley Tucker, of Virginia. Originally published in 1836, Now republished and edited by Rev. Thos. A. Ware. 8vo., pp. 220. Richmond, West & Johnson, 1862. U. Va.

    1844-1845. Gertrude; an Original Novel. So. Lit. Mess., 1844, pp. 512-519; 641-647; 705-713; 1845, pp. 178-186; 219-230; 257-265; 377-382; 434-441; 690-694; 705-712.

Tucker, St. George H., 1828-1863. Va.

    1857. Hansford; a Tale of Bacon's Rebellion. 12mo., pp. 356. Richmond, Va., George M. West. Congress; U. Va.

1878. Reprinted as: The Devoted Bride; or, Faith and Fidelity. A Love Story, by St. George Tucker of Virginia. 12mo., pp. 370. Phila., T. B. Peterson, 1878. Congress. See a good review in So. Lit. Mess., April, 1857, pp. 260-272.

Tyler, Robert, of Virginia.

1842. Ahasuerus, a poem by a Virginian. 8vo., pp. 46. New York, Harper & Brothers. U. Va.; Harris. An excellent review in So. Quar. Rev., October, 1842, pp. 312-321; also, So. Lit. Mess., March, 1842, pp. 237-240.

1843. Death; or, Medorus' Dream, by the Author of Ahasuerus. A Poem in three parts. 12mo., pp. 66. New York, Harper & Brothers. Congress; Harris.

Umphraville, Angus, of Baltimore, Md.

1817. The Siege of Baltimore, and the Battle of La Tranche; with other Original Poems. By Angus Umphraville, aged nineteen. 12mo., pp. 144. Baltimore. Printed by Schaeffer and Mound. Harris. The Siege of Baltimore, a poem in six cantos, pp. 1-57. Each canto is dedicated to some famous person such as Decatur, Perry, &c. Each dedicatory letter is dated Baltimore, May, 1817.

Vail, Thomas Hubbard, 1812-1889. Va.

1839. Hannah the Mother of Samuel. A Sacred Drama. Published anonymously. 12mo., pp. XIII, 94. Boston. Harris.

Walker, Miss Susan. (Nasus of Fredericksburg, Va.)

1843. The Vow. So. Lit. Mess., 1843, pp. 205-224.

1843. Lona D'Alvarez. A Tale of the South. So. Lit. Mess., 1843, pp. 531-545.

1844. Pretension. So. Lit. Mess., 1844, pp. 159-165; 217-228; 298-303.

1844. The Sciote Captive. So. Lit. Mess., 1844, pp. 592-599; 652-661.

1845. Prize Tale. The Wheel of Life. So. Lit. Mess., 1845, pp. 129-137; 213-218; 288-294.

1846. Worth Versus Beauty. So. Lit. Mess., 1846, pp. 136-145; 219-231.

1848. The Noted Firm. A Tale. So. Lit. Mess., 1848, pp. 111-123.

Wallace, Wm. Ross. 1819-1881. Ky., N. Y.

1837. The Battle of Tippacanoe, Triumphs of Science and Other Poems. 12mo., pp. 106. Cincinnati. Published by P. McFarlin. Harris. The Battle of Tippacanoe. Delivered on the Battle Ground, November 7th, 1835, pp. 11-25. The Triumphs of Science, pp. 30-54.

1848. Alban The Pirate, A Romaunt of the Metropolis. By William Wallace. Author of "The Gods of Old" &c. 12mo., pp. 82. New York. Published by Bedford & Co., 2 Astor Place. Harris.

Warfield, Mrs. Catherine Anne Ware, 1816-1877. Miss., Ky.

1860. The Household of Bouverie; or, The Elixir of Gold. A Romance, by a Southern Lady. 2 vols., 12mo., pp. 373-413. New York, Derby & Jackson. Congress. Reviewed in So. Lit. Mess., April, 1861, pp. 323-325.

Watkins, Tobias, 1780-1855. Md.

1821. Tales of the Tripod; or a Delphian Evening. By Pertinax Particular. 16mo., pp. 162. Baltimore. See Wegelin: E. A. F.

Watterson, George, 1783-1854. N. Y., D. C. First librarian of Congress.

1808. The Lawyer, or Man as he ought not to be. A Tale. 12mo., pp. 236. Pittsburg, Z. Cramer. Congress.

1809. The Child of Feeling. A Comedy in five acts (*scene Philadelphia time 14 hours*). 16mo., pp. 113. George Town, Published by Joseph Milligan, Dinmore and Cooper Printers. Congress.

1810. Glencarn; or, The Disappointments of Youth. A Novel, by George Watterson, Esq., Author of the Lawyer &c. Two volumes in one (paged continuously). 12mo., pp. 265. Alexandria (Va.), Cotton & Stewart. Congress.

Webber, Charles Wilkins, 1819-1856. Ky.

1848. Old Hicks The Guide; or, Adventures in the Comanche Country in Search of a Gold Mine. By Charles W. Webber, Author of "Jack Long; or The Shot in the Eye," &c &c. 12mo., pp. 356. New York, Harper & Brothers. Congress. See So. Lit. Mess., May, 1848, pp. 334-335.

1849. The Gold Mines of the Gila. A Sequel to Old Hicks The Guide, by Charles W. Webber, Author of "Jack Long; or, The Shot in the Eye," &c, &c. Complete in two volumes. 12mo., pp. 263. New York, Dewitt & Davenport. Congress. See So. Quar. Rev., October, 1849, p. 252.

1852. Tales of the Southern Border. Part I. Phila., Lippincott, Grambo & Co. See So. Quar. Rev., July, 1852, p. 250.

1853. Tales of the Southern Border. 8vo., pp. 400. Phila., Lippincott, Grambo & Co. Congress (card).

1856. Edition of 1856: Tales of the Southern Border, by C. W. Webber. Author of "Shot in the Eye," "Old Hicks the Guide," "Charles Winterfield Papers," "Gold-Mines of the Gila," &c &c. 8vo., pp. 400, illustrated. J. B. Lippincott & Co. U. Va. Contents: Jack Long; or, The Shot in the Eye; The Border Chase; A First Day with the Rangers; ·

Gonzaleze Again: or, The Bravo's Stratagem; Adam Baker, the Renegade; The Texan Virago and the Tailor of Gotham; Death of Little Red-Head; Gabrielle, the White Mare of Chihuahua; The Wild Girl of Nebraska; The Fight of the Pinto Trace; Back from the Wilderness. On copyright page: Entered according to Act of Congress in the year 1852, by Lippincott, Grambo & Co.

1868. Another copy. 8vo., pp. 400. Phila., J. B. Lippincott & Co. Congress. Contents same as edition of 1856.

1853. Spiritual Vampirism: The History of Etherial Softdown and Her Friends of the "New Light," by C. W. Webber, author of Old Hicks the Guide, "Charles Winterfield Papers," "The Hunter Naturalist," "Tales of the Southern Border," &c. 12mo., pp. 254. Phila., Lippincott, Grambo & Co. Congress. A satirical story, the chief personages of which are the Mesmerites, Grahamites, Fourierites, and Jebusites of New York and the neighboring country.

Weir, James, 1821-   . Ky.

1850. Lonz Powers: or, The Regulators. A Romance of Kentucky. Founded on facts. 2 vols., 12mo., pp. 364-319. Phila., Lippincott, Grambo & Co. Congress. Time after 1800. See Harper's Mag., 1:860.

1852. Simon Kenton; or, The Scout's Revenge. An Historical Novel. 12mo. Phila. Congress (card).

1854. The Winter Lodge: or, Vow Fulfilled. An Historical Novel. The Sequel to Simon Kenton. 12mo., pp. 231. Phila., Lippincott, Grambo & Co. Congress.

Wells, Helena. S. C.

1799. The Stepmother, A Domestic Tale from Real Life. By Helena Wells of Charleston, S. C. Second

Edition. 2 vols. London. See Gentleman's Magazine, July, 1800.

1800. Constantia Neville: or, The West Indian. By Helena Wells Author of the Stepmother. Second Edition. London. See Loshe: Early American Novel.

Welsh, Miss Mary, of Shuqualak, Miss.

1858. The Model Family.

1859. Aunt Abbie. See Owen: Miss.

Wharton, E. C. La.

—— War of the Bachelors (novel).

1851. Toodles, A Young Couple (comedy).

—— Dick the Newsby and other Comedies.

Anonymous.

1848. Where is She? A Tale. By a Cohee. So. Lit. Mess., 1848, pp. 486-502.

Anonymous.

1839. Whigs and Democrats, or Love of no Politics; a Comedy in three acts. 12mo., pp. 80. Richmond. Printed and published by T. W. White. Harris. See review in So. Lit. Mess., August, 1839, pp. 571-572.

White, John Blake, 1781-1859. S. C.

1806. Foscari, or, The Venetian Exile; A Tragedy, in Five Acts, as performed at the Charleston theatre. 12mo., pp. 52. Charleston. Printed for the Author. Congress. Scene: In Venice.

1807. The Mysteries of the Castle; or, The Victim of Revenge. A Drama in Five Acts. 16mo., pp. 65. Charleston.

1812. Modern Honour; or, The Victim of Revenge. A Tragedy. 12mo. Charleston.

1819. Triumph of Liberty; or Louisiana Preserved. A National Drama. 12mo. Charleston.

1825. The Forgers, A Drama played in Charleston, 1825. Published in the Southern Literary Journal, vol. 4, new series vol. I, 1837, pp. 118-125; 218-226; 354-362; 435-443; 509-518. Congress.

1839. Intemperance.

For reliable information about White's dramas, see Southern Literary Gazette (Charleston, S. C.), new series vol. I, 1829, pp. 150-155; also Southern Literary Journal, vol. 4, p. 190, *et seq.* Congress.

Whittlesey, Sarah Johnson Cogswell, 1825-   . N. C., Va.

1860. The Stranger's Stratagem; or, Double Deceit and Other Stories. New York, M. W. Dodd. Noticed in So. Lit. Mess., November, 1860, p. 399.

Wiley, Calvin Henderson, 1819-1887. N. C.

1847. Alamance; or, The Great and Final Experiment. 8vo., pp. 151 (double column, fine print). New York, Harper Brothers. Congress. See Sartain's Union Magazine, May, 1849, p. 352. Congress; U. Va.

1849. The Haunted Chamber; or, How They Chose a May Queen in the School of Parson Cole. Published in Sartain's Union Magazine, January, 1849, pp. 45-53. Congress; U. Va.

1849. The Poor Student's Dream; or, The Golden Rule. Same magazine, January, 1849, pp. 107-112.

1849. Roanoke; or, Where is Utopia? This historical novel was published in Sartain's Magazine for 1849, vol. IV, pp. 189-195; 241-249; 305-312; 369-376; vol. V, pp. 5-12; 80-88; 145-152; 208-216; 273-282; 339-352. Sartain's Mag., 1849, Congress; U. Va.

1852. Life in the South. A Companion to Uncle Tom's Cabin. 8vo., pp. 144 (double column, fine print). Phila., T. B. Peterson. Congress. This is identically the same work as the one published in Sartain's Magazine for 1849. Allibone gives the following additional titles by Wiley: The Adventures of Old Dan Tucker and His Son Walter, 12mo., London, 1851; and Utopia, a Picture of Life in the South, 12mo., Phila., 1852. All four of these are one work under different titles. In Roanoke, or Where is Utopia? and in Life in the South, the protagonists are Old Dan Tucker, generally known as Pocosin Dan, and his son Walter, Little Pocosin Dan. The scene is in North Carolina, but "Utopia" appears in the headings of most of the chapters, and is the place described.

Williamson, J. B.
  1800. Preservation; or, The Hovel of The Rocks: A Play in Five Acts: interspersed with part of Lillo's Drama, in Three Acts, called Fatal Curiosity. By J. B. Williamson Director of the Theatre in Charleston. Performed in London, and Boston ('Massachusetts') with the most flattering Success. (Copy-right secured according to law). 12mo., pp. 75. Charleston. Printed By T. C. Cox, No. 137 Tradd Street, one door from the Bay. MDCCC. Harris. Preface dated, Charleston, March 20, 1800.

Wilmer, Lambert A., 1805-1836. Md., Penn., N. Y.
  1836. The Confessions of Emily Harrington. 12mo., pp. c. 200. Baltimore. See review in So. Lit. Mess., February, 1836, pp. 191-192. "Among his longer pieces we may particularize *Merlin,* a drama, some portions of which are full of the truest poetic fire. His prose tales and other publications are numerous."

Wilson, Augusta Evans, 1835-1909. Ga., Tex., Ala.
  1855. Inez: a Tale of the Alamo. 12mo., pp. 298. New

York, Harper & Brothers. Congress. See So. Quar. Rev., April, 1855, p. 241.

1882. Another copy, 12mo., pp. 298. New York, G. W. Carleton & Co. Congress.

1899. Another copy, 12mo., pp. 303. New York, G. W. Dillingham Co., Publishers. U. Va.

1859. Beulah. A Novel. 12mo., pp. 510, New York, Derby & Jackson.

1887. Beulah. A Novel. 12mo., pp. 510. New York, G. W. Dillingham, Successor to G. W. Carleton & Co. Congress.

1899. Another copy, 12mo., pp. 492. New York, G. W. Dillingham Co., Publishers. U. Va. Reviewed in So. Lit. Mess., September, 1860, pp. 241-248.

Anonymous.

1851. Winderhaus—A Tale of Richmond 30 Years Ago. M—. Va. So. Lit. Mess., 1851.

Windle, Mrs. Mary Jane, 1825-   . Del., D. C.

1850. "A collection of her sketches was published in a volume, and was favorably received." Davidson, 629. It appears that this volume was entitled: Legend of the Waldenses, and Other Tales. 12mo., Phila., 1850. See Allibone III, 2790; also Hart's Female Prose Writers of America, p. 463.

Woodson, Mary E., of Goochland Co., Va.

1859. The Way It All Ended. A Novel. 12mo., pp. 375. Author's Edition. Richmond, Va. Printed by Charles H. Wynne. U. Va. See So. Lit. Mess., November, 1859, p. 398.

Workman, James.

1803. Liberty in Louisiana. A Comedy. 12mo. Charleston. Played at Charleston Theatre in 1803. Wegelin, E. A. P.

Worthington, Mrs. Jane Tayloe (*née* Miss Jane Tayloe Lomax of Virginia). Died 1847.

> Contributed the following tales to the So. Lit. Mess:

1839. The Poet, March, pp. 194-205; The Poet's Destiny, May, pp. 305-309; The Missionary, September, pp. 581-587.

1842. Love Sketches, pp. 337-342; 379-380; 430-438; 620-624.

1843. Love Sketches, pp. 33-36; 442-446; 632-635.

1844. Love Sketches, pp. 303-306; 545-547; 616-618; 731-734.

1845. Love Sketches, pp. 9-13; 299-303; 478-481.

1847. Ravenel Hall. A Tale in two parts. Pp. 31-37; 89-95.

Yellott, Coleman, 1821-1870.

1856. The Professor of Insanity; or, A New way to make a fortune. A Drama, in five acts. 16mo., pp. 36. Baltimore, Congress; Harris.

A CHRONOLOGICAL LIST OF SOUTHERN FICTION FROM 1765 TO 1860.

1765.
Godfrey, T., Jr.: Juvenile Poems on Various Subjects. With the Prince of Parthia, a Tragedy.

1776.
Brackenridge, H. H.: The Battle of Bunker Hill.

1790.
Anonymous: The Battle of Eutaw Springs.

1792.
Johnson, John: The Rape of Bethesda.

1793.
Imlay, G.: The Emigrants.

1797.
Burk, J. (D.): Bunker-Hill; or The Death of General Warren.

1798.
Burk, J. (D.): Female Patriotism; or, The Death of Joan D'Arc.

Munford, Col. Robert: A Collection of Poems and Plays.

Munford, William: Poems and Compositions, in Prose and Verse.

1800.
Williamson, J. B.: Preservation; or, The Hovel of the Rocks. A Play.

1803.
Workman, James: Liberty in Louisiana, a drama.

1804.
Anonymous: Delavel, a Novel.

1805.

Ioor, W.: Independence; a Comedy.

1806.

White, J. B.: Foscari; a Tragedy.

1807.

Brown, Wm. H.: Ira and Isabella.

Burk, J. (D.): Bethlem Gabor.

Anonymous: The Female Enthusiast, a Tragedy.

Harby, Isaac: Alexander Severus; The Gordian Knot; or, Causes and Effects.

Ioor, W.: The Battle of Eutaw Springs.

White, J. B.: The Mysteries of the Castle.

1808.

Botsford, E.: Sambo and Toney.

1809.

Hall, Everard: Nolens Volens; or, The Biter Bit.

1810.

Robinson, John: The Savage of Piomingo.

1812.

White, J. B.: Modern Honor, a Tragedy.

1813.

Bryan, Daniel: The Mountain Muse.

1814.

Anonymous: The Power of Christianity; or Abdallah and Sabat.

1816.

Harney, J. M.: Crystalina; a Fairy Tale. (Written as early as 1812.)

1817.

Umphraville, Angus: The Siege of Baltimore.

1818.

Anonymous: Essays, Religious, Moral &c.

1819.

Crafts, Wm.: The Seaserpent; or Gloucester Hoax.
Harby, Isaac: Alberti; a Play.
White, J. B.: The Triumph of Liberty.

1820.

Crafts, Wm.: Sullivan's Island.

1821.

Anonymous: Nature and Philosophy, a Drama.
Anonymous: The Land of Powhatan.
Simmons, J. W.: The Maniac's Confession.

1822.

Simmons, J. W.: Blue Beard; or, The Marshal of France; The Exile's Return.

1823.

Doddridge, Dr. J.: Logan, a Drama.

1824.

Sawyer, L.: Blackbeard, a Comedy.

1825.

Robertson, J.: Virginia or The Fatal Patent.
White, J. B.: The Forgers, played in Charleston.

1826.

Royall, Mrs. Anne: The Tennesseean.

1828.

Custis, G. W. P.: Indian Prophecy. A National Drama.
Anonymous: Donald Adair. See Lorraine 1841.
Heath, J. E.: Edge-Hill; or, The Family of the Fitzroyals.

1829.

Harby, Isaac: A Selection from the Miscellaneous Writings of.
Simms, W. G.: The Vision of Cortes.

1830.

Custis, G. W. P.: Pocahontas; or, The Settlers of Jamestown.
Dimitry, A.: Short Stories (1830-1835).

1831.

Lees, T. J.: The Musings of Carol, &c.

Pise, C. C.: The Indian Cottage; a Unitarian Story; Father Rowland, a North American Tale.

1832.

Kennedy, J. P.: Swallow Barn.

Simms, W. G.: Atalantis; A Story of the Sea.

1833.

Hentz, Mrs. C. L. W.: Lovell's Folly.

Pise, C. C.: The Pleasures of Religion and Other Poems.

Simms, W. G.: The Book of My Lady; Martin Faber.

1834.

Caruthers, Dr. W. A.: The Kentuckian in New York.

Chivers, T. H.: Conrad and Eudora; or, The Death of Alonzo. A Tragedy.

Gilman, C. H.: Recollections of a New England Bride and Housekeeper.

Nott, H. J.: Novelletts of a Traveller.

Simms, W. G.: Guy Rivers.

1835.

Caruthers, Dr. Wm. A.: The Cavaliers of Virginia.

Ingraham, J. H.: The Southwest.

Kennedy, J. P.: Horse-Shoe Robinson.

Longstreet, A. B.: Georgia Scenes.

McCabe, J. C.: Scraps.

Poe, E. A.: Berenice; Morella; Some Passages in the Life of a Lion; Hans Pfaall; The Assignation; Bon-Bon; Shadow, A Parable; Loss of Breath; King Pest.

Simms, W. G.: The Yemassee; The Partisan.

Thomas, F. W.: Clinton Bradshaw.

1836.

Collens, T. W.: Martyr Patriots, A Tragedy.

French, J. S.: Elkswatawa; or, The Prophet of the West.

Ingraham, J. H.: Lafitte; or, The Pirate of the Gulf.

Poe, E. A.: Metzengerstein; The Duc De L'Omelette; Four Beasts in One.

Anonymous: Rose-Hill, A Tale of the Old Dominion.

Simms, W. G.: Mellichampe, a Legend of the Santee; The Spirit Bridegroom.

Wilmer, L. A.: The Confessions of Emily Harrington.

1837.

Anonymous: The Dade Asylum.

Anonymous: The Age of Humbugs.

Chivers, T. H.: Nacoochee, &c.

Ingraham, J. H.: Spheeksphobia (in So. Lit. Mess.).

Poe, E. A.: The Narrative of A. Gordon Pym.

Simms, W. G.: Blondeville.

Wallace, Wm. Ross: The Battle of Tippacanoe.

White, J. B.: The Forgers; a Drama, published in the Southern Literary Journal, 1837.

1838.

Alexander, J. W.: The American Mechanic.

Drake, Benjamin: Tales and Sketches from the Queen City.

Duke, S. R.: Osceola; or Fact and Fiction.

Gilman, C. H.: Recollections of a Southern Matron.

Ingraham, J. H.: Burton; or, The Sieges.

Kennedy, J. P.: Rob of the Bowl.

Anonymous: Mexico *versus* Texas.

Poe, E. A.: Ligeia; How to Write a Blackwood Article; A Predicament; the Scythe of Time.

Simms, W. G.: Richard Hurdis; or The Avenger of Blood; Ipsistos (in So. Lit. Jour.); Pelayo; a Story of the Goth; Carl Werner, an Imaginative Story.

1839.

Anonymous: Florence; the Maid.

Gilman, C. H.: Tales and Ballads.

Ingraham, J. H.: Captain Kyd.

Ingraham, J. H.: A Legend of the Mountain of the Burning Stone (in So. Lit. Mess.).

Janney, S. M.: The Last of the Lenapé.

Meek, A. B.: Florence Lincoln.

Milward, Mrs. M. G.: The Bachelor Beset (in So. Lit. Mess.).

Mitchell, J. K.: Indecision; a Tale of the Far West.

Poe, E. A.: The Devil in the Belfry; The Man That Was Used Up; The Fall of the House of Usher; William Wilson; Silence (Siope); The Conversation of Eiros and Charmion.

Anonymous: The Prediction, A Tale of the Huguenots.

Ruffner, Henry: Judith Bensaddi, in So. Lit. Mess.; Seclus-aval, a Sequel to Judith Ben Saddi, in So. Lit. Mess.

Simms, W. G.: The Damsel of Darien.

Vail, T. H.: Hannah, the Mother of Samuel. A Sacred Drama.

Anonymous: Whigs and Democrats, a Comedy.

Worthington, J. T. L.: Love Sketches (in So. Lit. Mess.).

1840.

Anonymous: Abbot; or, the Hermit of the Falls, in So. Lit. Mess.

Calvert, Geo. H.: Count Julian; a Tragedy; Cabiro, A Poem, Cantos I and II.

Gilman, C. H.: Love's Progress.

Kennedy, J. P.: Quodlibet.

Lee, Mary E.: Social Evenings; or Historical Tales for Youth.

Lehmanowski, L. F.: The Fall of Warsaw. A Tragedy.

Longstreet, A. B.: Georgia Scenes.

Milward, Mrs. M. G.: Mrs. Shooter's Party (in So. Lit. Mess.); The Yellow Blossom of Glynn (in So. Lit. Mess.).

Mosby, Mrs. M. W.: Pocahontas, a Legend.

Anonymous: The Motherless Daughters (in So. Lit. Mess.).

Poe, E. A.: The Journal of Julius Rodman; Mystification; Why the Little Frenchman Wears His Hand in a Sling; The Business Man; The Man of the Crowd.

Simms, W. G.: Border Beagles; a Tale of Mississippi.

—8

1841.

Anonymous: Don Paez.

Allston, Washington: Monaldi.

Ingraham, J. H.: The Quadroone; or, St. Michael's Day.

Lorraine, Miss A. M.: Donald Adair, second edition.

Milward, Mrs. M. G.: Country Annals (in So. Lit. Mess.).

Poe, E. A.: The Murders in the Rue Morgue; A Descent into the Maelström; The Island of the Fay; The Colloquy of Monos and Una; Never Bet the Devil Your Head; Three Sundays in a Week.

Simms, W. G.: The Kinsmen; Confession; or The Blind Heart.

1842.

Anonymous: Florence Courtland (in So. Lit. Mess.).

Flagg, Edmund: Carrero, or the Prime Minister.

Hayward, Ann: Emma Stanley, A Novel.

Ingraham, J. H.: Edward Austin.

Jones, J. B.: Wild Western Scenes.

Anonymous: Mrs. Latour (in So. Lit. Mess.).

Poe, E. A.: Eleonora; The Oval Portrait; The Masque of the Red Death; The Landscape Garden; The Mystery of Marie Rogêt.

Requier, A. J.: The Spanish Exile.

Rives, Mrs. W. C.: Tales and Souvenirs of a Residence in Europe.

Robertson, J.: Riego; or The Spanish Martyr.

Simms, W. G.: Beauchampe.

Sims, A. D.: Bevil Faulcon.

Worthington, J. T. L.: Love Sketches (in So. Lit. Mess., 1842-1845).

1843.

Alexander, J. W.: The Working Man.

Anonymous: The Clairwoods. A True Tale. So. Lit. Mess.

Colcroft, H. R.: Alhalla, or the Land of Talladega.

Dupuy, E. A.: The Conspirator.

Harris, G. W.: Humorous Stories contributed to the New York "Spirit of the Times."

Hentz, Mrs. C. L. W.: De Lara; or, The Moorish Bride, a Tragedy.

Ingraham, J. H.: Jemmy Daily.

McIntosh, M. J.: Conquest and Self-Conquest; Woman, An Enigma.

Milward, Mrs. M. G.: The Winter Nights' Club (in So. Lit. Mess.).

Minor, Mrs. B. B.: The Fatal Effects of Insincerity (in So. Lit. Mess.).

Poe, E. A.: The Pit and the Pendulum; The Tell-Tale Heart; The Gold Bug; The Black Cat.

Shindler, Mrs. M. S. B. P.: Charles Morton.

Simms, W. G.: Donna Florida.

Walker, Miss Susan: The Vow (in So. Lit. Mess.); Lona D'Alvarez.

1844.

Anonymous: The Age of Brass.

Anonymous: De Mortier; A Tale of the French Revolution (in So. Lit. Mess.).

Goulding, Rev. F. R.: Little Josephine.

Ingraham, J. H.: The Midshipman; Arnold; or, The British Spy; The Miseries of New York.

Lewis, John: Young Kate; or, The Rescue.

Longstreet, A. B.: Darby Anvil (in So. Lit. Mess.).

Minor, Mrs. B. B.: The Prize Tale. Stephano Colonna (in So. Lit. Mess.).

Poe, E. A.: The Premature Burial; The Oblong Box; Thou Art the Man; The Literary Life of Thingum Bob, Esq.; The Angel of the Odd.

Shindler, Mrs. M. S. B. P.: The Young Sailor.

Simms, W. G.: The Prima Donna.

Walker, Miss Susan: Pretension (in So. Lit. Mess.) ; The Sciote Captive (in So. Lit. Mess.).

1845.

Caruthers, Dr. W. A.: The Knights of the Horse-Shoe.

Hentz, Mrs. C. L. W.: A Legend of the Silver Wave (in Simms' Monthly Magazine).

Ingraham, J. H.: Montezuma, The Serf; Norman; or, The Privateersman's Bride; Rafæl; or, The Twice Condemned.

Jones, J. B.: Wild Western Scenes.

Ladd, Mrs. C. A.: Emma Clifford.

McIntosh, M. J.: The Cousins; Praise and Principle.

Anonymous: Onslow; or The Protegé of an Enthusiast.

Poe, E. A.: The Purloined Letter; The System of Dr. Tarr and Prof. Fether; The Thousand and Second Tale of Scheherazade; Some Words with a Mummy; The Power of Words; The Imp of the Perverse; The Facts in the Case of M. Valdemar.

Shindler, Mrs. M. S. B. P.: Forecastle Tom.

Simms, W. G.: Castle Dismal; Helen Halsey; Count Julian; The Wigwam and the Cabin.

Thorpe, T. B.: The Big Bear of Arkansas and Other Sketches.

Walker, Miss Susan: Prize Tale. The Wheel of Life (in So. Lit. Mess.).

1846.

Dorsey, Mrs. A. H.: Tears of the Diadem.

Elliott, Wm.: Carolina Sports by Land and Water.

Anonymous: Gertru; or, The Maid of Charleston.

Hentz, Mrs. C. L. W.: Aunt Patty's Scrap Bag.

Hooper, J. J.: Some Adventures of Captain Simon Suggs.

Ingraham, J. H.: Bonfield; Grace Weldon; Leisler; The Mysterious State-Room; The Odd Fellow; The Spectre Steamer.

McIntosh, M. J.: Two Lives; or, To Seem and To Be.

Milward, Mrs. M. G.: Mrs. Sad's Private Boarding House (in So. Lit. Mess.).

Nourse, J. D.: The Forest Knight.

Poe, E. A.: The Cask of Amontillado.

Requier, A. J.: The Old Sanctuary.

Rhodes, W. H.: The Indian Gallows.

Walker, Miss Susan: Worth versus Beauty (in So. Lit. Mess.).

1847.

Arrington, Alfred W.: The Desperadoes of the Southwest.

Cooke, P. P.: Froissart Ballads (a translation).

Anonymous: Don Paez &c.

Dorsey, Mrs. A. H.: The Student of Blenheim Forest.

Farmer, C. M.: The Fairy of the Stream.

Field, J. M.: The Drama in Pokerville.

Ingraham, J. H.: Beatrice; the Goldsmith's Daughter; The Dancing Feather; Neal Nelson; Edward Manning; Paul Perril; Ringold Griffitt; The Truce.

Jones, J. B.: Book of Visions.

McSherry, J.: Père Jean.

Moore, J. S.: Abrah, the Conspirator, a Tragedy.

Poe, E. A.: The Domain of Arnheim.

Robb, J. S.: Streaks of Squatter Life.

Wiley, C. H.: Alamance.

Worthington, J. T. L.: Ravenel Hall (in So. Lit. Mess.).

1848.

Anonymous: Where is She? a Tale.

Brisbane, A. H.: Ralphton; or The Young Carolinian of 1776.

Cooke, P. P.: The Two Country Houses (in So. Lit. Mess.); The Gregories of Hackwood (in So. Lit. Mess.); John Carper; the Hunter of Lost River (in So. Lit. Mess.).

Cutter, G. W.: Buena Vista and Other Poems.

Dorr, J. C. R.: Isabel Leslie.

Flagg, Edmund: The Howard Queen.
Hentz, Mrs. C. L. W.: The Mob Cap.
Hunter, Mrs. M. F.: Sketches of Southern Life.
Ingraham, J. H.: Mark Manly; Jennette Alison.
McIntosh, M. J.: Charms and Counter Charms.
Nourse, J. D.: Leavenworth.
Phelps, Mrs. A. H. L.: Ida Norman.
Walker, Miss Susan: The Noted Firm (in So. Lit. Mess.).
Wallace, Wm. Ross: Alban the Pirate.

1849.

Anonymous: Alfred and Inez.
Arrington, Alfred W.: The Lives and Adventures of the
    Desperadoes of the Southwest.
Cooke, P. P.: The Crime of Andrew Blair (in So. Lit. Mess.);
    The Chevalier Merlin (in So. Lit. Mess.).
Anonymous: Cordora; A Poetical Romance.
Dupuy, E. A.: Celeste. The Pirate's Daughter.
Flagg, Edmund: Edmond Dantes, a Sequel to Monte Christo.
Hunter, Mrs. M. F.: The Seldons of Sherwood (in So. Lit.
    Mess., 1849-1851).
Jones, J. B.: Rural Sports; a Tale.
Leigh, J. E.: Lilenhorn; a Dramatic Poem (in So. Lit. Mess.).
Miles, Geo. H.: Loretto; or, The Choice.
Poe, E. A.: Mellonta Tauta; Hop Frog.
Simms, W. G.: The Cassique of Accabee.
Southworth, E. D. N.: Retribution.
Wiley, C. H.: The Haunted Chamber; The Poor Student's
    Dream; Roanoke; or Where is Utopia? (in Sartain's
    Mag.)

1850.

Carpenter, W. H.: Ruth Eversley.
Cobb, J. B.: The Creole; or, The Siege of New Orleans.
Dupuy, E. A.: The Conspirator.
Elliott, Wm.: Fiesco; a Tragedy.

Flagg, Edmund: Blanche of Artois.

Hentz, Mrs. C. L. W.: Linda; or, The Young Pilot of the Belle Creole.

Ingraham, J. H.: Forrestal.

Jackson, H. R.: Tallulah and Other Poems.

Miles, Geo. H.: Mohammed; a Tragedy.

Marks, Elias: Elfreide of Guldal.

Simms, W. G.: Flirtation at the Moultrie House; The Lily and the Totem.

Southworth, E. D. N.: The Deserted Wife.

Thompson, W. T.: Major Jones' Courtship.

Windle, M. J.: A Collection of Sketches.

1851.

Carpenter, W. H.: The Regicide's Daughter.

Cobb, J. B.: Mississippi Scenes.

Cooke, P. St. George: Scenes Beyond the Western Border, in So. Lit. Mess. 1851-53.

Falkner, W. C.: The Spanish Heroine; A Tale of War and Love.

Gregory, James: Bertie; or, Life in the Old Field.

Hentz, Mrs. C. L. W.: Rena; or, The Snow Bird.

Hooper, J. J.: Widow Rugby's Husband.

Hulse, G. A.: Sunbeams and Shadows.

Ingraham, J. H.: Nobody's Son; or The Adventures of Percival Mayberry.

Lamar, J. B.: Polly Pea-Blossom's Wedding.

McCord, L. S.: Caius Gracchus.

McIntosh, M. J.: Evenings at Donaldson Manor.

McSherry, J.: Willitoft; or, The Days of James I.

Miles, Geo. H.: The Governess.

Shreve, T. H.: Drayton, a Story of American Life.

Simms, W. G.: Norman Maurice; or, The Man of the people; Katharine Walton.

Southworth, E. D. N.: The Mother-in-Law; Shannondale.

Wharton, E. C.: Toodles, a Young Couple.

Anonymous: Winderhaus, a Tale of Richmond 30 years Ago.

1852.

Alexander, J. Bell: Malice.

Baldwin, J. G.: Sketches of the Flush Times of Alabama and Mississippi (in So. Lit. Mess.).

Cabell, Julia M.: An Odd Volume of Facts and Fictions.

Cooke, J. E.: Pine Fork Plantation; Chronicles of the Valley of Virginia.

Dorsey, Mrs. A. H.: Woodreve Manor.

Dupuy, E. A.: The Adventures of a Gentleman in Search of Miss Smith; Florence; or, The Fatal Vow.

Eastman, Mrs. M. H.: Aunt Phillis' Cabin; or, Southern Life As It Is.

Goulding, Rev. F. R.: Robert and Harold.

Hentz, Mrs. C. L. W.: Marcus Warland; or, The Long Moss Spring; Eoline; or Magnolia Vale.

Hunter, Mrs. M. F.: The Clifford Family.

Jones, J. B.: The Spanglers and Tingles; The Adventures of Col. Gracchus Vanderbomb, &c.

McIntosh, M. J.: The Lofty and The Lowly.

Randolph, J. T.: The Cabin and the Parlor.

Simmons, J. W.: The Greek Girl.

Simms, W. G.: Gleams After Glooms (in So. Lit. Mess.); The Golden Christmas; As Good as a Comedy; or The Tennesseean's Story; Michael Bonham; or The Fall of Bexar; The Sword and the Distaff.

Southworth, E. D. N.: The Discarded Daughter; Virginia and Magdalene; The Foster Sisters.

Wiley, C. H.: Life in the South; A Companion to Uncle Tom's Cabin.

1853.

Baldwin, J. G.: The Flush Times of Alabama and Mississippi.

Bennett, Mrs. M. H. B.: Antifanaticism.

Chivers, T. H.: Atlanta; or The True Blessed Isle of Poesy.

Falkner, W. C.: Henry and Ellen.

Hentz, Mrs. C. L. W.: Wild Jack; or, The Stolen Child; The Victim of Excitement, &c.; Helen and Arthur; or Miss Thusa's Spinning Wheel; Ugly Effie; or The Neglected One and the Beauty.

Jones, J. B.: The Monarchist.

Miles, Geo. H.: De Soto, a Tragedy.

Page, J. W.: Uncle Robin, in His Cabin.

Robinson, Fayette: Wizard of the Wave, a Romance.

Simms, W. G.: Poems, Descriptive, Dramatic, &c., &c.; Marie De Berniere.

Southworth, E. D. N.: The Curse of Clifton; Mark Sutherland; Old Neighborhoods.

Strother, David H.: The Blackwater Chronicle.

1854.

Bowen, Mrs. S. P. K.: Busy Moments of an Idle Woman.

Cooke, J. E.: Leather Stocking and Silk; or, Hunter John Myers and His Times; The Youth of Jefferson; The Virginia Comedians; or, Old Days in the Old Dominion.

Dorr, J. C. R.: Farmingdale, a Novel.

Dupuy, E. A.: Emma Walton; or, Trials and Triumphs; Asleigh; a Tale of the Olden Time.

Gayarré, C. E. A.: School for Politics; a Dramatic Novel.

Hentz, Mrs. C. L. W.: The Planter's Northern Bride; Love After Marriage and Other Stories.

Holmes, M. J. H.: Tempest and Sunshine.

Jones, J. B.: Life and Adventures of a Country Merchant; Freaks of Fortune; or, The History of Ned Lorn.

Anonymous: The Only Son (in So. Lit. Mess.).

Phelps, Mrs. A. H. L.: Ida Norman (complete edition).

Simms, W. G.: Vasconselos: Southward Ho! A Spell of Sunshine.

Smucker, S. S.: The Spanish Wife.

Southworth, E. D. N.: The Wife's Victory; The Lost Heiress; Hickory Hall.

Thorpe, T. B.: The Master's House; a Tale of Southern Life.

1855.

Bowen, Mrs. S. P. K.: Lily, a Novel.

Bradley, Mrs. M. E. N.: Bessie, a Story for Girls.

Cooke, J. E.: Ellie; or, The Human Comedy.

Cutler, Mrs. L. P.: Light and Darkness.

Dupuy, E. A.: The Country Neighborhood.

Hentz, Mrs. C. L. W.: The Flowers of Elocution, &c.; Robert Graham; a Sequel to Linda.

Holmes, M. J. H.: The English Orphans; The Homestead on the Hillside and Other Tales.

Jones, J. B.: The Winkles; or, The Merry Monomaniacs.

Ketchum, A. C.: Nelly Bracken.

McIntosh, M. J.: Emily Herbert; Rose and Lillie Stanhope.

Meek, A. B.: The Red Eagle.

Neville, Laurence: Edith Allen.

Peacocke, J. S.: The Creole Orphans, A Novel.

Simms, W. G.: The Forayers.

Anonymous: A Southern Home.

Southworth, E. D. N.: The Missing Bride.

Wilson, A. E.: Inez.

1856.

Adams, F. W.: Justice in the By-Ways.

Arrington, Alfred W.: The Rangers and the Regulators of the Tanaha.

Bradley, Mrs. M. E. N.: Bread Upon The Waters.

Calvert, Geo. H.: Comedies.

Clemens, J.: Bernard Lyle.

Cooke, J. E.: The Last of the Foresters; or Humors on the Border.

Cooke, P. St. George: Scenes and Adventures in the Army.

Cutler, Mrs. L. P.: Household Mysteries.

Cranch, C. P.: The Last of the Huggermuggers.

Dorr, J. C. R.: Lanmere.

Dorsey, Mrs. A. H.: Conscience.

Dupuy, E. A.: The Huguenot Exiles; or, The Times of Louis XIV.

Eastman, Mrs. M. H.: Sketches of Fashionable Life.

Gilman, C. H.: Poetry and Prose for the Young.

Hentz, Mrs. C. L. W.: The Lost Daughter and Other Stories of the Heart; Courtship and Marriage; Ernest Lindwood; The Banished Son and Other Stories of the Heart.

Holmes, M. J. H.: Lena Rivers.

Jones, J. B.: Wild Western Scenes. Second Series.

Levy, S. Y.: The Italian Bride; A Play in five acts.

Anonymous: The Literary Wife (by F. G. D. R. of Charlottesville, Va.)

McIntosh, M. J.: Violet; or, The Cross and the Crown.

Neville, Laurence: Lilias, a Novel.

Preston, M. J.: Silverwood.

Simms, W. G.: Charlemont; Eutaw; a Sequel to the Forayers.

Southworth, E. D. N.: India; the Pearl of Pearl River.

Yellott, C.: The Professor of Insanity, a Drama.

1857.

Barrow, Mrs. F. E. M.: The Lost Found and Clara C.; The Pious Mother and Her Dutiful Daughter.

Bradley, Mrs. M. E. N.: Douglass Farm.

Campana, G. S.: Mora; or The Mysterious Child (in So. Lit. Mess.).

Cooke, J. E.: Estcourt (in Russell's Magazine).

Cranch, C. P.: Kobboltozo, a Sequel to the Last of the Huggermuggers.

Dorsey, Mrs. A. H.: Oriental Pearls.

Ford, Mrs. S. R.: Grace Truman.

Holmes, M. J. H.: Meadow Brook.

Homes, Mrs. M. S. H.: Carrie Harrington; or Scenes in New Orleans.

Hulse, G. A.: Mine and Thine.

Ingraham, J. H.: The Prince of the House of David.

Lamar, Mirabeau B.: Sally Riley, Canto I. 1825; Canto II. 1843.

McCoy, Mrs. C. W. T. B.: The Three Golden Links.

Miles, Geo. H.: Mary's Birthday, a Play.

Peck, Wm. H.: Antoinette De Bordelaire, A Tale.

Smythe, James M.: Ethel Somers, or the Fate of the Union.

1858.

Anderson, Florence: Zenaida.

Bagby, George W.: The Letters of Mozis Addums to Billy Ivvins (in So. Lit. Mess.).

Chivers, T. H.: The Sons of Usna.

Clemens, J.: Mustang Gray.

Cooke, J. E.: May Days at Rackrack Hall (in So. Lit. Mess.).

DuBose, C. A. R.: The Pastor's Household.

Harris, G. W.: Sut Lovingood Papers, contributed to Nashville journals, 1858-1861.

Jervey, Mrs. C. H. G. G.: Vernon Grove; or Hearts as They Are (in So. Lit. Mess.).

Miles, Geo. H.: Senor Valiente, a Comedy.

Southworth, E. D. N.: The Three Beauties.

1859.

Bennett, Miss M. H. B.: Leisure Moments.

Blount, Annie R.: The Sisters.

Blake, Mrs. L. D.: Southwold.

Bowen, Mrs. S. P. K.: Sylvia's World, and Crimes Which the Law Does Not Reach.

Clemens, J.: The Rivals, a Tale of the Times of Burr and Hamilton.

Cooke, J. E.: Henry St. John Gentleman; Greenway Court; or, The Bloody Ground (published in So. Lit. Mess.).

French, Mrs. L. V.: Iztalilxo, a Tragedy.

Furman, Richard: The Pleasures of Piety and Other Poems.

Holmes, M. J. H.: Dora Deane; or, The East India Uncle.

Hungerford, J.: The Old Plantation.

Ingraham, J. H.: The Pillar of Fire; or, Israel in Bondage.

Jones, J. B.: Wild Southern Scenes.

Ketchum, A. C.: Rillo-Motto (a romance contributed to the Lotus of Memphis, Tenn., 1859-1861).

McCoy, Mrs. C. W. T. B.: Tales for the Freemason's Fireside.

McIntosh, M. J.: Meta Gray.

Newman, B. J.: The Eagle of Washington; a Story of the Revolution.

Peck, Wm. H.: The Brother's Vengeance.

Robb, John S.: The Swamp Doctor's Adventures in the Southwest.

Seawell, J.: Valentia, a Play in Five Acts.

Simms, W. G.: The Cassique of Kiawah.

Skitt (pseud.) Fisher's River.

Southworth, E. D N. The Lady of the Isle.

Thorpe, Thomas Bangs Major Thorpe's Scenes in Arkansas.

Wilson, A. E Beulah.

Woodson, M. E. The Way It All Ended.

1860.

Anonymous: The Mock Auction.

Anonymous: Ida Randolph.

Anderson, R. H.: Bricks.

Bagby, George W.: Blue-Eyes and Battlewick.

Barrow, Mrs. F. E. M.: Little Pet Books.

Bien, Herman M.: Samson and Delilah.

Bradley, Mrs. M. E. N.: Arthur and Other Stories.

Calvert, Geo. H.: Joan of Arc, a Poem in Four Books.

Cowden, Mrs. V. G.: Ellen; or, The Fantastic's Daughter.

Dupuy, E. A.: Autobiography of a Skeleton (in the "Ledger" of New York).

Ford, Mrs. S. R.: Mary Bunyan.

Grayson, W. J.: Marion; a Narrative Poem.

Holmes, M. J. H.: Cousin Maude and Rosamond.

Ingraham, J. H.: The Throne of David; The Sunny South.

McIntosh, Maria J.: A Year with Maggie and Emma.

Miller, Stephen F.: Wilkins Wilder; or, the Successful Man.

Peck, Wm. H.: The Conspirators of New Orleans.

Requier, A. J.: Poems.

Schoolcraft, Mrs. M. H.: The Black Gauntlet.

Skitt (pseud.): Ducktown (in So. Lit. Mess.).

Smith, Wm. R.: As It Is.

Anonymous: Southern Sketches.

Southworth, E. D. N.: The Haunted Homestead; The Mother-in-Law.

Whittlesey, S. J. C.: The Stranger's Stratagem.

WITHDRAWAL